S0-BRG-127

TRUE-LOVE

Contents

Acknowledgments

My profound thanks, first, to Susan Stewart for her constant friendship and the support that has been vital to the project of making this book. Even more, she gave precious time and her polymathic range of insight to editing the incomplete text of "Poetry and Enlightenment."

The generous sponsorship of the Humanities Center at Johns Hopkins University, and of the English departments there and at the University of Chicago, has enabled the development of several of the essays. I thank especially Michael Fried, friend and colleague, for his vital engagement with the arguments here presented.

Andrew Albin gave expert research assistance with "Figuring the Real: Wordsworth's 'The Solitary Reaper.'"

I thank Alan Thomas and Randy Petilos for shepherding this book through to publication, from its tentative beginnings.

SPRICH AUCH DU	SPEAK YOU ALSO
Sprich auch du,	Speak, you also,
sprich als letzter,	speak as the last,
sag deinen Spruch.	have your say.
Sprich—	Speak—
Doch scheide das Nein nich vom Ja.	But keep Yes and No unsplit.
Gib deinem Spruch auch den Sinn:	And give your say this meaning:
gib ihm den Schatten.	give it the shade.
Gib ihm Schatten genug.	Give it shade enough.
gib ihm so viel,	Give it as much
als du um dich verteilt weisst zwischen	as you know has been dealt out between
Mittnacht und Mittag und Mittnacht	midnight and midday and midnight.
Blicke umher:	Look around:
sieh, wie's lebendig wird rings—	look how it all leaps alive—
Beim Tode! Lebendig!	where death is! Alive!
Wahr spricht, wer Schatten spricht.	He speaks truly who speaks the shade.
Nun aber schrumpft der Ort, wo du stehst:	But now shrinks the place where you stand:
Wohin jetz, Schattenentblösster, wohin?	Where now, stripped by shade, will you go?
Steige. Taste empor. . . .	Upward. Grope your way up. . . .[3]

I assume, then, that *"something has happened to us"* bearing upon poetry or poetic practice: an enlightenment—our enlightenment. Kant's definition or motto for his enlightenment is in the imperative: *Sapere aude* (literally, "Dare to be wise"), taken from Horace's *Epodes,* 1.2.40. Kant's translation of this phrase in his essay "An Answer to the Question: What Is Enlightenment?" is "Have courage to use your *own* understanding"—an expression associated with German response to the French Revolution.[4] *Audere:* to venture, to be bold, courageous. *Sapere aude:* to be courageous, in the light of one's "own" knowledge, against opposition. It is the modal opposite *but moral equivalent* (what Kant would call the "incongruous counterpart") to Blake's very Low Church response, as a poet, to a sudden conviction about the truth of the Christian promise—the now at last certain knowledge— *that something promised has in fact happened.* You will remember Blake's poem that acts out "enlightenment" beginning in astonishment, "And did those feet . . .":

And did those feet in ancient time,
Walk upon Englands mountains green:
And was the holy Lamb of God,
On Englands pleasant pastures seen!

And did the Countenance Divine,
Shine forth upon our clouded hills?
And was Jerusalem builded here,
Among these dark Satanic Mills?

Bring me my Bow of burning gold:
Bring me my Arrows of desire:
Bring me my Spear: O clouds unfold!
Bring me my Chariot of fire!

I will not cease from Mental Fight,
Nor shall my Sword sleep in my hand:
Till we have built Jerusalem,
In Englands green & pleasant Land.[5]

In the light of now *certain and own knowledge* ("enlightenment" is not knowledge but "own" knowledge, recognition) *something has happened*. Someone
says in effect, "Now I know for certain, as a result of experience, that what
is written is true about *me*, in my world, is my own." Therefore the Blake
speaker vows its fulfillment, in the final stanza on the sword (*sapere aude*).

Kant's and Blake's texts perform the same archetypal narrative—the
reception of enlightenment. The archetypal identity of these two kinds
of texts was clearly acknowledged by the authors, unknown to one another. *Something has happened* and the response requires control—that's the
sense of regulative precaution in Blake's remarkable predication of fight by
"Mental." Likewise is Kant's restriction to spectatorship of the world's relation to the catastrophe of the "sublime" subject.[6] Blake would have called
Kant's enlightenment, as he called Swedenborg's, "the linen clothes folded
up";[7] and Kant would have called Blake's enlightenment *Schwärmerei*.[8] But
they are of the same mind.

We (you and I) also respond to the world as we can, in the kind of cultural work—mental fight—to which we have been called and about which
we *know*, as we suppose, not only the technique of it but also something
of the relations of it and responsibilities. But, for my part, I have felt, for
a long time, that whatever I have to say—as a poet and about poetry—is
out-of-date. It is as if something had happened: a great enlightenment had

passed over the world and something had been brought to light for which poetry, always and only what is seen somehow in the light (*lumine naturali manifestum*);[9] has no categories, no way of knowing, because what is seen was never seen before. Is not "in the light."

How then to respond to what Kant calls, as if it were in crisis, the "right of the need" of reason, that is, reason's need? How then to say anything if there is nothing like it, no analogy, no scripture. If there were anything in the biblical witness like it (this enlightenment that I feel but cannot name), it would be that FALL into consciousness—the biblical archetype of enlightenment—new knowledge: new knowledge that always entails, logically entails (<if *a* then not *b*>), ratios of gain and loss—as, we are in no doubt, conscious knowledge of "being" inevitably entails loss of immediate life and entails also, for the same reason, that what is lost will be incommensurable with what is gained. The first loss in biblical Eden is loss of immediacy, and the gain is a recovery in another kind, for what is lost is, as it were, light, and what is gained is "knowledge"—not light, but that other thing: seeing or enlightenment. Another name for that other thing given us instead is poetry (fallen redress or compensation of distance), poetry *in all the already existing instances and forms.*

As a consequence, the study and practice of poetry seems now to have no other concern, in the light of its purposes, than the question of the constraints upon variation of its kinds. In our time, there is, in fact, a disposition to project or pretend to practice *impossible* poetries—to reconstruct a making of the "new" that would undo the Fall, the traumatic enlightenment, that Celan's language of *Wirklichkeitswund* (a reality-wounded language) construed more or less in the biblical sense.

As an example of an impossible poetry, D. H. Lawrence wrote in 1918: "There is poetry of this immediate present, instant poetry, as well as poetry of the infinite past and the infinite future. The seething poetry of the incarnate Now is supreme, beyond even the everlasting gems of the before and after. . . ."[10] But does such a poetry, in fact, occur? Thinking about Whitman's *project* of free verse, Lawrence thought it did. Writing about the accomplished fact of *The Leaves of Grass*, he thought it did not. Such an accomplishment as *The Leaves of Grass* required, he found, a person so general, in its terms of address and reception, that there was no possibility of encounter. And the opposite idealism is also the case among poets— the projection of a personhood (after the Fall, after the Enlightenment, after Auschwitz) so particular, so *redemptively* particular it may be thought, that its reality blocks the possibility of not only acknowledgment, but also even knowing. This is the poet whom Derrida constructs in his essay dedicated to Paul Celan, "Shibboleth"—a poet of the irreducibly, the infinitely particular, self (a Celanian idea), a construction that makes true person-hood unaccountable, a non-recurrent date—a kind of life identical to the always already dead, the ultimate and bottom of corporeal particulariza-tion, because it defeats generality. Such life is real at the cost of being un-representable.[11]

Let me say, as a poet and, for the moment, as a thinker, that *the idea of the NEW is at this moment under pressure.* That is my subject here. An enlighten-ment has passed over us. It may be we should consider whether we can say what we have seen or, in any case, *whether we have rightly construed the poetic means.* We know we are no longer in Marvell's garden. So my question—a question that was Whitman's question in the mid-nineteenth century and Celan's question in the mid-twentieth century—is the following: Is there another poetry than the one I know? Is there another, a new, art? Or are we somehow inevitably, and yet too soon, at the logical limit (that was Hegel's idea) of the variation of a practice?[12] In any case, the idea of novelty is, as I say, *under pressure.* Milton's "pastures new" are drenched.

Adorno's proscription with which I began—"No poetry after Ausch-witz"—repeats Plato's proscription in the tenth book of the *Republic* (but in Plato's case, "after" what?) and is a recurrence (as I have said) of Hegel's speculation on limits, above, that art "has a limit in itself" and that "the manifestation of truth in a sensuous form" is not truly adequate to the claims of experience. Is there another poetry than the one I know? *That seems to me an inescapable question*—about the constraints of representation of the poetic kind and in general about the adequacy of the communica-tive structures we know how to make, and construe, to the weight of what needs to be said, however the claims of knowledge upon practice may be stated—either in Plato's or Hegel's sense, or Adorno's, or Hart Crane's, whose poetry (like modernist poetry in many instances) was built on the theme of the inadequacy of our communicative *structures* (in Crane's ex-pression, these were *bridges, towers, hands,* and *tears*) to bear the burden of our communicative traffic.

Immanuel Kant (whom, as I've said, I get along with) thought every-body in the world was right-handed—a priori; and Immanuel Kant discov-ered and stated the "nebular hypothesis."[13] These two judgments are not unrelated. When Kant saw the sky, he saw it with extraordinary clarity and could feel where he stood on the earth in relation to what he saw, and where the earth and the sun's universe really *was*—in eccentric relation to the vast disk of the nebula and in centric relation to his own body. Kant was a great spectator. You will remember, when you hear it, what Kant says at the end of *Critique of Practical Reason*:

Two things fill the mind with ever new and increasing admiration and reverence, the more often and more steadily one reflects on them: *the starry heavens above me and the moral law within me.* I do not need to search for them and merely conjecture them as though they were veiled in obscurity or in a transcendent region beyond my horizon; I see them before me and connect them immediately with the consciousness of my existence. The first begins from the place I occupy in the external world of sense and extends the connection in which I stand into an unbounded magnitude with worlds upon worlds and systems of systems, and moreover into the unbounded times of their periodic motions, their beginning and their duration. The second begins from my invisible self, my personality, and presents me in a world which has true infinity but which can be discovered only by the understanding, and I cognize that my connection with that world (and thereby with all those visible worlds as well) is not merely contingent, as in the first case, but universal and necessary.[14]

Kant was an oriented mind—a Protestant spirit, from a Pietist family, accustomed to a clear and immediate intercourse between mind and its God. Recall Edward Taylor's "Meditation 8":

> I kenning through astronomy divine
> The world's bright battlement, wherein I spy
> A golden path my pencil cannot line,
> From that bright throne unto my threshold lie
> And while my puzzled thoughts about it pore
> I find the bread of life in it at my door.

But Kant, going Taylor one better, tells us in a 1786 essay called "What Does It Mean to Orient Oneself in Thinking?" how this is possible (without the deluded enthusiasm of *Schwärmerei*):

In the proper meaning of the word, to *orient* oneself means to use a given direction (when we divide the horizon into four of them) in order to find the others—literally, to find the *sunrise*. Now if I see the sun in the sky and know it is now midday, then I know how to find south, west, north, and east. For this, however, I also need the feeling of a difference in my own subject, namely, the difference between my right and left hands. I call this a *feeling* because these two sides outwardly display no designatable difference in intuition.[15]

On this feeling, for the stated reason that external intuition gives no guidance, Kant builds the *legitimacy* (everybody is right-handed) not only of spatial, but also of mathematical, logical, and theological orientation. Orientation is given us a priori by the body (and everybody is a body) in order to respond to what he calls "the right of the need of reason" (*das Recht des Bedürfnisses der Vernunft*). This right and need of reason is the universal social requirement of communicability. Thus, truth in Kant's world (the ground of critique, sociability, and all possible knowledge of the highest human good, the moral *summum bonum* and explicitly God) is built (a ground without metaphysical requirement) upon the perishing basis of our common life—our corporeal singularity, our physical subject nature, our body as it is the bearer of recognition and intelligibility: a kind of knowledge, in my view, of the same order as poetic knowledge. This body secures the *sensus communis* and makes it possible for us to find the way—*die Richtung*—of which the only authority is the sunrise.

Narration of the loss and intended recovery of the orienting a priori of the body (assurance of mind-body connection, imagination—*Einbildung*—that Kant in some measure built[16]) is, in my view, the principle motive of strong poems of the post-Enlightenment modernity: for example, Hölderlin's "Patmos"; Rimbaud's "One soul in one body" ("Adieu"); Mallarmé's "Un Coup de Dés" oriented toward the pole star ("Septentrion aussi Nord"); Eliot's boat responsive "to sail and oar"; Stevens's "palm at the end of the mind."

But my attention was directed to Kant's text by Paul Celan's "Bremen Rede." As is well known, Celan—a Jew born in 1920 in the Eastern European province of Bukovina, died in Paris in 1970 (chose to die—for he was a suicide like many survivors of somebody else's Final Solution)—is the great European poet of the second half of the twentieth century. When the Nazis came for his parents, Paul was not at home. His parents were taken east and killed by Germans. He was taken west to a camp run by the Romanian Iron Guard but survived. The central narrative of his life—this not being at home—he never told in a coherent way: this unnarrated and unnarratable moment of the disappearance of his mother's body holds the never-to-be-healed traumatic enlightenment—*Wirklichkeitswund*—from which poems flow. His mother's tongue was German; his native language was Romanian. After the war he emigrated to Paris via Vienna and became a notable poet and translator—writing in German. His work is analytic of, and keeps on uttering, the traumatic enlightenment of which I speak. He stands for the difference of enlightenment in our time. Celan makes of his mother's tongue, not his own mother tongue, a poetic language—from the language of those who killed his mother. When he speaks of poetic language, he speaks of it *as* language (and this is the term I have centralized) now seen in context of a traumatically enlightened mind: language of the poetic kind precisely because it is wounded by reality and in search of reality—*Wirklichkeitswund und Wirklichkeit suchend.* The wound is on the body of the mother who has disappeared, and it is the body of his mother—her speaking tongue—that poetry seeks to reconstruct. This reconstruction of the *possibility* of poetry—which is very different than poetry (not possibility but its doubt)—is one response to the traumatic enlightenment of which I speak.

Most of Celan's prose was composed in response to public acknowledgment of his poetic distinction *in Germany.* The following is an autobiographical passage from "Bremen Rede: A Speech on the Occasion of Receiving the Literature Prize of the Free Hanseatic City of Bremen 26 January '58."[17]

This is Celan's voice:

> Only one thing remained reachable [*blieb unverloren*], close and secure amid all losses: language. Yes, language. In spite of everything, it remained secure against loss. But it had to go through its own lack of answers, through terrifying silence, through the thousand darknesses [*Finsternesse*] of murderous speech. It went through. It gave me no words for what was happening, but went through it. Went through and could resurface, "enriched" by it all.
>
> In this language I tried, during those years and the years after, to write poems: in order to speak, to orient myself, to find out where I was, where I was going, to chart my reality.

Please note, then, that what Celan intends to reconstruct by poetic language—the mother's tongue, but not the mother tongue—is precisely that utterly secure Kantian body: the body that knows exactly its location in the universe and the location of the universe among the stars. This is the body, not of the senses, aesthetic, but the body of meaning—the hermeneutic body, the body that makes sense. Celan continues:

> It [poetry as the work of orientation] meant movement, you see, something happening, being *en route* [*Unterwegsein*], an attempt to find a direction [*Richtung zu gewinnen*]. Whenever I ask about the sense of it, I remind myself that this implies the question as to which sense is clockwise. . . .

A poem, being an instance of language, hence essentially dialogue, may be a letter in a bottle thrown out to sea.... In this way, too, poems are *en route*. ...

Toward what? Toward something open, inhabitable, an approachable [*ansprechbares*] you, perhaps, an approachable reality.[18]

Poems in Celan are instrumental, dialogic, orientative, because the East is always and only the vanished other person. Poems are intended to engage in the recovery of orientative possibility—the mother's body, let us say, which has disappeared—by putting language (the competence for which is the specifying difference of humanity) in service of *Richtung*, orientation in space and time. Enlightenment has inflicted upon language a wound—a reality wound (*Wirklichkeitswund*—wound, trauma of knowledge, darkness inflicted by light). In Celan it was this language *Wirklichkeitswund* that put the "new" under pressure. I believe we are in Celan's position. Only language, the reality-wounded hero hand, can signify the direction, recover time and space. And what will constitute that recovery? It will be encounter with another (*Entgegnung*, reply), a second person who makes reason, communicative relationship, possible—response to the need of reason. The right of the need of reason. Kant is clear about the danger of not responding to that right. Celan understood, in Kant's sense, the need. Does poetry answer to that right, or does it baffle that right? Does art enlarge or diminish the communicability of persons? In Paul Celan's "The Meridian" (1960), the character Lucile, from Georg Büchner's play *Danton's Death*, is cited as speaking "the word against the grain"—utterance that is "homage to the majesty of the absurd which bespeaks the presence of human beings."[19] For Celan, her utterance fulfills the essential demand: "*Élargissez art*," enlarge art (*Die Kunst erweitern*), a demand, Celan says, that strikes us with a new uncanniness, as he writes in his "Meridian" speech.[20] He means here an unresolvable modal ambiguity, consequent upon the inability of a subject to ascertain whether the object of concern is living or dead. There is a strong sense that the art in Celan has, as Hegel predicted, reached a limit and is now cast out upon, can only be intended to produce, an encounter that is certainly not a possibility of language and is inconsistent with the logic of the poetic kind.

"Sprich Auch Du" *is a lyric.* In lyric there is never another who speaks—only the speaking self, the subject who says You. Formal lyric is, precisely, not dialogic. The other, in the lyric convention, is silent, or is she silenced—her word not wanted? The "you," other to the "I," orients the "I," as the muse of tradition (Sing, muse!) orients the singer and produces song in him. But the muse never sings. The desire that the disappeared mother speak is negated by unwillingness of the son to hear her say, "I am dead." This search for response and the endless deferral of response is a salient characteristic of the poetry of our time—right now.

My point is that the traumatic enlightenment of the postwar world compelled recognition of the loss of the meaning-bearing body, and of the vulnerability of all bodies. I emphasize that I am not talking about the body of the senses, but about the body that makes human, is orientative, recognitional, hermeneutic—the body that grounded Kant's confident orientation or Whitman's *confiance au monde*. The general function of the poem as stated in Celan's "Meridian," his most mature formulation, is not to produce an artifact or delight an emperor, but to give birth in language to the possibility of orientation that requires that there be an East—to sing a new song, not by means of but toward a resurrection. But apostrophe, as such, in the postwar world, has become an embarrassment. The practice of apostrophe, the figure of address, seems to entail the shame of acknowledgment that there is no Thou.

In "Sprich Auch Du," the voice of the dead mother addresses her living son. (It is found in Celan's third book, *From Threshold to Threshold*—the problem of the book is the question of getting across, that is, channeling.) The other talks back, in "Sprich Auch Du"—the artifact addresses the maker. Something that has no life, or other life, speaks. It is, strictly, uncanny. At the very least, we may say that the lyric speaker in this poem speaks from within the life of the artifact, in the sense of the artifact ("Don't split No from Yes" we are told is what the artifact always says), driven by the realization of an unutterable solitude, having waited ten thousand years to address the one who is responsible for this decorum, this form. Mobility of the speaking subject, the subject position, is a characteristic of Celan's practice and gives readers some difficulty. Here, at last, the artifact, the poem, addresses the maker, the poet, *in the sense of the artifact*. She says: "I am dead." The model is Rilke's "Archaic Torso of Apollo."

I offer you this essay in order to call attention to a state of affairs—how the new, and the idea of the new, is under pressure, *Wirklichkeitswund*, reality wounded, and to offer the merest beginning of an analysis *Wirklichkeit suchend*—in search.

What, then, have we learned from listening to Kant the philosopher and Celan the poet on orientation? Let us say that the grounding or authority both of philosophy and poetry may be discussed not in terms of relationship to thought, which always require further authority, but to materials, which did not. The Walt Whitman originality (out of Lucretius, and the Epicurean mind—but that is another story) was intended to overcome both the disability of constitution and accomplish the enlargement of art. Both of the eighteenth-century revolutions promised what "only poetry after Auschwitz—the something that happened"—promised: they put the idea of the new under pressure. The always-present-to-mind "something that happened"—by which euphemism I have referred (we have grown accustomed to refer) to, the ever-recurrent traumatic enlightenment for which there is no name or many names, the *Wirklichkeitswund* that threw Celan back upon language—was the holocaust of the body, the ruin of the only resource of meaning of orientation in the universe. Let us say that the maxim "only poetry after Auschwitz" means that the culture orientation succeeding the theological is the poetological in which the body of honor is reconstructed from the body of shame, for that body—the body of generality, the body bearer of meaning—is the body of which I speak. That body offers a possibility of meeting and reply, *Entgegnung*, that is of highest value in Celan as it is in Whitman—the poetological World Cup. Here I will briefly further indicate the orientative function of poetic structures.

Whitman was a line writer. The Whitmanian line was devised to conserve order (the line is end-stopped) and by the same gesture repudiate hierarchy. It is not the blank-verse line of what he understood to be feudal England—rather, the line is the inscription in text of the universal abstract right/left orientation. The line is the poetological meridian along which the speaker goes from "I" to "you" and by this means obtains the encounter that is a reply to the Celanian highest value—the reconstructed scene in which the mother reappears. The two hands in Whitman are not precisely the incongruent counterparts of Kant, but the hand in hand of the Adam and Eve at the end of Milton's *Paradise Lost* ("hand in hand / Through Eden took their solitary way").

All poems begin with a reestablishment of relation reorientation within space and time, as in the beginning of Whitman's "Crossing Brooklyn Ferry":

> Flood tide below me! I see you face to face!
> Clouds of the west—sun there half an hour high—I see you
> also face to face.

Water below/cloud above—face to face: orientation over against; the signifier of heroic encounter (Homeric and biblical, as we find in Deuteronomy 10: "Moses whom the Lord knew face to face") takes place (in crisis, the *Sprich Auch Du* is initiated *am letzten*—in extremis). The speaker begins an action of crossing the tide at its only open moment—the full of the tide. The whole action of the poem is expressed in the rotation of ninety degrees that exchanges a right-angle relation for a relation of parallel flow: language that crosses the given changes to language that intends exactly what the world intends—is redundant in relation to reality as it is redundant to tell the turned tide to flow. In the course of this rotation, the speaker passes from distance to intimacy in relation to the other's face by way of recognition: I, too, received identity from my body. This is intelligible immanence obtained by knowing the way.

We end, then, with a series of Celanian paradoxes regarding the body, which I will list here:

1. Unqualified individuality is inconsistent with generality of any kind and therefore with communicative possibility—the most important constituent of meeting and reply, or *Entgegnung.*
2. Unqualified generality is inconsistent with difference and therefore acknowledgment.
3. Unqualified contingency can be represented only as abjection. The Celanian *Entgegnung* is signified by the Whitmanian exchange: "We understand then, do we not?"

So Kant, whose argument on orientation follows a trajectory from sunlight to the night sky, to the orienting of the mind in abstraction through the right of reason's need, reaches this conclusion following the passage cited earlier from *Critique of Practical Reason*:

The first view of a countless multitude of worlds annihilates, as it were, my importance as an animal creature, which after it has been for a short time provided with vital force (one knows not how) must give back to the planet (a mere speck of the universe) the matter from which it came. The second, on the contrary, infinitely raises my worth as an intelligence by my personality, in which the moral law reveals to me a life independent of animality, and even of the whole sensible world, at least so far as this may be inferred from the purposive determination [*zweckmassig Bestimmung*] of my existence by this law, a determination not restricted to the conditions and boundaries of this life but reaching to the infinite.[21]

Hard Problems in Poetry, Especially Valuing

There is the world dimensional for those untwisted
by the love of things irreconcilable.

Hart Crane, "For the Marriage of Faustus and Helen"

Frankie and Johnny were lovers, O, how the couple could love,
Swore to be true to each other, true as the stars above—
He was her man, but he done her wrong.

Anon.

Eternity, Presumption
The instant I perceive
That you who were Existence
Yourself forgot to live—

Emily Dickinson, #1260

I. Hard Problems in Poetry

Poetry is the means of last recourse, the artistic form of communicative action. The use of poetry in which I wish to interest you is its intention to interrupt the continuity of cultural understandings. That's what I think poetic "originality" means. That's what poetic novelty, the new thing, is.

First, I want to think about valuing. The action of loving expresses the intention to value anything. So I must in order to think about valuing think about love. Valuation seems precisely the act of conferring (or depriving) existence and also "truth." In that sense, it is the same as the action of loving. Loving surely intends the existence and also the actuality of the loved. But consider Nietzsche, in *The Will to Power* #507:

> The *valuation* [*die Wertschätzung*] "I believe that this and that is so" as the essence of "*truth*." In valuations are expressed conditions of preservation

* "Hard Problems in Poetry, Especially Valuing" was originally published in an earlier version under the title "Discovery of the Poetic Principle: True-Love Considerations," in *Poetry's Poet: Essays on the Poetry, Pedagogy, and Poetics of Allen Grossman*, ed. Daniel Morris (Orono, ME: National Poetry Foundation, 2004), 225–68.

and growth [*Erhaltungs- und Wachstums-Bedingungen*]. . . . Trust in reason and its categories, in dialectic, therefore the valuation of logic, proves only their usefulness for life, proved by experience—not that something is true.[1]

What is proved by experience is: (a) that the making of representations or depictions expresses power; and (b) that the valuation implied in the expression "true-love" is inconsistent with life, is not among the conditions of preservation and growth, because under its definitions "quick, bright things come to confusion."

It appears that the belief (*Glaube*) that maintains the "preservation and growth" is not the contingency of the truth of love. Or, to put it briefly, that in "poetry" the conditions (the preservation and maintenance) of life—the *Glaube* that maintains both logic and religious authority—are inconsistent with the kind of knowledge that makes love true. And that this inconsistency (the poetic principle) produces the worth of things and persons. This state of affairs is inside the general civilizational project of representation (as "knowledge" or "depiction"). The nature of its motive is adequately presented by Nietzsche subsequently in *The Will to Power* #511: "The *will to equality* [*Gleichheit*, correctness of representation] is *the will to power*—the belief that something is thus and thus (the essence of *judgment*) is the consequence of a will that as much [of what is experienced] as possible *shall be equal* [*so viel als möglich gleich sein*]."[2]

Within the borderlessness of the language of love, I have chosen the term "true-love," the crossing of knowledge (truth) and acknowledgment (love), the identity of contradictories both of which are maximal terms freighted not only with explicit value but, when conjoined, with the intention of the highest value. Needless to say, the identity or equality of contradictories violates possibility in a world subject to the Aristotelian Laws of Thought. Power is brought to bear in the production of the *tertium quid*. True-love intends an action that somehow authorizes the valid predication of truth upon love. And this "somehow" seems to cover over a counterlogical principle such as Kierkegaard's "either/or" (*concordia discors*), neither religious nor philosophical—the poetic principle.

Human beings desire by their nature to know, so Aristotle affirmed. The desire to know *is really what desire is*: the desire, identically, for the beloved, on the one hand, and truth, on the other. Insofar as a "passion" is a social form—a name—for desire, it is not clear to me that there is any other passion. True-love binds truth and love into one word, as in philo/sophia. (". . . To philosophize there is need of love"—Dante, *Convivio* III. xi.) Whether first judgment (the election of Aphrodite by Paris) or Last

Judgment (Christ's division of the world at the end of days), the action of true-love is *judging: the exercise of power on the grounds of knowledge of the highest value*—"Kisses are / The only worth all granting" (Hart Crane). What kisses grant is existence, and *existence is in question*, one way or another, in all matters of valuation. For example: "A case of contradictories which are true. God exists. God does not. Where's the problem? . . . We have to believe in a God who is like the true God in everything except that he does not exist . . ." (Simone Weil, *Gravity and Grace*).[3] Take also as exemplary P. D. Ouspensky's *Tertium Organum* (1920), in which he proposes to replace the Aristotelian axioms (specifically, the excluded middle term) thus:

> We may express the principle axiom of the new logic in our poor earthly language in the following manner:
>
> A is both A and Not-A.
>
> or
>
> Everything is both A and Not-A.
>
> or
>
> Everything is All.[4]

Here is the poem "Legend" by Hart Crane, who read Ouspensky. Crane means to say by his title that this poem is the founding text, the originary legendary narrative of a new consummate order, "bright logic," "noon"— the identity of truth and love, the real and the actual, "a perfect cry."

LEGEND

As silent as a mirror is believed
Realities plunge in silence by . . .

I am not ready for repentance;
Nor to match regrets. For the moth
Bends no more than the still
Imploring flame. And tremorous
In the white falling flakes
Kisses are,—
The only worth all granting.

It is to be learned—
This cleaving and this burning,
But only by the one who
Spends out himself again.

Twice and twice
(Again the smoking souvenir,
Bleeding eidolon!) and yet again.
Until the bright logic is won
Unwhispering as a mirror
Is believed.

Then, drop by caustic drop, a perfect cry
Shall string some constant harmony,—
Relentless caper for all those who step
The legend of their youth into the noon.[5]

II. Poetry Is, Philosophically Speaking, an Assurance of "Normative Realism"

True-love, "the only worth all granting," confers the power to transgress the threshold, however inscribed, between existence-not-yet and the *nunc stans*: existence-just-now. In the twenty-first century, the highest value is still existence itself (Being of beings, the *I am* of *Exodus*), but existence obtained after the catastrophe of creation produced by the power that reexpresses the world in terms of the *bright logic* of universal identity.

I adopt for speculative purposes Nietzsche's proposal that what power desires is knowledge, and knowledge is effective most significantly in the human world as valuing—making the difference that judgment specifies (distinction, selection, election, the right arm of Christ judge)—finally the granting and withholding existence, existence being the category of highest value. Not the "I think" but the "I am" is god. We note also Nietzsche's qualification of possibility with respect to the *truth* element: "Therefore, what is needed is that something must be held to be true. *Not* that something *is* true."[6] When, Plato speaks (in *The Republic*, mysteriously) of the ancient quarrel between philosophy and poetry, his sense of "quarrel" (*diaphora*) is in fact categorical difference (as between species)—elements discursively contradictory; and the difference issue is specifically a question of truth or truthlessness. (A second term that Plato uses for the difference between philosophy and poetry is *enantioseos*, which implies face-to-face opposition, as in heroic life/death combat or legal contention.)

Valuing (the granting or withholding of existence) is an action persons do to one another in the world; and one kind of valuing is loving. My particular concern is what is called in English "true-love" or the crossing of love and truth/actuality, persons and knowledge (with respect to the historical anxiety inside the predicate "true"). Here Plotinus is relevant:

For existing is not one thing and always existing another, just as a philosopher is not one thing and the true philosopher another, *but because there
was such a thing as putting on a pretence of philosophy, the addition of "true" was
made.* So, too, "always" is applied to "existing," . . . so the "always" must
be taken as saying "truly existing"; it must be included in the undivided
power which in no way needs anything beyond what it already possesses;
but it possesses the whole. ("Time and Eternity"; emphasis added)[7]

My question remains: Why does the course of true-love never run
smooth? Is it because "true-love" is a foundationalist error as all anxious
talk affirming truth must be, and therefore doomed to disconfirmation?
(Frankie constructs Johnnie—buys him a superior suit and a watch to go
with it, just as Marlowe's passionate Shepherd clothes his girlfriend—and
then must destroy him—*roota toot toot*—for practicing the autonomous
life she has confirmed.) Or is "true-love" a strong form of *knowledge* about
the destination of the will, which is indispensable to our culture of human
value? Or both?

An implication intended by setting these arguments together is the generality of the issue—the horizon of which is the whole of civilization. I
wish to show that poetry (the poetic principle however actualized) functions as a critique (from the point of view of consummation and expense)
of regulative prudence, the maintenance conception of truth, to which the
discourses of both philosophy and religion defer. The conclusion is that
poetry is neither identical nor coterminous with the poetic text. It occurs
wherever claims of truth are held in mind as prior to philosophy and religion and indistinguishable from love. The highest value flows from the
conjunction of truth and love—"true-love." But "logic does not derive
from the will towards truth [*die Logik stammt nicht aus dem Willen zur Wahrheit*]," says Nietzsche.[8] Poetry, as it is understood in this argument, is the
principle of discourse that is more serious and more philosophical than history (Aristotle)—and more realistic.

III. The Instituting Force of Loss in the Domain of Representation

To begin with: Something philosophical and serious *can* be said about
"true-love," if for no other reason than that there is a type of valid English
language text in which the word is at home and known. The practice of language being valid (the poem being good), it must have authority of some
kind that makes it reliable *as a host* of the term under investigation. That is
to say, if I am to affirm poetic text as a context authoritative in the matter
of "true-love," then I must concern myself with the authority of poetry as

witness to the term in question. In brief, "true-love" or the infallible discovery of the unmistakable object of love—the truth of love and also the
love of truth—is among the recurrent idealizations of civilization. It is also
a very constant subject of poetry and mingles itself with the most fundamental questions of relationship, representation, intentional consciousness, and valuation.

*It will be among the conclusions of these pages that the implications of the "true-
love" expression and the authority and particularity among discourses of poetry co-
incide and express one another;* that the true-love expression carries inside it
a story (cf. "Legend") about how the meaning of representations (or depictions) is produced and validated, that is, expressed as true. And that poetry
tells this story as a narrative of the establishment of poetry's own authority—the true-love story, *a story of the instituting force of loss,* as, for example,
the myth (or legend) of the empowerment of Orpheus' song—Orpheus,
the archetypal poet of the West—by the irrevocable death of Eurydice, his
true-love. Bourdieu speaks of this state of affairs, in "Rites of Institution,"
as a kind of blind fatality or curse:

> The veritable miracle produced by acts of institution [I presume he
> means institution as authorizing a discourse] lies undoubtedly in the fact
> that they manage to make consecrated individuals believe that their ex-
> istence is justified. . . . But, through a kind of curse, because of the essen-
> tially diacritical, differential and distinctive nature of symbolic power,
> the rise of the distinguished class to Being has, as an inevitable coun-
> terpart, the slide of the complementary class into Nothingness or the
> lowest Being.[9]

Indeed, the story of "true-love" is not *named* (even though it is present)
in all poems. The absence of the name and the presence of the structure
is normative and produces an effect of blindness neither tragic nor comic
that is thematized as fatality of a kind (a curse): the necessity of truth and
the contingency of its grounding.

"In short," says Nietzsche,

> the question remains open: are the axioms of logic adequate to reality
> [correct representations] or are they a means and measure for us to *cre-
> ate* reality, the concept "reality," for ourselves?—To affirm the former one
> would . . . have to have a previous knowledge of being—which is cer-
> tainly not the case. The proposition therefore contains no *criterion of
> truth,* but an *imperative* concerning that which *should* count as true. [*Der*

Satz enthalt also kein Kriterium der Wahrheit, sondern einen Imperativ über das, was als wahr gelten soll.][10]

No one speaks of "true-love" in *Antony and Cleopatra*. But *A Midsummer's Night Dream* and *King Lear* are texts where one can study the meaning of this expression—because "true-love" is in those plays a term in love's vernacular both necessary *and possible* to define—a factor of normative life that states itself. In *A Midsummer Night's Dream*, we find the following well-known exchange:

Lysander:	How now, my love? why is your cheek so pale?
	How chance the roses there do fade so fast?
Hermia:	Belike for want of rain; which I could well
	Beteem them from the tempest of my eyes.
Lys.:	Ay me! for ought that I could ever read,
	Could ever hear by tale or history,
	The course of true-love never did run smooth;
	But either it was difference in blood—
Her.:	O cross! too high to be enthralled to low.
Lys.:	Or else misgraffed in respect of years—
Her.:	O spite! too old to be engaged to young.
Lys.:	Or else it stood upon the choice of friends—
Her.:	O hell! to choose love by another's eyes.
Lys.:	Or if there was a sympathy in choice,
	War death or sickness did lay siege to it,
	Making it momentary as a sound,
	Swift as a shadow, short as any dream
	Brief as the lightning in the collied night,
	That, in a spleen, unfolds both heaven and earth;
	And ere a man hath power to say "Behold!"
	The jaws of darkness do devour it up:
	So quick bright things come to confusion.
Her.:	If then true lovers have been ever cross'd
	It stands as edict in our destiny.
	Then let us teach our trial patience,
	Because it is a customary cross.

(I.i.128–55)

There is a sublime and ominous de-creative implication in the line "So quick bright things come to confusion." The issue of true-love is profoundly human, *and not in human scale*. It brings the person close to a reality prior to world—chaos, "confusion." The paradox, as we shall see, is identical with the first event of sacred history—the creation of the world, theodicean in the sense that it is unaccountable in the light of the freedom of God. This true-love talk constructs a relation to suffering of a kind, reinventing it as customary or common, instituting loss as patience and pronouncing a judgment of proverbial authority, with respect to any narrative that predicates "true" upon love. True-love's course never did run smooth, and its not doing so makes it "a *customary* cross" (emphasis added). Since, indeed, the word *love*, wherever it occurs and in many different ways, accounts for the necessity and desirability *but not the possibility* of valid relationship among persons, the motive to understand the true or right form of love, its conditions of actualization and entailment, is profoundly reasonable. The substance of this essay concerns the implications of the regulative term *true*, as it is anxiously applied to love—no doubt the human world's most unstable signifier.

Hence we are also concerned with the supposition, love being after all *the generic* poetic subject, that the prestige of poetry derives from the dedication of language by poetic means to this (counter-logical) work of patience, the regulation or *trueing* of love.

> Then, let us teach our trial patience
> Because it is a customary cross.

IV. The True-Love Knot

The expression "true-love" and its material reexpressions and instituted accounts (e.g., the Eucharist, or the true-love knot) is constituted of a difficult union of contradictory discourses (like the poetic text, a *concordia discors*)—the *truth* discourse (abstract, general, masculine, regulative, formal, unchanging—the ever-constant turtledove) and the *love* discourse (concrete, particular, feminine, subject to regulation, without determinate form, and at the same time the preeminent force in the universe—the phoenix flame forever changing into itself). This (hypostatic) union of disparates is enigmatically both impossible and, as constituent of the person, necessary to the world. Although these disparates have no meaning except in relation to one another, it is as though they belong to utterly distinct cultures (e. g., phoenix, Eastern and mythical, but the turtledove, Western and a real-life bird).

Let us begin, then, with the most beautiful example of true-love in the written tradition—a story in which true-love has instituting or creative force (God so loved the world), for it founds the Davidic lineage and therefore the meaning of Davidic and subsequently Christian history. When Ruth the gentile, the Moabitess, in the biblical book of Ruth, contracts with Naomi, her mother-in-law, a Jew, she speaks across their difference with the intention of negotiating it. Ruth's power is power itself: the will to "equality" [*Gleichheit*]). Her song is a true-love poem everybody knows—a song of *intentional* identity in difference—power itself.

> Whither you go I will go
> And where you lodge I will lodge.
> Your people shall be my people
> And your God my God.
> Where you die I shall die
> And there I shall be buried.
> The Lord do his worst to me
> If anything but death part us.

This paradigmatic instance of true-love poetry is a contractual (a "covenanting") utterance (see below), which intends to join the impossible-to-join, the trueing of love: woman to woman, non-Jew to Jew, particular love (sentiment) to general destiny (history). Further, Ruth's poem is embedded in a prose narrative that situates it as a consequence of a particular catastrophic past (originally the creation of the world, but proximately famine and the death of men) to which it supplies a counter-natural outcome as a cause of a symbolic future of abundance and life—the messianic lineage of David and then Christ, which repeats the instituting sequence (life/death/ then life of another kind)—and the cursed providence of which Bourdieu spoke.

Of specific importance for the production of this effect by the true-love poem is that: (a) it is uttered in the wake of a preceding catastrophe (all the men are dead)—signaling a (re)newal like the "modern" world after the catastrophe of the Noachic flood, or the world of history after the catastrophe of Eden, or the world of Eden after the catastrophe of first creation; (b) it represents an autonomous will, since Ruth can have (we are assured) no economic motive: the will that authorizes a system of values precisely because it is without heteronomy; (c) it performs, as I have said, an instituting effect, specifically, the messianic genealogy (House of David, etc.).

This truth of true-love, then, is much like a contract, the free-will plighting of a troth or truth in clear view of the inevitable fact of the difference of interest between free agents. The other state of affairs to this true-love is when "love" (Lucretian, Schopenhauerian) is understood as a will heteronomous to the person, as in Samuel Beckett's "But there it is, either you love or you don't."[11] In a remarkable paper on love, the philosopher Harry Frankfurt observes in the course of his argument in "Autonomy, Necessity, and Love": "There is, I believe, a quite primitive human need to establish and maintain *volitional* unity [of the self]. Any threat to this unity—that is, any threat to the cohesion of the self—tends to alarm a person and to mobilize him for an attempt at 'self-preservation.' . . . The authority love has for us is closely related to this compelling and irreducible need to protect the unity of the self."[12]

But at the conclusion of his essay, Frankfurt remarks: "In any case it is clear that the categorical requirements both of duty and of love are vulnerable to violation and betrayal. As the theoretical necessity of the one [that is, the categorical requirements of duty] cannot ensure that rational agents will be virtuous, so the volitional necessity of the other [that is, the indispensable autonomy of the beloved] cannot ensure that lovers will be true."[13] In other words, the enigma of true-love is seen when we reflect that love, true to its nature, can refer only to intentional and autonomous subjects (as Frankfurt wishes us to understand). Love requires the freedom of the subject, the volitional autonomy of the person. "True-love," in this sense, can be a state or predicate only of a subject, never of an object. And that is one way of stating the perpetual crisis of truth (both of relationship and of representation): the other—world or person—can be neither the same nor the self, which fact in itself ensures that the course of true-love never will run smooth. Hence, "true-love" stands (by reason of the true-love criterion that the true lover be autonomous, a law to herself) in a relation of virtual heresy (or treason) to every actual orthodoxy including its own. Lear says of Cordelia, "So young and so untender." And Cordelia, Lear's *true* lover—whose true-love intention, being free, has no already written representation ("Love and be silent")—says, under her breath, "So young, my Lord, and true."

The *true-love*, then, that is our concern is the *free* judgment of subject (or self-)consciousness as it identifies and intends an object. True-love is the boast of the adulterer, the martyr, also the assassin.

V. Shall There Be No More True-Love? The Walsingham Ballad: "As You Came from the Holy Land"

All representations of true-love are interrogative because true-love arises at crises of social knowledge (cf. Plotinus, cited above), which ironically specify the difference between heresy and orthodoxy (i.e., between the truth of the particular and the truth of the general, child and parent, knowing and not knowing)—difference that always involves a betrayal. One such *histori-cal* crisis was the English Reformation to which twentieth-century poetic modernism owes the structure of its discourse—consciousness as revision (cf. "repentance" in Crane's "Legend") and the de-commodification of the highest value. The authority of true-love, as of poetry, is always (as the example of Ruth brings to mind) a generative contingency—both origin and consequent presence—of institutions that true-love founds and that then bear it as an alien logic across time. (Indeed, it cannot be stressed too emphatically that neither love nor poetry are, strictly speaking, institutions.) *Institutions such as church, state, nature, law, two-factored logic, et cetera, supply the historical object of value that true-love (subject) consciousness intends.*

In England the Reformation of the sixteenth century problematized such objects or signs of value (the Eucharist being the sign of signs, Faustus's Helen being the secular correlative) by unfixing the institutions that specify, validate, lend the bearer of value its presence, regulate access to it and participation. Yet it is such objects (sacrament, god-term, image, and artifact) that permit satisfaction of "that quite primitive human need" to maintain the volitional unity of the self of which one name is "true-love" and of which one actualization is the poem.

The complexity of *true-love* in the early modern period is clearly articulated in the familiar sixteenth-century poem "As You Came from the Holy Land of Walsingham," a composite of traditional folk ballad elements and Elizabethan additions sometimes attributed to Sir Walter Raleigh. The poem is a dialogue between an old man, a true lover (cf. Hermia, "Too old to be engaged to young"), and a returning pilgrim. The old man's true-love object has been lost on the pilgrim way—as one might say, between particular or personal experience (the "quick bright things") and general or impersonal experience. The pilgrimage direction is from the particular to general and its motive epistemologically aggregative (all pilgrims to the same shrine come to know the same thing.) The *old* man (age here, as in the Shakespearean sonnet, signifies captivity to contingency—time—which renders the aging body incapable of practicing or conferring the true-love requirement of autonomy) first inquires of a returning pilgrim whether he has met his true-love. The pilgrim asks the old man for an identifying feature of his true-love. The old man gives a description in exalted terms so general that a reader suspects that no response to his question could ever serve to identify any particular person. The "truth" (*Gleichheit*) put in play by the true-love term is a self-identity inconsistent with classification, therefore recognition, *and also with mimesis, depiction in words.* Insofar as truth is correctness of representation, an old man being without power is without truth. Thus Heidegger on Nietzsche:

> The essential definition of truth that since Plato and Aristotle dominates not only the whole of Western thought but the history of Western man in general down to his everyday doings and ordinary opinions and representations runs, briefly: Truth is correctness of representation. . . . Representing adjusts itself to beings, assimilates itself to them. . . .[14]

"As You Came from the Holy Land," having begun with a question about the existence of a particular person, ends with a figure expository of true-love that makes inevitable the conclusion that *true-love has no actual form* and that it can exist only in the subject's (the lover's) willed persistence in projections of self-identity inconsistent with depiction. In the words of the primary speaker [A], "None hath her form divine / On the earth, in the air." Although the responding speaker [B] confirms a meeting with an unnamed "angel-like" beauty, she remains always lost, out of reach. The old man has at the end abandoned the hope of any personal finding in the other. Even so, "love it is a durable fire / In the mind ever burning. . . . / From itself never turning."

[A] As you came from the holy land
         Of Walsingham,
      Met you not with my true love
         By the way as you came?

[B] How should I know your true love
         That have met many a one
      As I came from the holy land,
         That have come, that have gone?

[A] She is neither white nor brown,
         But as the heavens fair;
      There is none hath her form divine
         On the earth, in the air.

[B] Such a one did I meet, good sir,
         With angel-like face,
      Who like a nymph, like a queen, did appear
         In her gait, in her grace.

[A] She hath left me here alone
    All alone, as unknown,
  Who sometime loved me as her life,
    And called me her own

[B] What is the cause she hath left thee alone
    And a new way doth take,
  That sometime did love thee as herself,
    And her joy did thee make?

[A] I have loved her all my youth,
    But now am old as you see:
  Love likes not the fallen fruit
    Nor the withered tree.

[A] For love is a careless child,
    And forgets promise past:
  He is blind, he is deaf when he list,
    And in faith never fast.

[A] His desire is fickle found,
    And a trustless joy;
  He is won with a world of despair,
    And is lost with a toy.

[A?] Such is the love of womenkind,
    Or the word love abused,
  Under which many childish desires
    And conceits are excused.

[A] But love it is a durable fire,
    In the mind ever burning,
  Never sick, never dead, never cold,
    From itself never turning.[15]

    Walsingham in Norfolk was, before the Reformation, a pilgrimage desti-
nation devoted to the Virgin Mary and a devotion of particular importance
to women. In 1538 (sixteen years before Raleigh was born) Walsingham
priory was ruined by iconoclastic Protestants who meticulously hacked
off the sculpted faces of imaginary persons representing the sacraments,

especially the sacrament of marriage, leaving those faces unrecognizable as faces or, in the words of the poem, "unknown." Such defacement did not, however, stop the pilgrimage of women to the shrine (cf. Eamon Duffy, *The Stripping of the Altars*[16]). We have a doggerel lament—remembered by Shakespeare, Wordsworth, Blake, Robert Lowell, and many others—which gives an account of the destruction of Walsingham. Doggerel is that style of poetic writing that signifies the unavailability of high-cultural consent. "The Arundel Ballad" reads, in part:

> In the wracks of Walsingham
> Whom should I chuse,
> But the Queen of Walsingham
> To be guide to my muse?
> . . . .
> Bitter was it, O, to viewe
> The sacred vyne
> (Whiles the gardeners plaied all close)
> Rooted up by the swine.
>
> Bitter, bitter, O, to behould
> The grasse to grow
> Where the walles of Walsingham
> So stately did shewe.
> . . . .
> Oules do scrike where the sweetest himnes
> Lately weare songe;
> Toades and serpents hold their dennes
> Where the palmers did throng. . . .

The chronological succession of these two texts is as follows: *first*, the "Lament" for Walsingham destroyed, the older poem, and *then* the Walsingham ballad first printed in 1593, though representing a historically earlier time when Walsingham was still standing.

The true-love narrative (true-love is a late-time concept) presented in the ballad text is constituted of the ratio of terms I have been describing, a subsequent generalization validated by reference to a prior (catastrophic) text. This sequence constructs a kind of authority that functions very like proverbial authority as in Lysander's proverb-like line: "The course of true-love never did run smooth." True-love (the intentional case of love that knows both the general and the particular life) is a virtual state of affairs always discovered, on the basis of prior text or experience, to be always already canceled as actuality ("The course of true-love *never* did run smooth").

Hence, we see once again, that the true-love term is here, as always, an allusion to an originary narrative, catastrophic in theme, of which the "Lament for Walsingham" is an example, or the martyrdom of a saint, or the death of the messiah, or the creation of the world. More precisely, true-love is an allusion to the intersection of two narratives—the love narrative of unqualified relationship (having no actual life except destruction or conflagration) and the truth narrative (truth that supplies the story) of qualified but possible life requiring patience, as the poetic imagination requires patience, because it is always a deferral of the truth or the real—*which at the same time it brings to mind.* First, the validating story is always a narrative of catastrophic loss (the phoenix immolation)—martyrdom. Second, the cult, the human world, is instituted as a consequence precisely of the loss of (the unqualified form of) everything. The sacrifice of the whole serves to obtain, in human scale, the use of the part. (Cf. Julia Lupton, *Afterlives of the Saints*: the hagiographic death story of the saint institutes the narrative structure of literary text.[17])

Two conclusions should be noted at this point: (a) Not two flames but one flame. The flame of the martyr (as represented in *Foxe's Book of Martyrs*, with its almost unendurable limnings of the death by fire of the heretic Protestant who chooses horrifying suffering because it is an instituting act entailed by true-love) and the consuming flame of the phoenix (which institutes the cult of the true and fair) *are the same flame.* Each bears witness to the freedom of the self ("durable fire"), which cannot tolerate the freedom of the other (hence the true-love inevitability of religious tyranny or heresy, and likewise the inevitability of coercion or unfaithfulness), and also bears witness to the logical necessity of that freedom. And (b) the poetic account (fundamentally the phoenix riddle, the "domain of representation") is a contingency of that well-functioning original that destroys itself without survivor and is only recovered by the successor (a spectator, not a participant): the reader who believes. (Cf. Hans Blumenberg's posthumous lecture, recently translated, *Shipwreck with Spectator.*[18])

But sacrifice is the master story inside representation—both thematized and theorized by poems. The question whether poetry as representation is—in the light of this state of affairs—defensible or indefensible is the question posed to judgment by poetry itself in the twentieth century. The strong poetry of the century says to me: Find another master story of representation than the sacrificial story—or there shall be no more true-love.

The central sixteenth-century poetic-theoretical text presenting this matter is Shakespeare's "Phoenix and the Turtle." It announces the ordering of the obsequy for true lovers, from whose ashes is articulated by appalled and prudent Reason (the representative of the poetic principle) the cult of the vanished unqualified form of relationship ("Death is now the Phoenix nest") to which cult, in postures of prayer, come the fair and true (human postures—for prayer is the gesture that confesses the contingency of the will, a truth not absolutely free and fair, a love not absolutely autonomous).

> Truth may seem, but cannot be;
> Beauty brag, but 'tis not she;
> Truth and Beauty buried be.

> To this urn let those repair
> That are either true or fair;
> For these dead birds sigh a prayer.

VI. Canonization

As a final illustration, let me introduce a Reformation poem everybody knows—Donne's "The Canonization"—which narrates the (re)institution of possible life after a reorganization of value from the domain of public visibility (the prior generality like Catholicism) to the yet unfigured domain of privacy, which stands precisely for that autonomy (including exemption from history) both of the self and also of the ethical subject, the dangerous problematicity that true-love posits. (One must note that Donne's poem—foundational for modernism—extended its instituting force into the twentieth century and became a pattern for the realization of situated presence in the poetry of my time.) In the "The Canonization," the unspeakable heresy of erotic privacy (the extinction but also the origin of the poetic subject) produces, beyond the martyr's funeral urn, the well-wrought urn of the (New Critical) word-artifact (reliquary of the subject burned alive), a hypothetically re-productive form of representation: the "pattern"—which is ethically powerful because of its difference from possible life.

Donne's word "pattern"—"beg from above / A pattern of your love"—exemplifies the instituting force of loss and expands somewhat the word *canonization*—in his sense: the authorization or validation of a person or an action as an ideal general model of a person or an action of another kind. Donne's speaker (the lecturer who says "For God's sake hold your tongue . . .") offers us a rant on the innocence of love, the inevitably totalizing (or enveloping) force of which is inscribed at the end of the first and last lines both of the poem and of each stanza. But the lecturer in the poem, as you will notice, concedes the persistence of incurable injuries in the public world juxtaposed with this performance of subjective autonomy, that is, "love." As recompense for the transgressive love that's unfit for the public world, he offers a solution from which he is absent like an author from his work. His practice, however, is instantiated in a *possible* form—as the *pattern of the literary culture*: that cult of the dead, the institution of which is the action of the poem.

THE CANONIZATION

For God's sake hold your tongue, and let me love,
    Or chide my palsy, or my gout,
    My five grey hairs, or ruined fortune flout,
With wealth your state, your mind with Arts improve,
    Take you a course, get you a place,
    Observe his Honour, or his Grace,
Or the King's real, or his stamped face
    Contemplate; what you will, approve,
    So you will let me love.

Alas, alas, who's injured by my love?
    What merchant's ships have my sighs drowned?
    Who says my tears have overflowed his ground?
When did my colds a forward spring remove?
    When did the heats which my veins fill
    Add one more to the plaguy bill?
Soldiers finde wars, and lawyers find out still
    Litigious men, which quarrels move,
    Though she and I do love.

Call us what you will, we are made such by love;
    Call her one, me another fly
    We are tapers too, and at our own cost die,
And we in us find the eagle and the dove,
    The phoenix riddle hath more wit
    By us; we two being one, are it.
So to one neutral thing both sexes fit,
    We die and rise the same, and prove
    Mysterious by this love.

We can die by it, if not live by love,
    And if unfit for tombes and hearse
    Our legend be, it will be fit for verse;
And if no piece of chronicle we prove,
    We'll build in sonnets pretty rooms;
    As well a well-wrought urn becomes
The greatest ashes, as half-acre tombs,
    And by these hymns, all shall approve
    Us *Canonized* for Love.

And thus invoke us; "You whom reverend love
    Made one another's hermitage;
    You, to whom love was peace, that now is rage,
Who did the whole world's soul contract, and drove
    Into the glasses of your eyes
    (So made such mirrors, and such spies,
That they did all to you epitomize),
    Countries, towns, courts: Beg from above
    A pattern of your love."[19]

VII. Two Genealogies

At the beginning of this true-love discourse, I observed that the word *love*, wherever it occurs and in many different ways, accounts for the possibility of relationship among persons, and that therefore the motive to understand the true or right form of love is profoundly reasonable and fundamentally a poetic concern. It should further be noted, for it is fundamental to an understanding of the poetry of the twentieth century, that the defenders of poetry generally, the Aristotles and Shelleys (and also its attackers, the Platos and Peacocks), *do not confine the meaning of the term* poetry *to the textual poem*, which Shelley calls "poetry in the restricted sense." Indeed, poetry for Plato, Aristotle, Horace, Longinus, Whitman, seems to include all discourse about conjunctive relations: all theory of how the elements of social formation—that is to say, persons—fit together. But poetics as the theory of how persons fit together in social formations must encounter the durable but murderously problematic flame of the true-love relationship, which is ironically "from itself never turning."

The "true-love" I am studying has two genealogies, one demotic (the love knot, like a four-leaf clover, that everybody in the sixteenth century knew how to tie), and the other an esoteric transformation of the true-love knot, commonly figured as the Seal of Solomon (pentangle). The first stems from Anglo-Saxon feudality. "True-love" is a Germanic expression (as still in *der Liebesknoten*). This true-love (AS *treowlufu*) implies in the first instance the *truth/troth of contract* (both social and cosmic on the *cosmos/polis gleichnis*) respecting the relationship of persons whether in the Homeric *hero/hetairos* dyad or the Aristotelian ethical/economic—as we see in Sidney: "My true-love has my heart and I have his, / A just exchange. . . ." This contract between unlike parties *stipulating likeness* (the logic of power within power) bears, like biblical covenant, upon the fundamental intelligibility of the world as personal other. We hear it in default as a true-love demand for autonomous reconstruction in Arnold's belated "Dover Beach":

> Ah love, let us be true to one another. . . .

And in the bitterly ironic voice of subaltern *ressentiment* in Keats's "La Belle Dame sans Merci."

> And sure in language strange she said
> I love thee true. . . .

The autonomy of the other (her freedom) is rewritten as uncertainty about the intelligibility of the world as ordered. The lament for the dead of the feudal *comitatus* (true-love as the fanatic loyalty of the warrior band to an vanished master or an untimely cause) is heard in the cry of Yeats's speaker as he (re-)inscribes the well-wrought urn of the insurrectionist dead of Easter 1916 as true-love martyrs:

> What if excess of love
> Bewildered them till they died?
> I write it out in a verse. . . .

The instituting act—the artisanal boast of the poet, perpetualization—illustrates the Horatian logic in which human value is produced by human sacrifice—no middle term.

The second genealogy of the true-love I am studying (the Seal of Solomon, esoteric version of the true-love knot that anyone could tie) implies the love of truth (objective genitive as in *philosophia*), not Germanic but Greco-Roman, indeed Platonic—as Foucault found it (*The Use of Pleasure*, part 5, "True Love"[20]), intending not the sufficient conditions of contract, but cognitive/amative unity with the real, that is to say, *knowledge*. Ontological in claim, it appears in the thick substantial (hypostatic) personifications such as the Amor of Dante's *Vita Nuova* who says, "Ego dominus tuus," or the Love of Herbert's "Love bade me welcome," or Crashaw's "Love thou art absolute sole lord." As is the case with any post-Platonic ideal fidelity, the loss, lamented upon the institution of this representation, is nothing less than the totality of the actual world. (Both Dante's text and Herbert's explicitly claim typological identity with the biblical book of Lamentations). In both cases, the production of value is a dependency of the sacrificial model.

VIII. Is There Another—A Third Model?

Whatever requirement of mind or world it is that drives perpetual recourse to the true-love model (the sacrificial) must lie very deep. Pilgrimage, as we have observed with respect to the Walsingham ballad, is the intentional search for meaningful general experience. The account of the search for the true-love includes interrogation of a third party—you cannot go for yourself—*because in language the road back from constructed generality* (everyone who bears the logos of the shrine may be said to know the same thing) *never ends quite here—in this self.*

Is there is no help for it?

It is evident that poetry shares with all speech that is language-like an incompetence with respect to consummatory states of experience. *All indicators of temporality—including the present tense—signify distance from the origin of experience.* Insofar as true-love imports a simultaneity (consistent with predication), it appears to intend a violation of what appears to be the logic of signification by language. As evidence of this, consider the following very simple observation: there are many poems of *not yet having* (petitional poems, as it were, or poems of seduction), and there are also poems (though proportionally to the first type many fewer) of *having had* (doxological poems as it were, e.g., the aubade). But there are no poems (certainly no Western poems) situated upon the zero point of *having*, of *union just so*. At that moment, the coincidence of consciousness and experience, language disappears and with it representation as depiction—for the same reasons, no doubt, that there are no private languages nor for that matter perfectly public languages. True-love like incest (as incest) is universally forbidden (e.g., the primal scene of Oedipus with Jocasta.) On the inevitability of this state of affairs, and the necessity of acknowledging it as such, the value of poetry rests on its power of deferral; and one name for value of that kind is "true-love"—that "durable fire" as the author of the Walsingham ballad has it—durable but not consummatory.

Poetry, like language itself, does not reach to the real. Prudence (an accurate understanding, a fundamental realism, with respect to the relation between the moral interest and the systematic requirements of representation) dictates that it must not do this, and indeed linguistic structure prevents it. The imperatives therefore of love (both to the search for true-love experience and its deferral) confront the poet with complex requirements of contradictory kinds—the fundamental transgressive logic that finds the figure of the poet's work (definitive of its structure—true-love) in problematic relation to any outcome that can be rationally chosen in the light of any defensible meaning of love or of truth.

There is required a willingness (the historical province of religion and philosophy) to ask questions not just about the comparative value of particular representations (this poem or that poem—good or bad), as we do, but about the value (the goodness or badness) of representation itself, the class of things (representation) to which poems belong—*as distinguished from representation's other, which is the moral real.* If there is no account of representation that does not yield the sacrificial model, then the project of representation—the poetic vocation itself—must be reconsidered. But the identification of poetry with representation as such may be a mistake (a misunderstanding of Plato's objection), as I think certain master poets of this century concluded—in particular Yeats, Rilke, and Stevens. Their example seems to me to require not a reconsideration of the poetic vocation (which is not in question) but of the nature of poetic means, which it is the poet's business to judge.

You will remember also Ophelia—a true lover—who in her grief asks first:

> Where is the beauteous majesty of Denmark?

and then sings,

> How shall I your true love know
> From another one? (*Hamlet* IV.iv)

IX. The Question of Truth and the Ancient Quarrel

As I observed at the outset, the Platonic imagination of the ancient quarrel seems to me a struggle for authority. The claim I wish to make is that the structures in which poetry is realized as poems are authoritative, and recognized as such by philosophers (hence the "quarrel") precisely because they preserve *and affirm* logically contradictory propositions, by contrast to the structures in which philosophy is realized as text subject to the constraints of a logic (the Aristotelian Laws of Thought) known to be necessary but without truth. Nietzsche is a guide, although not entirely consistent from the poetic point of view. I have already cited above Nietzsche's distinction between truth and what *must* (in the interests of peace of mind and the orderly conduct of life) be thought to be the case. Consider also *The Will to Power* #516, which begins: "We are unable to affirm and to deny one and the same thing. This is a subjective empirical law, not the expression of any 'necessity' but only of an inability."[21] To this inability—rewritten as power of a kind—the citation from Simone Weil speaks (see above), and the preference for a "bright logic," the instance from Hart Crane, attests.

In this light, the poet's authority is superior to the philosopher's precisely because the poet can assign significance to a larger range of experience than can the philosopher. The will to power is a way of pointing to highest value, and the name of that value in the twentieth century is existence. The advantage of poetic authority is the poet's confidence with respect to appearances (Stevens's *confiance au monde*) or the existence of what is seen to exist. This primacy of existence-experience (a revaluation or transvaluating—*Umwertung*—of the phenomenal by contrast to noumenal) also constituted the authority of patristic theology as represented by Thomas Aquinas in the twelfth century and was contributed from that source to Heidegger (educated as a Catholic) and thence to Sartre. Étienne Gilson says this, of Thomas's position: "The actual existence of a thing is that which causes it to be, and since apart from actual existence an essence is nothing, the act in virtue of which a thing is, or exists, is the supreme act of that thing. In Thomas's own words, it is the perfection of all perfections [*Summa Theologiae* I.8.1, etc.]. . . . The uniqueness of this property of being already points out its particular affinity with God."[22] Neither Kant nor Hegel, nor for that matter Quine, regards the principle of contradiction as other than conventional. But it is the poet whose art consists of labor subject to the resistance of the reality that Aristotelian Laws of Thought cover over. It is for this reason that I call attention to the poetic text as authoritative by reason of a superior realism that might well be called (borrowing a term of Thomas Nagel) normative realism. *Realism* because the poetic principle restates appearance, confident that there is something real that is like what is experienced. *Normative* because the poem is always built upon a double system of signifiers. To put it another way, the poem is always a discourse of one kind (existence discourse) about or intending and deferring a discourse of another kind (a true-love discourse). Plato tells the story about Socrates—the true lover—just as Homer tells the story about Achilleus—the true lover. Wordsworth's narrator hears the singing of the solitary reaper—the true-love song—and passes on, protesting no understanding. Keats's narrator hears the nightingale and refuses or defers the true-love estate. All poems are of this sort. The poem shows and validates both systems—one system of signifiers displays, as in a theater, another—without reciprocal cancelation, as is the case with the theologies and philosophies of the West.

The moral order of the actual language of a poem commits the reader to this double system as well: the textual poem and its reader must be constrained by the communicative ethic that governs intersubjectivity mediated by language. What is remitted in return for the discipline of the poem—the deferral of consummatory states—is another *askesis* to which the poem gives access—a tragic system, I think, which colors passion with the sense of irrevocable loss. A good poem presents this second system in a frame that defers its actuality.

The authority of the tragic—the true-love—passion is finally the gift of the poem to the conscious world. The world, in return, must know enough to know that the poem is an occasion of thought without alternative, and hold the poet to his work.

Why Is Death in Arcadia?

POETIC PROCESS, LITERARY HUMANISM,
AND THE EXAMPLE OF PASTORAL

Therefore, "I am original" means "I am mortal."

Jacques Derrida

Death is the mother of beauty, mystical,
Within whose burning bosom we devise
Our earthly mothers waiting, sleeplessly.

Wallace Stevens

And so it was I entered the broken world. . . .

Hart Crane

On the one hand, we feel You—John the hero—must live, or I shall be in the
depths of despair. On the other, we feel, Alas, John, you must die,
because the shape of the book requires it.

Virginia Woolf

Et in Arcadia ego.

I. What Kind of Knowledge Is Literary Knowledge?

The question with which I here experiment is simply stated: What sort
of witness to history and experience is art? A great part of literary culture
occupies itself with restating the testimony of literary works for various
purposes (on the authority of author N—we say that the world is a state of
affairs of a given kind); but can we say with clarity what sort of testimony
literary testimony is? With respect to what human state of affairs are works
of art witnesses? What is the nature of their report, and on the basis of
what authority does the vast and morally confident culture of statement
derived from the literary text found its truth?

The older answers to these questions are on the whole honorific. For
the sake of brevity, an elegant passage from I. A. Richards's *Principles of Lit-*
erary Criticism—a passage from 1928 that promulgates as a universal social

*"Why Is Death in Arcadia? Poetic Process, Literary Humanism, and the Example
of Pastoral" was originally published in *Western Humanities Review* 41 (Summer 1987):
152–88.

benefit the singular, and I think obscure, moral privilege that theorists from Aristotle through Longinus, Sidney, Vico, Coleridge, Schopenhauer, and Arnold assign to poetry—must stand for many others:

> We pass as a rule from a chaotic to a better organized state by ways which we know nothing about. Typically through the influence of other minds. Literature and the arts are the chief means by which these influences are diffused. It should be unnecessary to insist upon the degree to which high civilization, in other words, free, varied and unwasteful life, depends upon them in a numerous society.[1]

That literature is a means of influence of some minds upon one another in society, and that it forms part of what is called "high civilization," is unnecessary to dispute; but that such civilization and its mediations tend to facilitate "free, varied, and unwasteful life" in our "numerous society" is quite properly put in question since the time of Richards. It is the purpose here to show that in order to seek, with any probability of success, a good outcome for literature and literary studies, we must give renewed attention to the constraints upon meaning inherent in literary representations, by reason of their nature *as* representations.

The analysis here dwells upon what may already be a commonplace apprehension in the mind of the experienced reader—namely, that there is a specialization of the presented subject matter of literature (in this essay, for the sake of example, mostly poems of a certain kind), which arises as a consequence of the conditions under which things in the world become *representable* in literature, and perhaps by implication *representable at all*. My point, which I can hope to press only a shade beyond tautology, is that the world to which literature attests (and about which we speak when we make reference to the literary account) is not *the world at large* but just that state of the world that is susceptible to representation, and that the "meanings" of literature may in fact bear exclusively on the question "What must the world be like when we represent it?"—and not at all, or only indirectly, on the vast residual question "What is the world?"

The tendency of my analysis is toward a reconsideration of our knowledge that, prior to the constraints upon meaning that arise when literature is viewed as bound to situations and mortal interests such as Marx, or Freud, or Mannheim define, there is an intrinsic system, a "grid of rationality" (to borrow William Ivins's phrase)[2] inherent in the poetics of image construction, in the light of which the question of literature as a basis for advocacy or indeed world-construction of any sort, must be reconsidered.

My subject, then, is a branch of poetics—poetics regarded *not*, as is now common, as a guide for the making of texts (or the sorting of them), but as a part of the hermeneutic issue: the hermeneutics not of textual reference but of *text itself* as it attests reflexively to its own constructive processes, and its economic relationships to other forces operating in the world. This is of course to repeat a suspicion as ancient as the honor of poetry—a suspicion I shall attempt to deepen—that the medium of representation, which depends for its validation on the appearance of transparency, is at best highly colored, indeed tendentiously self-insistent and ideological, in unsuspected ways.

II. Representation as Post-Catastrophic

Plato thought poetry to be a repetition of those epistemological concessions that turn life into death, by contrast with philosophy, which he thought to be a means of turning that death into life again through the undoing, a dialectical "de-creation," of the prior negative displacement of the "viewless" idea into incarnate and therefore manifest existence. From another point of view, Barbara Smith has called attention to the implicit closural constraints upon representation that produce, in the modally characteristic way in which the structures of poetry become explicit in poetry as meanings, references to death as one sort of closural allusion.[3] And we find in Frank Kermode's analysis of the meaning of fictional estate, *The Sense of an Ending*, an account of closure as a "concord fiction. . . . A fiction designed to relate events that appear to be discrete and humanly inexplicable to an acceptable human pattern"—that pattern being death—"a matter of images, figures for what does not exist except humanly."[4] Kermode's analysis repeats the well-known doctrine of E. H. Gombrich. His dictum "no innocent eye" implies that representation is postlapsarian (after the Fall that brought death into the world) and even post-catastrophic, because the catastrophe of creation establishes that bondage of the will both of God and man, which is (as we shall see) the sufficient condition of narratability (the heart of representation) and which is ended only at the end of the world—the resurrection that concludes nature, death, history, and narration at a stroke.

In view of these and other analytic accounts, both ancient and modern—which suggest that *poiesis* produces the subject matter of mortality as an account of its own process, that indeed the first stage in the production of immortality, the traditional function of poetry, is the production of *mortality*—I turn to the specific issue of death in art.

III. Death as Artifactual

Neither in fictions nor experience are death and birth symmetrical events. In the Western system of representation, birth is both divine and natural; but death is human and artifactual. Birth or its hindrance (as in the Hebrew Bible) is a judgment upon another; but death (as in Dante) is a judgment upon the self. God created the world and man; but man "brought death into the world." When I speak, in ordinary parlance, of "my birth," I am referring to something that, as an expression of *my* will, is impossible and as an inference from *my* existence is both preempted and inevitable; but "my death" is a possible, counter-natural, constructible, prospective part of the project in which the self is *causa sui*—the test of the will, a goad to action, and expressive means, an occasion of self-realization, and a cause of art.[5] Birth is a fact, or alternatively the fiction of another; but death is a fiction in which I participate, my making, an instance of fiction as such. "Man has created death."

I do not wish to argue (nor did Yeats, the author of that last quoted statement) that death is man's creation—this would be to presume more than I know about "the vast residual question"—but I do wish to argue that death, as man is situated, is *in* man's creations (including consciousness itself) for reasons related to their nature as creations; and that the idea (or ideology) of mortality is identical with the fiction of order, which, as we saw in the citation from Richards, is a chief meaning of the order of words in fictions.

The first part of my exposition is theoretical. It offers a provisional theory of representation, or of manifestation—for it is manifestation as the outer skin of representation that is the region of concern—in terms of a possible set of constitutive rules of the manifestational process.[6] In the latter part of this essay, I offer as an extended example the pastoral and elegiac kind of poetry, because in the topography of pastoral in Arcadia, which is a continuing metonymy of the culture of representation, the etiology of death is an explicit—and as I think, inevitable—subject, offering itself for study.

In his well-known article of 1936, Erwin Panofsky acquainted us with the meaning of the expression *"Et in Arcadia ego."*[7] There remains for the theorist the subsequent question *"Cur in Arcadia Mors?"*

Like the greater literary kinds—Scripture, the Christian epic, and tragedy—pastoral and elegy are etiologies of death, histories of the coming of death, histories that address but do not settle questions of cause. The obscure theological dramas of Eden—the death-histories—that pastoral *repeats* give rise to an endless culture of justification, but are really unexplained (the unfolding of the etiology is, as it seems, internally preempted) since the explanations must disappear into the paradox of that first human use of freedom, which, having been granted one deathless world, creates another in which there is death. A paradox that is identical with the general paradox of art—indeed of all human self-presence—where the fact of being free is abolished in the urgency of being present, and regretted forever as the hidden subject of the death-fiction or image-life thus founded. In elegy we know even less than in Eden why, for example, Milton's Lycidas, Shelley's Adonais, Whitman's Lincoln, Yeats's Robert Gregory—or for that matter Melville's Bartleby, James's Milly Theale, and Woolf's Mrs. Ramsay—must die. What we know is that in the archetypal fictional space—the emanation of their will that somehow expels them—they died.

My argument will tend to show that, just insofar as Arcadia is a fictional place (not the landlocked, stony region, historically notable for its asses), death will be found because the fictional process generates death, generates it as a by-product of the manifestational life, in view of which it is sought; that fictions in general, not merely the Bible or *Paradise Lost*, are indeed etiologies or histories of death; and that they are so because they are *also* accounts of the process of their own production. Mortality is born twice out of immortality, once from the everlasting prior life of Eden, and a second time from the immortalizing or redemptive process by which Eden is re-obtained—that is to say, from fiction.

In the fallen world, we know that the will toward growth (described by Richards as recapitulating cosmogenesis: "We pass as a rule from a chaotic to a better organized state by ways we know nothing about") is related antinomically to—is mutually exclusive of—the will to wholeness both in experience and representation. (The more growth, the more loss; the more order, the more breaking.) The final outcome of this antinomy—totality/wholeness—is death, "the last stage of growth." In what Richards calls "high civilization," where, as we know, social privilege is founded in representation both as perquisite and power, the conflict lies between the natural order (wholeness) and the fictional (totality), so that the order of fiction—born as it were from the conflict of the inscribing will and the natural ground—is the *breaking* of nature inscribed posthumously (and as a consequence) in fiction as its subject.

Only if we can place ourselves at some distance from the customary values of the "high culture" can we ask the question whether this repetition of cultural process inside the apparent inevitability of historical, social, and even natural process is without alternative.

For death in nature and death in representation (the order of the world), though semantically parallel, are in no immediate or necessary sense the same process or accounts of the same process. This is borne out by our customary assumptions about the distinction between art and experience. To promulgate a humanism (which always involves a "high" culture or program of social legitimation) on the basis of the antinomic thematics of poetic construction (that is to say, a *literary* humanism) is to presuppose, and indeed to will, a tragic content for moral life. Either the structure of representation and the life imaged is produced by rules of its own nature, which tend to impose their meaning through the prestige of representation upon history and mind; or, as the following argument will suggest, the structure of representation is produced by the *same rules*, and in the process of the *same enterprise* by which we produce, as manifest, what we know as the common worlds both of things and of selves. In either case, the distance of theory is required to prevent the customary values of the high culture (and indeed the compulsive orientations of the common life) from obscuring the difference between the questions "What appears?" and "What is?" In the difference between these questions lies the true authority of human freedom.

When, as we have done, we raise the question "What kind of knowledge is literary knowledge?" in the form of the question "What kind of witness, and witness to what, is the literary text?" we are seeking to establish literary culture in the context of real knowledge by making it responsive, as explicitly as possible, to the as-yet-unrealized obligations of its own terms—the obligation, such as it may be, of "love" to love, of "freedom" to freedom, of "death" to death.

IV. The Constitutive Rules of Manifestation

The argument for the antinomic meanings of manifestation derives from two hypotheses: (1) That representations take the conditions of their production as a central subject—that they make thematic as content the history of their life as structure. With this hypothesis I see no difficulty, since it is commonly agreed that art—for example, poetry in its endless metrical paronomasias—discourses about its own processes. (Some—like Roman Jakobson—would take this fact to be definitional of artistic by contrast to other forms of discourse.) (2) That the conditions of producing representations (what I here call manifestation—the threshold of the likeness of presence) are such that human value must appear, insofar as it *appears* at all, in binary distributions constituted of sets of negatively complementary terms. What I shall be saying is that the structuralist analyses of narrative into sequences of binary oppositions, for one example, or the Marxist analyses of existing orders in dialectical terms, for another—or for that matter the alchemical *solve et coagula*, or our several modernists' archetype and displacement, or the linguists' competence and performance, or the prosodists' pattern and actualization—are all fundamentally congruent accounts of the inner generative processes of any "real" presented state of affairs.[8] It follows that states of affairs that do not incorporate these complementarities are not capable of being represented: are non-narratable. Such merely virtual worlds are innocent or null *topoi*, the true u-topias, by contrast to those of which an account can be given, which can come to mind as story.

According to this view, there are at least four sets of opposed powers that include in a rough way the central conditions of manifestation, and therefore inhere as meanings in representations of all sorts. These are not, I would add, the "causes" of manifestation. They are merely one way of pointing to its constitutive and sustaining processes: the states of affairs necessary to produce it. Note: It is of great importance to separate the meanings of representation—which are its reasons *for being as it is*—from its causes. For it is at the level not of cause but of meaning, of which these constitutive rules are as it were the scheme, that we really encounter objects in the world; and our adductions of "cause" (again, "the vast residual question") are for the most part meanings that we have attempted, for whatever reason, to take out of the hermeneutic realm.

The four sets of opposed processes to which I refer are: (1A) construction/destruction; (1B) inclusion/exclusion; (2A) symbolic/organic; (2B) narration/participation.

(1A) Construction/destruction (cosmogenesis). All stories about creation are also stories about destruction. The *world that arises* (section VI, below) does so on the ruins of prior states of affairs: Tiamat, Rahav, Yam, Behemot, Canaan, Carthage. The function of the obliterative cosmogenic rhetoric (the prototype of the obliterative political rhetoric associated with Western revolutionary *praxis* from the Bible and Virgil to Milton, and on to Lenin[9]) is to devalue the oppositional element. In consequence, the manifest world is established in a hierarchical relation to that prior state of affairs, which becomes thereby formally unmanifest (that which is without value is unmanifest) but never loses substantial subsistence (like the sea or darkness of the Bible, or the buried Titans of Hesiod). The etiology of the manifest as real is a history of injustice followed by an endless *apologia* (representation or art), the entelechy of which is the ethical devalorization of the injured realm. Death enters the world as an "explanation" (the ideology of mortality) of the constitutive rules of creation, that is to say, as the promulgation and enforcement of the laws by which manifestation is produced. And these laws are exclusionary: "Thou shalt not eat. . . ."

In other words, death is a consequence of conditions internal to the production of text itself. In this sense, death is not irrational. It is an expression, by reason of entailment, of the inherent process of manifestation—that is also to say, of birth. I will argue, therefore, that where the text is the world (in representation, art), as where the world is text (cosmogonic myth, Bible) death arises as a result of the creational process; and that the ethical rationality assigned to death (e.g., the death-etiologies of legislation: "Thou shalt surely die") is really a law of manifestation, a poetics of the distinction and hierarchical ordering of realms.

(1B) Inclusion/exclusion (perception). Cosmogenesis in the Hesiodic, the priestly (biblical), and the Mesopotamian accounts is, as everyone would agree, an etiology of the world as experienced. The particular way in which the world is built up is accountable in these texts in terms of the sufficient conditions of ocular perception—beginning with the establishment of the horizon (the space of ocular perception) and the promulgation of light (the medium of ocular perception). The world is prior to man, the object prior to the subject. Wherever in the subsequent history this heteronomy is conceded, the human person is conserved. ("In His will is our peace.") In biblical history, ocular perception is the repetition of the creative event. All other forms of experience (especially auditory) are sanctioned insofar as they repeat the conditions of ocular experience—and in particular its heteronomy to the perceiver, its subordination of the subject to the suzerainty of the object-as-subject (God). In this way, the priority is asserted of language as legislation or text, eye-recovered, over language as discourse. When Moses climbs the mountain, he is blinded by storm, lest his eye establish an alternative world; and he receives legislation as text. The voice of God (as in Deuteronomy 4), which is received within, is more external to the hearer than the external world—just in proportion as it is, in fact, the principle of that external world in the mind of its Author. In ordinary experience the subordination of the subject to world takes the form of focus, the narrowing of the field from the *Ganzfeld* (the unseeable "image" of the whole), where all is taken in and nothing is perceived, to the bright circle of manifestation (the "totality"), which is constructed through the exclusion of the whole, the prior infinity. Perception is mounted on the ruins of the whole.

In perception, the distinction of realms established through cosmogenesis, perception's myth, is experienced in the form of the mutual exclusiveness of realms—as meaning or depth perception ("profundity") is obtained through the accretion and occlusion of conceptual edges in the eye's recovery of the world.[10] Death or mortality, the "human" version of life, is obtained therefore in exchange for the whole, or is visited upon the perceiver as the functional equivalent of achievement of the whole, of the seeing of all.

By way of illustration of the inclusion/exclusion antinomy, note the functional equivalence as reduction of "immortality" in lyric, death in tragedy, and marriage in comedy. The effort to internalize the whole, which would if consummated defeat the paradoxes of the horizon, is the ultimate (and not actual) Faustian or apocalyptic realization of the *lyric*. In lyric, the world flows from the "I" without that preliminary willed concession ("Sing, Muse . . .") that is customary in the epic formulas of invocation and the dramatic convention of *persona*. It is in fact the textual wedding of resonance to *vision* (in John Hollander's terms)[11] that puts the mark of finitude, the eye's horizoning of the I's horizonless claims, upon the lyric excursion. The drama of immortality in lyric is a repetition of cosmogenesis in which the beloved (the lost wholeness) is received as image, after having been expelled from mortal existence as a precondition of the coming-to-be of image-life at all. Similarly, within the dramatic paradigms of comic and tragic, the tendency of plot—the Aristotelian theory of tragic plot, for instance—is toward the reduction of the whole as a repetition and fulfillment of the manifestational criterion of cosmogenetic *praxis*: the tragic hero who claims too much, violating the horizon, always (according to Aristotle) dies. Likewise, comedy ends in the "measured consummations" of marriage, which is fundamentally a pluralizing event over which ceremony casts fiction's apologies of unity. Death in tragedy, marriage in comedy, and immortality in lyric are the notational equivalents of the abrogation of the whole; and the abrogation of the whole is a function of the constitutive rule of manifestation—that negative complementarity of human powers, which takes the perceptual form of the distinction of realms, and which has inside it the tragic implication of the mutual exclusiveness of worlds.

(2A) Symbolic/organic (envalorization). Perception, then—the process (or *dromenon*) of which cosmogenesis is the myth (or *logion*)—is post-catastrophic; and the catastrophe is read back into the subject matter of representation as the death of the whole—the death of the hero where the hero is at the center (paradigmatic tragedy), and the death of the center where the hero is at the periphery (paradigmatic comedy). But the obedience of the subject matter of representation to the conditions of its production as manifestation is repeated in all the dimensions in which manifestation is experienced, and manifestation is inseparable from meaning; or, more precisely, manifestation is being at the point of meaning. Manifestation is the world as it is intelligible, and in intelligibility repeats the process

of perceptibility. *For being in representation does not become meaningful but rather is exchanged for meaning.* The exchange of being for meaning—the process of semantic actualization—as it is thematized in the subject matter of art is perhaps the most familiar moral spectacle of Western representation.

A paradigmatic instance is the death of Socrates, where "death" stands as a notation of the negative complementarity of truth (symbol) and organic life—the point of the exchange of being for meaning. Socrates by choosing death enacts the bitter exclusionary process of symbolization. Socrates, like Jesus, becomes the living word. Obedient to the laws of meaning, both Socrates and Jesus will their own death, the final heteronomy of selfhood as meaning, in the interests of manifestation. Being at the point of meaning is life at the point of death. From a systematic point of view, this can, of course, be seen as a consequence of the fact that the source of meaning is in the unmanifest; and the choice of manifestation constitutes a postponement of life, a separation of life from meaning (an exchange of meaning for life) that entails death. When Jesus chooses to be born, he commits himself to die (as Adam died), or rather to bracket by death and manifestation the continuity of the life as meaning that is *prior* to world, *posterior* to world, and *inconsistent* with world. Manifestation, or world, is brokenness or deferral of meaning. And apocalypse, or the disclosure of secrets, is the breaking of world. Hence, the apocalyptic style makes meaning manifest by bits and orts—the brass, the clay, the wool—of the life it has superseded. Manifestation is not merely the brokenness or deferral of meaning: it is meaning's fiction, the world.

The fictionality with which Plato invested the Socratic discourses (their status as "dialogues") is an extended commentary on the irrationality of manifested life and on the use of manifested life or "fiction" for the postponement of truth. Within that discourse (centrally in the biographical dialogues), we see the paradigmatic version of death in art, the extinction of the natural or organic life for the purpose of validating meaning (martyrdom is death as validating witness) and for the purpose also of binding fiction (and by analogy of the life it represents) *back* into the realm of rationality. Hence, death in art will appear to be irrational from the point of view of the life represented (Socrates need not have died), and rational from the point of view of the life of representation (the death of Socrates validates the meaning of the images of his life). The poetics of this dramaturgy may be called "philosophy," as in the case of Socrates, or "law" in the biblical culture, or "manners" in the novel, or "prosody" in poems. *But it will always respect, as constitutive rules, first of all the mutual exclusiveness of distinguished realms, and then a hierarchy of value in which a mutual exclusiveness of realms will be seen to be stabilized within a vertical system that defers the mutual extinction of the antinomies, and thereby accounts for the stability of the manifest fiction: the world as it is perceived.*

The hierarchy in which the symbolic dominates the organic is expressible in an indefinitely large number of ways (e.g., as sky over earth, form over matter, male over female . . .); but the universality of the structure thus formed constitutes a destiny that bears upon those countless histories, natural and social, in intimate ways, and that compels in its net the major deaths in fiction. Indeed, the representation of human affairs seems founded or covenanted upon this version of order that is, therefore, laden with predictions. Thus at the oath moment near the end of the *Aeneid*, Latinus (repeating *Iliad* I.233ff.) narrates the life of his scepter (the oath stick) and thereby expresses the nature or the covenant of *foedus* with Aeneas promulgated by the oath, the myth of fiction here functioning as central performative:

> ". . . nor shall any force turn aside my will, not though, commingling all in deluge, it plunge land into water and dissolve Heaven into Hell: just as this sceptre"—for by chance in his right hand he held his sceptre— "shall never sprout with light foliage into branch or shade, now that, once hewn in the forest from the lowest stem it is bereft of its mother, and beneath the steel has shed its leaves and twigs. Once a tree, now the craftsman's hand has cased it in fine bronze and given it to the elders of Latium to bear."[12]

The covenanted intelligibility of persons (the established totality, imperium, state) is based on the death of the whole and is as strong and of the same irreversible nature as that death. (Here we see clearly the administration of death, death as the ideology of the irreversible ordering of social process, sanctioned by the apparent authority of natural process.) The manifestation of that covenant takes the shape of the sufficient conditions of social language (hierarchy) promulgating themselves as the necessary form of world order (empire). The living tree has not *become* meaningful; it has been transformed or caught in the *exchange of life for meaning*. Death has entered the Arcadia of Latium as the antinomic dialectic of envalorization or culture.

(2B) Narration/participation (discourse). The fourth antinomy (like the preceding three) points to the exclusion, by the process of manifestation, of wholeness in the space of appearance that is the one human world. As the symbolic/organic antinomy indicates the *myth* of envalorization with its scenario of meaning as the eschatology, or afterlife of organic totality, so

the narration/participation antinomy elucidates the *process* therein represented—the process of discourse as it is characterized by what everyone
will recognize as "the paradox of storytelling."

That discourse is a death is notoriously affirmed whenever the pros-
pect of participatory life is viewed from its domain, as in the love poem—
perhaps in particular the *alba* or *aubade*, the poem of the rediscovery of
the destiny of the self in the vexations of consciousness and difference.
To speak about something is no longer to be a part of it. Narration is posthumous, and the serious person—the agonist—must hate his narrator precisely in proportion as he realizes his bondage to him, a realization that
may—perhaps must—be expressed as more or less compelled love. Like
Dante among the dead, the narrator wanders among the cursing and bless-
ing souls, the derelict reality—his own—upon which the narrator's "point
of view" is founded. Biblical creation, for example, was the beginning of
narrative, the birth of death; while the end of the biblical narrative is the
return of all being into the book—the opened scroll—leading to the dissolution of antinomy, the death of death, and the perfection of the world
beyond story. Don Quixote is the modern prototype of a narrator seeking
to become a participant, and failing. As a narrator he cannot die, for he is
dead; he can only change the nature of the tale so that death overtakes him
in Arcadia. The life of the tale is a contingency of the incompleteness of
the moral will of the narrator—his concession, with whatever tranquillity
or furious reluctance, of the wholeness of his moral will.

Narration, then, implies incompleteness, and narration is a requirement
of manifestation. This final structural entailment of that negative complementarity that is the constitutive rule of manifestation may be described
as a strategy toward continuity through pluralization: in effect a repetition
of creation in the diminishing perspective of discourse—the Seventh Seal
of the text.

In the process of traversing four antinomic distributions as expressions
of the basic rule of negative complementarity that underlies representation, we have produced in an illustrative way: construction/destruction
(cosmogenesis) as a mode of *separation* (1A); inclusion/exclusion (perception) as a mode of the *mutual exclusion of realms* (1B); symbolic/organic (envalorization) as the *hierarchicalization of realms* (2A); and finally narration/
participation (discourse) as the paradox of storytelling or *continuity through
pluralization* (2B). It is, I think, clear that the experimental side of modern
poetic art founds its method squarely upon the last of these, the paradox
of storytelling.

Indeed, nowhere in the stream of texts is a death more clearly a consequence of the constraints of the production of representation than the

world-death of modernism. Where in modernism we find the apparent disappearance of the narrator, it is because the world itself, object and central authenticity of the protagonist, has driven out the narrator in the interests of manifestation. The paradox of storytelling has become a violent principle of world-existence. In the text that has become the narrator of itself, the paradox of storytelling includes the death of the human world. In Yeats—as also in Pound, Eliot, Stein, Joyce, Crane, and Beckett—the world tends toward the merely manifest. What is thematized in the text is the non-participation of the narrator whose place is taken by the process of manifestation itself—the manifest seeking continuity with the ruthlessness not of an individual but a race.

> All things fall and are built again
> And those who build them again are gay.

Literary modernism, in this aspect as in others, exhibits the intensification of an underlying scarcity in existence. Here, the whole state of affairs characterized as negative complementarity and antinomy depends on a fundamental sense of economic conflict within the nature of representation itself, which modernism thematized as central fact. For example, style, the great fetish of modern literary value, flourishes on uniqueness and founders on that synonymity that would allow the innocent multiplication of presences in the space of appearance.[13]

In order to understand the principle that digs out the grave in the Arcadia of traditional art—and the deepening of which "usurps the soil" of modern experimentation like Empson's Chinese tombs—it is necessary to explore more thoroughly the privative economics of poetic construction.

V. Representation and the Economy of Scarcity:
Art and the One World

What I have called the general conditions of manifestation are economic in character. Our four sets of negatively complementary terms yield states of affairs (separation, mutual exclusion, hierarchy, and pluralization), all of which are expressive of an economy of scarcity that drives the whole into fragmentation, in the interest of the will to become manifest—the embittered will toward immortality pitted against mortality, which is paradoxically its own principle of realization. Insofar as humanism (at this point in the argument the assertion can be repeated with a somewhat more articulated weight) founds itself on literature—one class of manifestational instruments serving humanity's stern tropism toward life in the light—

humanism is thereby committed to repetition of the conditions of the economy of scarcity implied in the manifestational process.

One characteristic modernist version of the entailed moralities of poetic process is the grave that Yeats labored all his life to make speak in Arcadia ("Our Arcadia is become Ireland of the four bright seas") and that speaks, when in the end it does speak, the language of the paradox of storytelling: "Cast a cold eye / On life, on death. . . ." Much of postmodern humanism takes its spring, either by aversion or repetition, from this grave-sentence, which may define at once the point at which the motive of art and the motive of all immortality projects intersect, and also the inherent unworkability of art and art processes as a basis for future morality. The question that I have raised—whether the thematization of the art process in representation *need* be promulgated as a thematization of experience by personal, ethical will—seems to be the prior question to all questions about the viability of humanistic values. The moral comes at the end. It establishes the alliance of art with the world ("Absent thee from felicity a while . . ."; "Beauty is truth . . ."; "Cast a cold eye . . .") on the basis of the closural imperative, the need to make an end. It is the text, the grave, the dying man as epistemological witness that speaks. We question not what the text says, for the text says what text has to say; but rather the implications for the nature of the world that flow from the fact that the text says what it says.

To begin with, we must put in question the Romantic aesthetic ideology of art as reconciling and unifying, which obscures the commitment of art to the world as inherently finite, and to its contractile and non-theoretical nature. The repudiation of wholeness in the interest of narration is a major subject of Romantic art and of the histories of auto-fictionalization (lives subjected to the manifestational process as a form of "wisdom"), which come down to us as biographies from the period. As praxis it is repeatedly thematized with deliberated naïveté in the stereotype of the Romantic poetic life as, for example, in Shelley's "Adonais."

The principal deformity of the Romantic *kerygma* lies in the expectation (inherited as a nominal resource from the authentically transcendental economics of evangelical Christianity) that the inner life is non-economic in character—one error at least that the Freudians have corrected. The repeated and compelled realization in the poems themselves of the severe, indeed deadly, divisions within being entailed by the identification of life with the privative dynamics of manifestation ("Die / If thou would'st be with that which thou dost seek") is in marked contrast with the irreality (irreal because univalent) of the status assigned to poetry, when poetry as text is juxtaposed to other cultural institutions (i.e., that poetry is divine, that it redeems, restores justice, reconciles disharmonies, is innocent of the exploitative brutalities of industrialism). No more "extreme situations" exist in representation (outside of the literature of atrocity) than the scenarios of Blake's "prophetic books," which have as their very scheme and subject the constitutive laws of manifestation, the shattering privations of the heroic slave laboring at the human image. Everywhere symbolic life feeds on organic life; and interiority driven by the will toward manifestation as immortality exhibits the human terror of this process.

What we must infer from the Romantic array of manifestational narratives—the Romantic account of image production, which is after all its major thematic presentation—is that justice in art is broken justice, and that the poem as a deed of presence is a death-implicated ethical paradigm. Insofar as *Romantic poetic theory* did not give a truthful account of the Romantic art process, it stands as an as-yet-unassimilated theoretical critique of its own enterprise. Insofar as the *Romantic poem* thematized retrospectively the conditions of its own production, and by implication the production of the manifest world, it correctly noted the antinomic nature of the principles and powers of cultural life—a nature that is produced by the same criterion of unity (that there will be but one world) that is sometimes proposed as the basis of the peace of art.

VI. Actuality as the Principle Both of Scarcity and Artistic Validity

Among all possible things that could happen—the myths, the worlds not "created," the plenitudes undisplaced—the poem, like the person of which it is inferential, is the one actual thing (one of the actual things) that did happen in the situation at hand. The poem is not the unconstrained child of preterition, of the experiential *esprit d'escalier*; nor does it consist of experimental counterfactuals with respect to a given state of affairs (the poetic imagination, that which comes to mind as image, is the defeat of the heterocosmic theoretical intelligence); it is the one thing that could be done. It *is* the one thing that *was* done, and its excellence derives from its retrospective inevitability—its cosmic "fitness." Consequently, poetry is a hostage in the one world where finally and unexchangeably the thing that happens, the very thing, comes to reside.

Actuality, by contrast to possibility, is the principle of scarcity that renders manifestation paradoxical, that drives the powers of the real against one another in negatively complementary relationships and predicts the triumph of structure, the defeat of hope. For, as was earlier stated, another way of reducing the antinomies of manifestation is by stating them in terms of the negative complementarities of structure (the life of the object) against hope (the life of the world):

A. Consciousness   B. Value
or structure   or hope
(cosmogenesis,   (envalorization,
perception,   discourse,
totality)   wholeness)

The precondition of narration is the limitation of the will. Autonomy, as the hypothetical free will of God before creation—the only autonomous will in the Judeo-Christian universe—is not a narratable state. The God prior to the qualification of his will by world has no stories. The perfectly free man would have no history. Man must improvise servitudes in order to be seen. He must create death, as Christ chooses death, in order to have a history. The Christian Bible is in fact the end of the story of the progressive manifestation of God (God's progressive concession to the manifestational constraints)—God as the initially undisplaced power of the imageless whole human hero, doubled in Genesis on his own nature as manifest in man. The final event is the Incarnation, the merging of archetype and displacement on Golgotha, the space of appearance. Christ, as man who has chosen history as story, dies of manifestation (betrayed and opened) in the cause of history. The redemptive monumentality of the Christ story depends on the possibility of the final *delegation of the lethal entailments of manifestation* so that death may finally be shaken out of history as story—*in his will toward death is our peace.*

The redemptive goal of Scripture, and of the Christ-life as living scripture, is the execution of the obligations to death of all history and all persons through the improvisation of a single master story or totalizing act. But the inclusion of *all* story into one story is alien to the nature of the separated consciousness. The existence of art, which the Bible anticipated only as the betrayal of human peace, endlessly reflects the secular destiny of each will toward the birth and death of the individual existence. The brokenness of the will is now as always the precondition of narratability, the triumph of consciousness-as-structure over value-as-hope, or the interminable postponement of wholeness (when the two terms of the antinomy as the lion and the lamb will lie down together). The content of history, which as we shall see is only the thematized struggle to enter history, is overdetermined by the same constraints that qualify all narratability and that seem to underlie *in a theoretically independent way* both history and story, and story (art proper) as repetition—but not necessarily representation—of history.

VII. Manifestation as the Reduction of Ambiguity

The discovery of the dynamics of the anti-theoretical nature of manifestation for our present purposes can be fathered, like so much else, on E. H. Gombrich's *Art and Illusion*, where it is noted that we cannot perceive ambiguity—we can only gather or collect it from discrete occasions of manifestation and perception.[14] The laws of manifestation, and hence of art, are antinomic precisely because we cannot perceive things as this way *or* that. That which is this way *or* that belongs to the general *aporia* of undisplaced theory or myth. Manifestation requires determinate outcome (the slaughter of the innocents). The great primary works of representation are constructed, as we have seen, in such a way as to *thematize the reduction of ambiguity*, as by the rule (in what Nietzsche calls "the Homeric contest") that two must become one in order to produce an image. "Legion" must be cast out. The poem as manifestation, mounting on the ruins of excluded possibility, competes within the horizon of human attention for the one spatiotemporal moment. From the point of view of the relentless economics of manifestation, true ambiguity (Achilleus and Paris alive at the end of the one story) is a mere myth about experience, a *post festum* mentalization having nothing to do with art.

In these respects, the work is like the human body. Wittgenstein remarks: "The human body is the best picture of the human soul."[15] But the soul is a creature of the plurality of metaphysically possible worlds, while the body—a case of representation (a picture), the soul as *manifest*—is bound to the one world. The body is psychophanic, the picture of the soul, and as displacement of the soul, its betrayal. As body, the soul competes for space in the museum of the human world. Like the body, the poem is subject to the law of the one world, as it comes to mind through the eye; and the entailment of that law is scarcity whose human name is death: the destiny of the body. From that law, the appeal to mercy takes the form of strategies of interpretation—the founding of the culture of human value not on bodily presence but on the inference of presence from absence.

1. Interpretation as the Reconstitution of Ambiguity. Here, interpretation in which the plurality of the pre-text is reconstructed ("The innocents," as Yeats says, "relive their death, their wounds open again") functions as the will to life in the realm of death. The identification of the person not with the body but with the soul recovers, by a gesture of beneficent inference, the immortality of the person. The letter kills, and the spirit of hermeneutic friendship gives life. The proper freedom of persons lies in the realm of inference, and the realm of inference is neither constructive nor destructive, but rather deconstructive, not closural but rather anti-closural—taking its stand precisely at the point of the disintegration of literary culture itself—the culture of the self-insistent text—and of the denumerative rationalities of commutative justice.

2. *The Reinterpretation of Origin as Difference, Presence as Absence.* That the ideology of mortality (*Et in Arcadia ego*) is inseparable from the processes of representation, and hence from the subject matter of poetry, is a notion that arises in Derrida, aspects of whose work (anticipated in this matter by William James) intersect our constitutive laws of manifestation at the antinomy of narration/participation.

> My death is structurally necessary to the pronouncing of the I.... The statement "I am alive" is accompanied by my being dead, and its possibility requires the possibility that I be dead; and conversely. This is not an extraordinary tale by Poe, but the ordinary story of language. Earlier we reached the "I am mortal" from the "I am"; here we understand the "I am" out of the "I am dead."[16]

In this connection, Derrida calls attention to the illusional character of the substantial one origin, for which he substitutes the scanning of the trace, or *différance*. Indeed, the illusion of the one origin and the related illusions of the unmediated presence and the nuclear self seem part of that ideology of mortality by which structure or consciousness obtains its dominance over human hope in Romantic poetic theory. The counter-ideology to the ideology of mortality is not immortality, which is its mere reciprocal; but rather an ideology of value and hope for which there is no name, the innominate and non-manifest plenitude that, as Hillis Miller has shown (and Bergson before him), can come to mind only catachrestically like the sun.[17] So long as humanism is literary, is founded on the letter and the merely notational vocalities of the letter as speech, on the culture of absolute origin, its meanings are bound to the catastrophic nature of creation and perception, and to the paradoxical structure-dominated hierarchies of valorization and narration. Neither Eden nor Arcadia, nor the topical space of art in general, is a true image of the repose of hope; they are the space of negative differentiation governed by the economics of scarcity, inseparable from manifestation in the one world.

3. Two Models of the Fate of Arcadia. The evidence for all this is embedded in poetic discourse itself. Arcadia, like fictional world-systems in general, is always encountered at the point of dissolution. This dissolution is a stage in one of two linear processes: Either (a) the devolution of the ideal into history, that is, into the antinomic system; or (b) the evolution of the historical, the antinomic system, toward the ideal or eschatological. Either the birth that follows death (the second death, or Fall), or the death that follows birth (the second birth into the eschatological dissolution of the manifestational paradox). In other words, the point of manifestation of the fictional moment is either the moment of entrance into the antinomic system or the moment of exit outward into the eschatological reals. The two sovereign models in Western discourse for these processes are, first, the Hebrew Bible ending in Kings II (or Chronicles II) and reproduced as prototypical poetic structure in *Paradise Lost*; and second, the Christian Bible ending in Revelation and reproduced as prototypical poetic structure in *The Divine Comedy*.

The second, eschatological, type just mentioned is apocalyptic. It incorporates manifestation as theme in the form of a birth following upon death. (Apocalypse, or the disclosure of secrets, means of course "manifestation" and is conventionally mimetic of manifestation as catastrophe.) In this model the new creation puts an end to the antinomic character of experience by destroying the terms of experience. (In eternity, as Dante reminds us, natural law is of no effect.) In general, this new creation is now understood as the completion of the old creation through the final abolition, or permanent delegitimation, of the Satanic or antithetical element. More concretely, we may say that the terms of manifestation are *analyzed* in the eschaton, and thus suspended. Particularly in the Judaic tradition that yields the doctrine of the bodily resurrection, the antinomic pairs (construction/destruction, inclusion/exclusion, symbolism/organism, narration/participation) cease, as it seems, to be antinomic in the day of the Lord, and become corroborative. The lion lies down with the lamb. *But nowhere in Western representation does this occur in the realm of nature.* (The "day of the Lord" is darkness, the darkness of deconstruction, not of destruction; but it is also not light, which is the signature, as it were, of natural life.) The ideology of mortality precludes the reconciliation of the terms of manifestation within history as story. Consciousness and value, structure and hope, are reconciled only outside of time. No conception of human possibility founded on this idealism can remain secular.

Virgil's Fourth Eclogue, for example, which records the birth of the mysterious child who smiles preternaturally on its mother, portends rather than exemplifies the higher song (*paulo maiora*), which, like the "unexpressive nuptial song" of *Lycidas* and the "new song" (*shir hadash*) of the Bible, has no secular text, indeed no text at all. Simplification is post-catastrophic; and the program of the catastrophe is de-creation. The cosmogenetic antinomy has been resolved through the annihilation of the medium, space and time, in which it worked—the final dominance of structure, symbol, figure—narration, the *word* ("Heaven and earth will pass away, but my word will not pass away"). Dante's vision (for after the simplification of catastrophe comes clarified perception) occurs after almost all the people who will ever be are dead. The difference between the number of places in the white rose and the number of dead is a very small difference, as we are led by St. Bernard to believe. But it is just the difference between the completion of the world system that would bring together value and structure, and by contrast that necessity of returning to history, that pressing apart of the beginning and end (Kermode's tick and tock), which makes literature and history possible, and which both enables and also requires the return of the journeyer to the world of narration and its paradoxes, where he tells his tale.

The eschatological analysis and suspension of the paradoxes of manifestation lead invariably to the question "Why history?" which is the same as the question "Why fiction?" or "Why poetry?" And this question repeats the astonishment of the shepherd in Arcadia that death should be there as well. (One sees the question, recognized as theodicean and in this sense superlatively poignant, in the center of Milton's "On the Morning of Christ's Nativity." The answer is irrational and final: "The wisest judge says no.") But in the eschatological system, as we have noted, everything is dead. The reconciliation of structure and value in the totality is a mere theory about being which reduces being to the terms of manifestation; or to put the matter another way, it is the idealization of the theory of perception—the totalization of all being in terms of that theory, the consummation of antinomies rather than their transcendence.

The alternative secular model, by contrast, interprets immanence as exile. The eschatological model, characterized as just described by post-catastrophic participatory consummation, is transgeneric and almost without instances in the tradition of texts. The immanent and secular model, by contrast, associated earlier with the Hebrew Bible, is vastly productive of texts. It is exilic, lamentational, indeed a discourse-myth. Its narrative is the story about narrative. That is to say, the birth into history, in which the paradox of value and structure (particularly structure as closure—the secular model is pre-closural as the eschatological is post-closural) remains sovereign in its experiential form, thus giving rise to poems. This is the realm of the narrator, the desolate survivor, and also, therefore, a realm of death. It is the realm of the pastoral as Empson defines it: the pastoral that is a false enterprise—inherently a "false surmise"—where the antinomies of narration and participation preclude the completion of the generic premise—the pastoral that is impossible, the grin without the cat. Indeed, when Empson declares pastoral to be impossible, he is rediscovering the tomb in Arcadia, giving reasons for its presence, and wide room for fiction.

For the shepherd's problem remains: the cause of death in representation. Blake labored throughout his work to redeem the human image from the catastrophe of birth as manifestation, which he so deeply understood, being himself a master theorist of the craft processes of representation. The great figure of Los "laboring and weeping" bears the burden of the contradictions until the dissolution of nature (the extreme resolution of the paradox of creation and destruction) releases humanity from the one real world of death. This Christian apocalyptic (or eschatological) model we also find in other familiar Romantic pastoralist poems such as Wordsworth's "She Dwelt among the Untrodden Ways" or "A Slumber Did My Spirit Seal." In these poems death in Arcadia, the shepherd's problem (from which Blake's Thel, as type of the will to wholeness, recoils with consciousness of her woman's role as the delegated sacrifice) is encountered directly as a function of the paradoxes specifically of perception (inclusion/exclusion) and envalorization (symbolic/organic).

> No motion has she now, no force;
>   She neither hears nor sees;
> Rolled round in earth's diurnal course,
>   With rocks, and stones, and trees.

Beyond the antinomies of perception ("She neither hears nor sees"), the beloved has descended the ladder of creation into the earth, where the symbolic has been subsumed or taken back into the organic. Wholeness or value is conserved through (traded against) the loss for her—of that life back into which the speaker is pitched across the threshold of difference ("the difference to me"), which is the finite perceptual horizon. The residual legatee of the hierarchicalization is the text and its (male) custodian and sponsor.

These deaths are "caused" by the *obligation* of the speaker (the notation in narration of a functional necessity in poetic construction) to stay within the paradoxes of narration, and at the same time to make alliances with the culture of hope. No cause of death is stated in these poems (and that is in effect the hermeneutic problem toward which all of these remarks are addressed) because the whole reference of the poem is to the relationship between death and the bitter urgencies of the creative process.

VIII. Death and the Collective

Another way of stating the theme of this essay is that *the subject matter of representation, and consequently of history considered as record, is the struggle to enter history through representation*. The Latin word *fama* means susceptible to description, describable; the Greek word for honor as report, *kleos*, is the same as the word for deed of glory. But the hero obtains fame by the loss of life—and this is true whether the vehicle of representation is considered to be the historical collective, as in Homer, or the transcendental collective, the mind of God—as in the Christian manifestational paradoxes, which trade life lost (organic) to gain life forever (symbolic). Wherever one looks through the window of representation at the landscape of history, one finds the actors in history engaged in deeds of presence under the constitutive rules of manifestation; and these deeds tend to be deeds of blood, murder, or marriage. For what is at stake is presence and absence in the light of acknowledgment, which is to say human life and human death.

Manifestation may be restated as a function of sociability and therefore language. From this point of view, the paradoxes of manifestation can be restated as versions of sociability.[18] Insofar as persons are individuals, they are doomed to the final discontinuity that is an entailment of bodily singularity (note Wittgenstein above, on the textual status of the body as "the best picture of the human soul"). Insofar as persons are assimilated to the species, they obtain continuity but lose individuality. The death that obtains presence as image-life in history destroys the subject consciousness. It is for the separated individuality a form of life that follows on a bitter death indeed. In the death poems of the great image-masters, to die is to pass into the collective; and to pass into the collective is to die. To reexpress the paradoxes of consciousness and value as the paradox of individual and collective is merely to deepen slightly the identification of manifestation with language, and in particular with poetic language as it is both the consummation and surrender of selfhood. Thus Donne:

> Since I am comming to that Holy roome,
>   Where, with thy Quire of Saints for evermore,
> I shall be made thy Musique; As I come
>   I tune the Instrument here at the dore,
> And what I must doe then, thinke here before.

In Donne's construction, the grave inside the representational system is a reminder of the necessary mutual exclusiveness of individuality and continuity that takes, in the social world, the form of crime (negative individuation as the basis of antinomic narration) and justice (the reassertion of narrative in terms of the criterion of continuous collective life), and in the analogous religious world the form of sin and salvation. Antinomic narrative based in crime constitutes the arrogation of narrative for private purposes—the death of the collective. Justice, on the other hand, recovers the narrative privilege for the life of the whole community. Pastoral, with its emphasis on dyadic relationships, tends to experiment with conditions intermediate between being one and being many. Art, as we have said, is not an imitation of these social states of affairs but a repetition of the central manifestation process that is common both to society and art. It is at the outer face of representation that all these processes meet and are restated in the one language of language, which is the social covenant—the form in which the relationships both of men and gods pass from possibility to actuality in the one world. Arcadia is, therefore, both the space of fiction and the space of society—the space of social appearance—where the paradox of individual and collective, of property and freedom, may be rightly said to subsume the array of antinomies by which we have entered the central principles of appearance—fiction and society—as manifestation. More particularly for our argument, we note how deep is the association in Western culture of sin and individuation, on the one hand, and salvation and collectivity, on the other—and each term is a version of death.

Art and freedom remain as continuing problems of presence. Humanity as individual person is visible to other persons and to itself; and humanity as collective person is visible to God, or to others, but not to itself. Yet to be perfectly or merely individual (*individuum ineffabile*) is to cut oneself off from humanity and God (infernal man), and to be merely collective is to be extinct to self, even though one may then live in the light of God and in the undistinguishing sustenance of collective acknowledgment. There is no formulation of the paradox of sociability that does not repeat the negative complementarities of manifestation. *For social persons are humanity manifested.* The problem of art and the problem of freedom are founded on the same conflict between the scarcity of existence in the space of the one world and the relentless demand of humankind for continuity through presence in that space. A person is both individual and collective; yet each term is a claim on the whole horizon of appearance. Under the rules of manifestation, you cannot compose a whole person; you can at best provide a text in which imperial structure arrests immanent value and holds it suspended upon the vanishing point of citation—the dead poet, the dead child, the dead beloved—phantom worlds. Consciousness (the life of the separated individual) and hope (the life of the participatory collective) are co-present, reciprocally generated, and internally uncommunicating states of affairs.

No hero in Western representation down to the eighteenth century fears obliteration. What is feared is the loss of subject consciousness, the consequence of becoming an image to another altogether; or the loss of object status, by becoming an image to oneself and nothing else; or the loss of the subject-object difference in the metamorphosis from singular to plural. Each of these feared states is at once a strategy toward continuity (a version of image-life) and at the same time a death. Each represents the subversion of the quest for immortality by its processes; and each is repeated in the stratified homologies of art and society, which, we contend, align along the axis of manifestation.

IX. The Paradoxes of Sociability and the Pastoral Elegy

Having reexpressed our problem in terms of the social person and the project of entering history, I now carry the argument toward the cultural present, noting briefly the invariance across time of the processes that are my subject. The texts cited are among the most familiar pastoral elegies in English: Milton's *Lycidas*, Shelley's "Adonais," Yeats's "In Memory of Major Robert Gregory," and Stevens's "Sunday Morning."

So far as the Yeats poem is concerned, external documentation informs us that Robert Gregory was shot down in the air war over Italy in 1915. Internal to the poem, however, the cause of death is the antinomic character of manifestation, a reinterpretation of World War I as world construction (as cosmogonic rhetoric) that was common to both Yeats and Pound.

> Some burn damp faggots, others may consume
> The entire combustible world in one small room
> As though dried straw, and if we turn about
> The bare chimney is gone black out
> Because the work had finished in that flare.
> Soldier, scholar, horseman, he,
> As 'twere all life's epitome.
> What made us dream that he could comb grey hair?

Gregory as poet, painter, soldier, statesman, aristocrat, horseman is the archetypal master dwelling at the bitter intersection ("bitter" is Yeats's term

for the inner registration of the paradoxes) of the mutually exclusive powers constitutive both of art and history. He is man caught at the moment of
death, which is the portal to story. Gregory has died because he was whole,
because the conflict between his ideal completeness of nature and the one
real world of life could not be mediated by any concession (any concession would have changed the terms of the conflict) and also because the
paradox of culture, the strange conservational hierarchy placing symbolic
over organic life, is invariable. Perception is mounted on the ruins of the
infinity of the world. Gregory, like the pastoral singer in general, is not so
much perceiver as the world's central object, the world as whole, where
perceiver and perceived are one. And perception is left behind as world and
the world-vestige of art, in the wake of the ruin of this impossible simultaneity of singer and song.

In Yeats's preliminary and specifically Arcadian version of the Gregory
poem ("Shepherd and Goatherd"), we find a formulation of his well-known
visionary system, a manifestational philosophy pitched into consciousness
as response to the grave in Arcadia. Yeats's *A Vision* lays out a systematiza-
tion of the constitutive rules of manifestation in terms of the antinomic
character of image-life. At the full and the dark of the moon, where the
image is complete, there is no life. Wherever there is possible life, there is
some brokenness. Indeed both the first and the last poems of Yeats's care-
fully managed *Collected Poems* repeat the motif of the discovery of the grave
in Arcadia. All his work through *The Wind among the Reeds* seeks to solve the
problem of manifestation by reference to the Christian apocalyptic model,
the breaking of the actual in view of the completion of the self in eschatological space. Thereafter, he devotes himself with such consistence as he is
capable of, to the breaking of the self in view of the conservation of that
world in which manifestation is possible.

In Yeats we see the carrying of the shepherd's problem into the modern
world in its most atavistic form, the prioritization of structure over value
and hope, under the auspices of the authority of art. Also in Yeats we see
the inner sensibility to the cost of art, as in the man for whom, in "The
Grey Rock," to become visible is to die, and to die is to betray the destiny
of the visible. It is important to note that Yeats's politics, which are well
known, are a repetition of the hierarchical imperative—not merely a generalization from art, but a repetition, in the realm of the social order, of the
processes by which art is generated.

Yeats's early master was Shelley. In Shelley's "Adonais," the manifestational reduction by "life" of the undifferentiated whole produces the
perceptible world ("a dome of many-colored glass"), a distorting lens destroyed by its inherent instability as a structure composed of antinomic

fragments—shattered along the fault line of the principle of difference that constitutes its perceptibility.

> The One remains, the many change and pass;
> Heaven's light forever shines, Earth's shadows fly;
> Life, like a dome of many-colored glass,
> Stains the white radiance of Eternity,
> Until Death tramples it to fragments.

Shelley's dead shepherd has been destroyed because he could not control the whole of the social world in view of the "unity" of his motive. The "last critic" is a notation of the paradox of sociability in which the self is actualized and obliterated by the counter-freedom of the Other—and has therefore drunk poison (cf. Moschus). The antinomies of narration and participation into which the cosmogonic hero is thus precipitated are finally resolved in the extinction of the conditions of actual life ("He is made one with Nature"). The one world of manifestation (the metonymic totality that we now see as the contradiction of the wholeness of man's proper infinity) is inconsistent with the highest hypothesis of human life. Thus the ethic of transcendence is defined in terms of the inadequacy of art (and indeed of all manifestations of structure) as a basis of human value.

> . . . Die
> If thou wouldst be with that which thou dost seek.
> Follow where all is fled!—Rome's azure sky,
> Flowers, ruins, statues, music, words, are weak.
> The glory they transfuse with fitting truth to speak.

As poetry is typically discourse of one sort (finite, structural, at hand) about discourse of another sort (infinite, hopeful, receding), so in all these poems the poet as epigone discourses, asserting the paradox of discourse, upon the master of image-life—Bion, Thyrsis, Gregory, Adonais, Lincoln (and the case is the same for Christ, as for Milly Theale, or Mrs. Ramsay)— who has become an image by dying, thus fulfilling the rule of brokenness and affirming the hierarchies required for manifestation. Such are the obligations entailed by mastery. The death of the master of the image is explained by the successor, the survivor as narrator, as the defeat of the ideology of mortality through its fulfillment. In this way, the master completes the establishment of continuity, on the terms allowed, by substantiating the epigonal narrator's rationalization of his own dominance. For each successor takes his predecessor as a substantiating image. Hence each narrator becomes in his turn the doomed master of the image (Bion for Moschus, Virgil for Dante, Keats for Shelley, Baudelaire for Swinburne, Dante for Eliot, Yeats for Auden); and the survivor takes on the role of victim in the struggle for the local habitation and the name. There is neither peace nor . innocence in the deadly vexations of displacement.

For our purposes, the most prominent version of this scenario is found in Milton's *Lycidas*, although it may be seen in various displacements to form the basic structure of all Milton's poems.

> So may som gentle Muse
> With lucky words favour my destined urn
> And as he passes turn
> And bid fair peace be to my sable shroud.

The succession of persons, the succession of regimes, the succession of civilizations are all reduced in Milton to the manifestational urgencies that require destruction for creation. His subject was the troubled threshold of emergence into history. In "On the Morning of Christ's Nativity," the preparation for dawn, for the illumination or visibility of things, is the destruction of prior civilizations, not on ethical grounds finally but on the functional grounds of the requirement of antinomic reduction for manifestation. We note that Milton wrote the mythology of revolution—practiced the obliterative rhetoric of cosmogenesis—in the same terms both prior to, and posterior to, the onset of Cromwell's regime. He did so because the subject matter of revolution was not historical except insofar as history *really is* the account of the struggle to be present in history. That is to say, except insofar as the poet, the priest, the politician, and the warrior are engaged in the same manifestational task.

The death of Lycidas—the grave in Arcadia as the pure problem of the obliterative paradox of anthropogenesis (Lycidas disappeared at sea)—sets the speaker in the poem the task of rationalizing his dominance as a narrator, of justifying his place in the hierarchy of survival. To do so, he read back into the narrative the process that produced his image-life. Lycidas dies of the disordering of the binary terms of the manifestational paradox; he is redeemed by their reordering, in particular by the eschatological subordination of the individual to the collective. His elegist performs a functional reexpression of death that reverses a prior subordination of the collective to the individual, which is the first cause of the death thus reexpressed. We are told that the perfidious bark rigged in eclipse was the cause. But what had occurred was that the master of the image had lost his power to remain manifest, as a consequence of the inversion of the preferred hierarchy of the individual/collective antinomy. Lycidas was swallowed up by one vortical term of the paradox of sociability and will be rescued by the other. The ship of eclipse (obliteration) is the participatory subjectivity that is the very principle of the unmanifest (the invisible inwardness) over which the powers of symbolic culture—the university, the church, and the arts—no longer exercise rule. As a consequence of this descent into psychological subjectivity (Yeats's Phase One, the dark of the moon), the principle of representation was weakened in the cosmos at large. All phenomena—and above all Arcadia as an instance or frame of the *topoi* of perception—became "surmise."

Lycidas is redeemed by passage through the extreme individuation of natural subjectivity (on the model of Jonah) into the collective realm, of which the manifestational form is choral song. Death and the collective are (as I have said) identified. More specifically, death as obliteration is identified with radical individuation, and death as manifestation is identified with the collectivization of the self. Since, however, the collectivization of the self does not yet produce a local habitation or a name (Lycidas has passed from nameless participatory immanence to equally nameless participatory transcendence), the assertion of structure (the final octave) is required to establish the dominance of narration—and the substance of the poem is enclosed within the further globe of rational distancing: "Thus sang the uncouthe swaine."

In the early modern period, the destabilizing of representation enters through the equivocation of structure. Conspicuous throughout Milton's work is the sentiment that the functional rules of image production (God's creation by classification is an instance) require justification. The prerequisite brokenness of the whole life, which manifestation exacts (the Fall), is not intuitively compensated by the consequences of presence (Christ's incarnation). Indeed, there is in Milton the finally countervailing sense that the post-catastrophic nature of real life, the loss of Eden, *is* uncompensated by any possible consequence. This sentiment enters the modern poetic tradition with Milton—that the destruction inherent in creation is too great, that the organic life that must be traded for symbolic life finds no sufficient remission in structure, that the participation lost in view of the narrative record is too precious to be restored by any possible value of history. Subsequently in modern poetry, and modern representation in general, the brokenness of the world in record becomes the dominant feature of all record; and the thematization of the process of record with its attendant losses becomes virtually the whole subject of representation. History as presence becomes, as we have seen, predominantly an account of its own production. Under such conditions, literary humanism is subdued to the singularly limited witness of a reduced artistic enterprise, for without confidence in the transcendental remissions of structure, there is little funding back of value from the phantom realms of hope. Representational systems, which multiply upon the ground, become machines for the mere production of death, once the by-product only of image-life.

The last justification of the dominance of structure was encoded in the functional rationality advanced for the much-discussed political feudalism of modernity. It took the form of the constant argument that the perfection of justice would destroy manifestation at its root in difference—that the masses, or the middle class, or the ill-born, or the impure of blood had no death and therefore no image-life. Inevitably, the conflict between the value of structure and the value of life was mediated by the removal of art from the realm of reference. ("A poem should not mean, but be.") The final remedy and the most progressive was the effort to equivocate the status of structure altogether. This we see in Stevens, whose management of the issue confirms his superior originality.

In Stevens's "Sunday Morning," the pastoral couple, now come indoors, contemplate like Poussin's shepherds the grave in Arcadia—here, "the tomb in Palestine." The male speaker expounds the ideology of mortality as the founding principle of perception and world presence:

> Is there no change of death in Paradise?
> Does ripe fruit never fall? . . . .
> . . . .
> Death is the mother of beauty, mystical
> Within whose burning bosom we devise
> Our earthly mothers waiting, sleeplessly.

Of utmost importance is that reversal of the valence of death in Stevens, following Whitman, which is deeply explored elsewhere in *Harmonium* and beyond, in terms of an abandonment of the culture of closure, or (what is the same thing) in terms of the equivocation (the word is precise) of the culture of difference. This equivocation involves an assertion of the real possibility of the perception of ambiguity and reflects an effort that has persisted into the postmodern period to appease the antinomies of manifestation by holding the constituent terms suspended.

In this way, there is advanced the salvific idea of an immanent (open) culture of images in which death becomes value, and the prior dominant culture of death as structure becomes a phantom civilization taking its place as all predecessors at the point of vanishing. Thus we may see a true culture of inference ("nuance"), in which the human image is released from the privative economies of the body as picture, portended in the fearless anti-closural glide "downward to darkness." Indeed, already in Yeats there is a clearly defined impulse toward a civilization in which consciousness and hope are not involved in those paradoxes of construction that he himself of all moderns most explicitly described.

> Labour is blossoming or dancing where
> The body is not bruised to pleasure soul,
> Nor beauty born out of its own despair,
> Nor blear-eyed wisdom out of midnight oil.
> O chestnut-tree, great-rooted blossomer,
> Are you the leaf, the blossom, or the bole?
> O body swayed to music, O brightening glance,
> How can we know the dancer from the dance?

Here the several antinomies of manifestation are reviewed, and the final question is merely whether the paradox of narration and participation is inescapable. The answer is an equivocation. It is and it is not.

Whether there is a possibility of representation, and therefore of a "humanism" based in representation, which is neither a reassertion of the antinomies nor an equivocation that holds them in suspension or reconstitutes them in a different form—whether there is a version of art free from the obliterative rhetoric of cosmogenesis, an art that derives its authority from the dominance of hope—is the central question that lends interest to the critical enterprise in our time.

X. The Present Crisis in Representation and the Human Interest

There remains of course the question, scarcely touched on here, as to why the brokenness of value in the realm of manifestation has become acute in modern and postmodern times. The answer lies in the facts of historical life.

Modernism was historically a post-catastrophic moment. Its great instances in literature were postwar efforts to reassert continuity, works that, like *The Waste Land*, thematized history as a story about perception abolished and re-obtained—as perception is always re-obtained—from ruins. Between 1919 and 1946, history as catastrophe became increasingly involved with terminal factors such as nuclear war. Hence, the effort to sublimate history in Arcadian realms, where catastrophe is consistent with continuity, was correspondingly urgent. *Just in proportion as art was an enterprise distinct from history, art became an occasion of cognitive heroism.* World War II, however, destroyed the ability to distinguish between the two realms. Nuclearism, above all—the founding moment of postmodernism—effected an implosion of mind upon world (imagination upon history) that dissolved the category of difference upon which representation is founded. Nuclearism rendered the paradox of creation and destruction potentially, and therefore effectively, complete. It provided the excluded wholeness—the titanic vestiges of the cosmogenesis of Western civilization—with immanence and a terrifying and de-creative bearing upon the world from which the regulatory ethic of the past had withheld it.

From all of which, I must conclude here that the culture of representation is founded in an inescapably antinomic construction of value. Naive quasi-ethical generalization toward a humanistic idealism based in the culture of representation will repeat those antinomies in the actual human world. When taken as indication toward social truth, the inherited hierarchy of the counterposed elements of which the antinomies are constituted predicts an oppressive and banal version of social and psychological order. In view of the postmodern historical situation, both extreme and actual, as noted above, an enterprise capable only of constructing a prior state of affairs—just that state of affairs to which normative criticism would know how to address itself as wisdom—has about it a dangerous inappropriateness. Only if text can be placed in the context both of its function—which can only be the advancement of the human interest—and also of its nature as representation can discourse about text obtain sufficient conscious magnitude to include within its scope any problem as important as a human problem. If this essay has made some advance toward discovering where the literary subject lies, it will have achieved all that it could reasonably intend.

The Passion of Laocoön

WARFARE OF THE RELIGIOUS
AGAINST THE POETIC INSTITUTION

Solus sapit hic homo / Only this man knows[1]

*Though the objects themselves may be painful to see we delight to view the most
realistic representations of them in art. . . . The explanation is to be found in a
further fact: to be learning something is the greatest of pleasures, not only to the
philosopher but also to the rest of mankind. . . . For the reason of delight
in seeing the picture is that one is at the same time learning—
gathering the meaning of things.*

Aristotle, *Poetics*, III.4 (trans. Bywater)

*What if excess of love
Bewildered them till they died?*

Yeats, "Easter, 1916"

Originally, and particularly in Aristotelian usage, the word pathos (Latin passio)
*meant an affliction or seizure; it always implied suffering, passivity, and it was
ethically neutral. . . . The new and, in a way, active element in the Christian
conception is that spontaneity and the creative power of love are kindled by
passio. . . . But passio always comes from the superhuman powers above or
below and is received and suffered as a glorious or terrible gift.*

Erich Auerbach, "Gloria Passionis," *Literary Language and Its Public*

I. A New Laocoön

Laocoön was a Trojan priest who was destroyed because he knew the truth
(*Aeneid* II). His knowledge of the truth, if acknowledged by his people,
would have saved his city from destruction by the Greeks. Laocoön *saw
through the harmless appearance* of the Trojan horse. He threatened to make
his knowledge of Greek deception known (the army concealed in the Trojan horse). He knew the truth ("Only this man knows") and was a true lover
of his people—a patriot who put his knowledge of truth in service of innocence. But he was, together with his two sons, atrociously destroyed *by
his own gods*. Why? In addition, Laocoön's story became the subject of a

* "The Passion of Laocoön: Warfare of the Religious against the Poetic Institution"
was originally published in the *Western Humanities Review* 56, no. 2 (Fall 2002): 30–80.

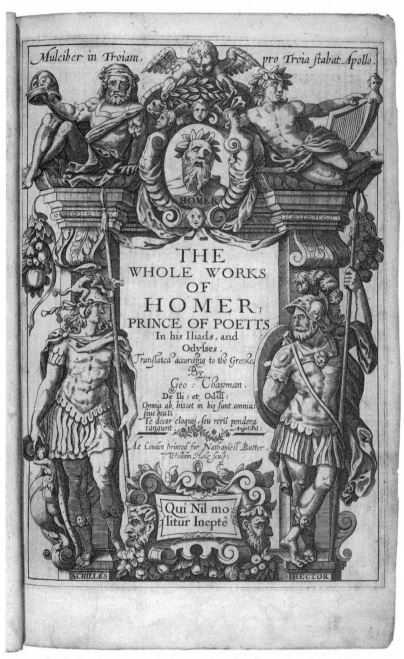

Fig. 1. Title page from *The Whole Works of Homer* (1616). *Solus sapit hic homo* (Only this man knows). Reproduced by permission of the Huntington Library, San Marino, California.

great work of Greek sculpture—in its own time (3rd–2nd century B.C.) and also in the century that followed its rediscovery in 1506, it was considered the supreme instance of its artistic kind. What is the interest of the image? Since, as we shall see, the face and predicament of Laocoön came to be understood as explanatory of the meaning of highest art, especially in Homer, the answering of that question—What is the interest of the image?—discloses much about the human interest in poetry and (representation) altogether.

In context of the *Laocoön* sculpture (following Gotthold Ephraim Lessing's precedent), I intend in this essay to say something about the interest or stake of men and women in poetry. In order to do so, I will need to supply, briefly, some of the propositions required to build a *non-literary* (a *true-love*) poetics. At the present time, two kinds of poetic theory are current. The one focuses solely on the reader's position with respect to the poetic text afforded by cultural membership, and is open, theoretic, and hospitable to desire. It seeks out what can in thought be devised to give satisfaction. It is a virtual poetics—a speculative comedy of enhancement. The second kind of poetics focuses solely on the position with respect to the poetic text afforded to one who engages in the labor of making (not the poet, but the person), one who encounters the resistance that materials oppose to the desires of the heart, and confronts also the difference between what can be conceived and what can be made. It is to this latter, perhaps tragic, kind of poetics—one that holds that "[constructional] artistic decisions provide the model for all actions"[2]—that what follows is a contribution.

This kind of poetics, the poetics of construction, is in my view a decisive critique of the former, the poetics of desire. At the very least, I wish to make as unmistakable as possible the conclusion that these two positions with respect to the poem should not be substituted for one another—the one, readerly poetics, for the other, the poetics of the maker. And that it is likely that in every age, after the Romantic, it has been and will be necessary to build ever new Laocoöns.

The specific appropriateness of the Laocoön image to a poetics of the kind I propose lies in the status assigned to the sculptural image as a "supreme" case of human construction. The first record of the *Laocoön* artifact presents it as the limit-case of sculptural representation. According to Pliny: "[The *Laocoön*] is a work to be preferred to all that the arts of painting and sculpture have produced."[3] In addition, Pliny *names the workmen* (sculptors, or copyists) who produced the *Laocoön* and expresses his wonder that human workmanship could fabricate such an object. "Out of one block of stone, the consummate artist, Hagesandros, Polydoros, and

Athenodoros of Rhodes made, after careful planning, Laocoön, his sons, and the snakes marvellously entwined about them." As a supreme instance of human making—a consummate negotiation of the resistances of materials by artisanal skill that affects the viewer as esoteric power—the *Laocoön* is situated at the limit of the imagined possibility of making and therefore full of new knowledge—what Aristotle calls "the meaning of things."

In addition, the subject matter of the Laocoön image exhibits, beyond expectation ("a work to be preferred to all that the arts of painting and sculpture have produced"), the capacity of the human body subjected to extreme experience to communicate human presence, and also the always previously untested *adequacy* of representation to transmit such a communication. Apparently, the great value of the *Laocoön* is in direct proportion to the extremity of the experience it represents. That representation as such was involved in the prestige of the Laocoön image was immediately seen by the Renaissance masters—particularly Raphael—who took Laocoön's head, *as antiquity had done*, for the likeness of Homer, the visible image of the pain of the invisible master. The decisive challenge of experience to representation (productive of the highest class of artifact in a medium) is mounted at the limit of human capacity to endure and to communicate the experience of pain. *The greater the pain, the greater the value of its credible representation.* More generally, the Laocoön narrative specifies the crisis that gives rise to new representation. Pain locates that moment: the moment of the superseding of one institution that grounds representation by another.

The most important event of this kind in the history of the human world is the unfixing of the otherness or difference of divinity—the putting in question of the boundaries (or what we name the "existence") of the domain of the sacred. This unfixing or problematization of realms of being—as old as the human world, as inveterate in human experience as the representation of human experience—makes poetic work both inevitable and, in fact, impossible. And precipitates the warfare between the religious and poetic institution that the Laocoön image specifies as the moment both of the greatest pain and its representation. In the biblical story about the beginning of pain, Adam and Eve are expelled from Eden because they have witnessed and put in question God's sanction against knowledge, the boundary between divine and human realms of being.

What facts, of all the facts that come to mind by reason of representation, "exist"? This is the question in dispute—the *casus belli.* The field of this war of the religious against the poetic institution is the scarce space of existence always contested—that is to say, significant life.

Now the crisis precipitated by the unfixing or problematization of the sacred (a crisis of the collective human power of imaging and valuing persons) is recurrent in history. The power of imaging (and therefore valuing) depends upon the difference of a transcendental term (a god-term, or *theologos*) that functions to effect *generality* in language. The questioning of this term—the dispute over proprietary control of it—results in crises of the justice of acknowledgment. *There is nothing metaphysical involved in the positing of the theo-logos.* All language and all imaging requires the difference of a principle the function of which is generality. The dispute over proprietary control of the god-term (as the principle of generality and generality's productive functions, among which are collectivity, intersubjectivity, intelligibility, recognizability, and therefore "immortality") generates the religious/poetic (in)distinction and the violence that attends it. "Credo" (I believe) is the prefix both of religious and also artistic reality.[4]

In biblical narrative once again, Adam's transgression attests to the primordiality of divinity's monopoly of "deathless" consciousness. The narrative of the reiterated re-grounding of Western religion (*covenant renewal* in Judeo-Christian language) is a thematic example of the recurrent need to renegotiate, as between God and creature, the terms of sacred difference in the interest of the manifest presence of persons. In the uncovenanted gentile world, and in later periods of Judeo-Christian civilization, such renewal takes the form of the reconstruction of secular means of representation (human-human acknowledgment), which, after the Reformation—the last of the great religious covenant renewals in the West—we may call the literary (or, better, the *poetic*) system.

II. *Laocoön* and the Human Interest

At the inaugural moment of the modern poetic system (which was driven into existence together with, and for the same reasons as, in England, the separation of the British church from Rome and on the Continent the failure of German Pietism), Lessing in his book called *Laocoön* (1766), and Lessing's approximate contemporaries (e.g., Kant, Hegel, Goethe, Schiller, Wordsworth, the American Federalists), undertook the (re-)discrimination of the instituted relations among métiers of discursive representation, including philosophy, government, poetry and religion and the kinds of art such as poetry and sculpture, in the light of *the renewed human need for depicted life*—the *justice* of acknowledgment, "the human interest."[5]

Among such human needs is the building and just distribution of the descriptive terms that specify the value of a person—such as nobility, beauty, visibility, and intelligibility. The science of this "building" and "distribution" is, in general, *poetics*. For our purposes, *the study of poetics investigates the human work peculiarly appropriate to generic poetic means (poems) and specifies those conjunctive capacities and resistances of the materials of poetic representation that bear on that work as fundamental constraints upon the constructive will to the self-description of the person.* It is Lessing's attention to the resistance of materials, as such resistance enters into the meaning of the representation of persons, that constitutes his contribution to poetics, as I understand poetics.[6] It follows that if you can answer the question *"What can be done by poetic means—given the nature of the materials of poetry—that cannot be done by other means?"* then you can decide when a poem is good. In any case, the work of the founding of the literary-poetic system—the profundity of which is discovered only in the urgency of the recurrent civilizational need for the (re)valuation of persons—now, at the end of the second millennium C.E., requires to be done over again.

But why? And why should a reconstitution of poetics always be an ever new *Laocoön*? Because the insight of Lessing—that the materials of representation and the logic of their relations determine the limits of imaging and the meaning of the image—needs to be extended in our time. There is no outside to the subjection of representation to the structure of its materials. And the meaning of terms central to the construction of human value has become increasingly absorbed in relations that the structure of materials repeats, as if that structure were experience itself—or perhaps value itself. In this sense, the passion of Laocoön (fig. 6) (for many reasons, as we shall see, an image that is *the type of the image*, caught as by serpents, in the death-hold of its own materiality) is what the poet knows—*Solus sapit hic homo*. The poet is the kind of maker who knows this.

The passion of Laocoön is what the archetypal poet, Homer, has witnessed. It is in his face (fig. 2).[7] We see Laocoön in the portrait of Homer—as we see in any face some trace of what that person has witnessed (his or her experience), and as in any portrait, we see, therefore, the *meaning* as it is supplied by the structure of experience of the otherwise unintelligible name the portrait bears (e.g., "Homer"). What experience do we see in the face of Homer—the poet's meaning? It is the same experience (as I shall show) seen in the face of Alkyoneus in the Pergamon frieze (fig. 8). After the first unrepresented moment (the beginning of the world), which unfixes the difference of divinity, there follows the cosmic (i.e., general) conflict—Olympian against chthonian—which, in order to restore that lost difference or its effect, supplies the (unstable) terms—race, class, and gender (let us say)—by which the recognizability of the face (its value acknowledged, its intelligibility determined) is narrated.

The capacity to value persons is dependent upon the intelligibility of experience. At the moment when experience ceases to be intelligible, experience produces (let us say, obtrudes) its own image for inspection. That is the moment of poetry. The *Laocoön* and its associated artifacts, including the portrait of Homer, constitute such an image and demand a text. My purpose is to look into the face of Laocoön once again, where the face of blind Homer can be seen (and the faces it sees seen) and some answer to the question of what poetry knows rearticulated.

III. The Face of the Poet

Someone has to exist in the world who is as old as the world.

Levinas[8]

The "text" that my argument addresses is not the Homeric poem, but an ancient Greek, *invented* portrait of Homer, the archetypal poet of the West, whom nobody ever saw (fig. 2).[9] This imagined face of Homer (conserved and repeated for centuries) I take to be a face intended as a representation, both of poetry's agency and of its effect portrayed (*protrahere*, draw out) to be *made visible*. Reading that stone face (itself a reading of the poetic vocation), I can say something about *what poets are called for* — or say something about what with respect to this matter can be invested in a face and perceived by looking at a face.

For on the imagined face of the blind poet is seen to be written *the meaning of a practice*.[10] Such a meaning, the result of a particular account of the making of the human world, can also be read, I dare say, in the represented face of other masters of a practice such as Socrates, Buddha, or Christ[11] — different as the practice is different and as the provenience of the image in time and space make it different, but always within each class of image bespeaking the same witness to the same practice: building the human world subject to the constraints of the same materials. In the case of the imaginary portrait of the poet, the world in question is the one made by poetic means, and the practice that determines the meaning of the world is poetic practice.

Among the propositions entailed by the practice of poetry is, first of all, that all speech implies a speaker. Therefore, within the practice of poetry, there is no theoretic position, because all speaking is interested speaking. All poetic speaking is within the *human interest*. Every person speaks, living or dead, and has a *face by reason of speaking*. From the lineaments of the face, it is not merely possible but necessary, in the human interest *that is the cultural reproduction of recognition*, to infer the means or métier by which

Fig. 2. Bust of Homer
(three-quarters view).
Museo Nazionale
Romano (Terme di
Dicleziano), Rome, Italy.
Photo credit: Alinari /
Art Resource, New York.

Fig. 3. Bust of Homer
(Sala delle Muse). Museo
Pio Clementio, Vatican
Museums, Vatican State.
Photo credit: Scala / Art
Resource, New York.

Fig. 4. *Laocoön* (detail of father's head). Vatican Museums, Vatican State. Photo credit: Alinari / Art Resource, New York. (See also fig. 7.)

Fig. 5. Raphael, *Parnassus* (detail of Homer and Dante). Late fifteenth or early sixteenth century. Vatican Museums, Vatican State. Photo credit: Scala / Art Resource, New York.

Fig. 6. *Laocoön* (Roman copy, perhaps after Agesander, Athenodorus, and Polydorus of Rhodes). First century C.E. Museo Pio Clementino, Vatican Museums, Vatican State. Photo credit: Archive Timothy McCarthy / Art Resource, New York.

Fig. 7. *Laocoön*. Vatican Museums, Vatican State. Photo credit: Alinari / Art Resource, New York. (See also fig. 4.)

the face comes to mind. From the face of "Homer" we infer (as I have said), not only a world, but the principle of the manifestation of a world—that is to say, the poetic principle. The imaginary portraits of Homer (e.g., figs. 2 and 5) are the poetic imagination considered as a face. That is to say, *the invented artisanal portrait exemplifies that kind of making, or poieisis, which supplies the means (and the theoretical conditions) of constructing faces.*

All portraits are imaginary—the constructed implication of speaking. But the *"invented"* portrait of the poet is portraiture conscious of the heterogeneous images of which it is composed. The practice of poetry makes faces manifest and is constituted of the faces it manifests.[12] Within the face of Homer, as in every face, is the whole history of the human world as it comes to mind—by which I mean, as it is representable (sayable, singable, seeable, knowable). As I shall show in what follows very particularly: In this Hellenistic face of Homer is the witness above all of Laocoön (fig. 6), whose catastrophe repeats the destruction of Alkyoneus (fig. 8) in the cosmogonic Gigantomachia (warfare establishing by violent differentiation the intelligibility of the world) that is inscribed on the Great Altar at Pergamon, and that depicts the moment of the Olympian institution of the human form. The face of Homer is therefore a legible account (as is every face) of the origin of the intelligibility of the world or (more specifically) the sublime knowledge of that origin that is recognized each time a person is acknowledged. In the face of Homer, we learn that the difference specified by a face is the same (and has the same value) as the difference that secures the intelligibility of experience altogether.

The importance of poetry, therefore, lies in the fact that poetic practice builds up an artifact *structured like* the human stake (or interest) in the world, *which is the production of just representations of persons.* Poems are valid when they serve that interest. However much one may be interested in the poet's *meanings*, nonetheless the rationality of poetry (its reason for being) in the civilization serves an interest of another kind. For that reason, I am interested in what is called poetic language (identical with the face capable of uttering it, of which Homer is the archetype). I view poetic language as the social memory of the prehistoric language of human beings—language prior to communicative ("messaging") speech—and the purposes it served as the most generally useful tool of the earliest human community, the first necessity of which was the transmission of the human image—the *eidos*[13]— the conditions of the construction of the portrait of the person. (See section VIII below.) Therefore, "Someone has to exist in the [human] world who is as old as the world." The "poet" is that kind of person.

Fig. 8. Athena Group, eastern frieze, Altar of Pergamon (post-restoration 2004). Hellenistic, 164–156 B.C.E. Antikensammlung, Staatliche Museen zu Berlin, Germany. Photo: Johannes Laurentius. Photo credit: Bildarchiv Preussischer Kulturbesitz / Art Resource, New York.

IV. The Secret of the God: *Verum Factum*

In our time, as in the modernist period, the poet and also the student of poetry seem to insist on uncanny or esoteric kinds of knowledge such as are inadmissible, both in the academic literary-theoretical and philosophical disciplines, and also in the sacred discourses of institutional religions. By reason of what relation to experience, inseparable from the poet's practice, arises this association of poetry and "false" knowledge?

I placed at the beginning of this essay the image of Teiresias from the first edition (1614–16) of Chapman's *Homer* (fig. 1). Teiresias's face is constructed by means of the Hellenistic portrait of Homer (fig. 2), itself a version of the face of the destroyed father-priest Laocoön. Further, Laocoön's image (fig. 6, the restored sculpture) is itself structured upon the Pergamon depiction of the Olympian destruction of the giants (fig. 8).

By this iconographic genealogy, we see that Teiresias's face (and Homer's) are situated on the battlefield, which founds the dominance of the Olympian representational establishment. This Homer-Teiresias was the only conscious man among the shadowy dead—*the only one who knows*. It is the Homer-Teiresias-Laocoön consciousness (*Solus sapit hic homo*) manifested as the superimposed faces of the poet, the priest, the prophet, the giant (and the narratives attending them) by which *the singular relation to experience of the poet's consciousness (Homer's face) becomes intelligible.* It is knowledge of origin—and particularly the kind of knowledge that results from the witness of consciousness in the place and moment of the origination of manifestation[14]—that distinguishes the poet as the only one who knows, and that commits the poet and the student of poetry to uncanny learning. For blind Teiresias—*unheimlich*, a cosmic androgyne—was both living and dead, both male and female, between worlds, the transcendent spectator.

Religion makes war against the poet, *because the poet knows the secret of the god*. What, then, is the god's secret that the poet knows? That secret that characterizes the poet and contributes the esoteric element to poetry, especially in the modern world, is at bottom the indeterminacy[15] of the human form. Knowledge of *the secret that the god keeps* governs the poet's practice; and the poet's practice, endlessly reproduced in history, is (not least by its relentless multiplicity) the poet's contribution to "the human interest."

More particularly: "The secret of the god" is not a figure of speech but a reference to the narrative that power promulgates (the secret that power keeps) with respect to the (in)determinacy of the human form. The narrative of creation or foundation disseminates, under the auspices of legitimate "existence," the determinacy that poetic knowledge intends to repudiate. The wisdom of Teiresias (the "cause" of his blindness) is precisely discovery of the arbitrariness of legislated difference—narrated in the case of Teiresias as the crossing of divinely defended boundaries: between life and death, male and female, the apparent and the real (he saw the naked goddess-mother).[16] These boundaries that delineate the determinate human form ("beauty") are defended by the gods, and the transgression of them punished by the gods. The poet knows Beauty is a groundless artifact.

But what logic renders inevitable the conflict of the poetic and the religious institution?

Both the poetic and the religious institution of reality are founded, as I have said, upon the transcendental term. The transcendental term is only the sufficient and effective condition of the making of general world-effects. The word "creation" (poetic or divine) indicates the effect of the god-term; and the god-term (the *theo-logos*, as we have called it), wherever it is found, means nothing more nor less than the sufficient condition of "creation"—that is to say, language itself insofar as it pertains to common (or general) life. The substitution, for example, of human for divine agency in the subject position of the verb created in the eighteenth and nineteenth centuries makes the point clear. "The priest departs, the divine literatus comes."

Both the religious and the poetic functions are included within the sacred; but the sacred (indistinguishable from the exclusionary difference that effects recognition) produces the archetype of economic scarcity (making clear what is scarce when scarcity is the case)—scarcity of what constitutes the human interest, the image.

Hence, poetry is *theo-logic* in nature—the "god-term" meaning only the sufficient condition of credible common existence. Poetic and religious institutions are always discovered in the violent practice of differentiation within the scarce space of manifest existence, where common possession of the god-term is subject to dispute. This is, as I have said, because the god-term constructed by exclusion is (tragic paradox!) the abstraction that is the effective condition of image-making—the determinator of generality as it is of intelligibility, and therefore the contested possession—the fundamental "interest." The secrets of the god who made the world are artisanal or industrial secrets—"mysteries" of artifice.

Representations, including poetic representation, are thus by their nature "political" for the reason that (like the cosmos as a whole) social formations are representations; and, therefore, have (1) the same (hierarchical) structure as representations, which they repeat as truth; and (2) are subject to the same possessive (hegemonic) social will: that is, are subject to scarcity.

Hence the warfare of which I speak is the same that crushes states, destroys the bodies of men and women, and betrays the goodwill of all humanity, not only within the community of persons, but between persons and the gods. At the end of *Une saison en enfer* (1873)—at the moment of summation ("Adieu")—Rimbaud says:

We must be absolutely modern.

No hymns. I must hold what has been gained. Hard night! The dried blood smokes on my face, and I have nothing behind me except that horrible stunted tree! . . . The spiritual fight is as brutal as the battle of men; but the vision of justice is the pleasure of God alone.[17]

The poet knows the secret of the god. Again, what is it? That the justice of *"le combat spirituel"*—note that what we are studying is the structure of Western spirituality—pleases only the god *who prevails*, in whose interest adjudication is invariably decided in history *by force*—Olympian over chthonian, Aryan over Dravidian, Christian over pagan, light over dark, young over old, same over different. The god who prevails, and the party of that god on earth, becomes as a consequence *the describer of the world* and its sole inheritor—the imperial describer. He who says, *"Il faut être absolument moderne."* The proscription of that "only emperor" is clear and widely promulgated: *You shall not make any images of anything I have made.* You shall not—without my permission—make images of anything.

The warfare, then, of which I speak is eidetic in character. The *eidos* of the person is always fundamentally a "face"—the (own) image of the person both particular and general, *but subject to scarcity.* The *eidos* is the final term of value in the violent economies of race, tribe, class, sexuality, gender, religion—in other words, existence as such. The secret of the god that the poet knows, what is called "spiritual warfare" (*le combat spirituel*), is *eidetic warfare*, the struggle to fix or establish a determinate form of the self—individual and collective—by means of the violent usurpation of predominant power of description in the scarce space of manifestation.

By *eidos* I mean (as in Homer *eidos* means) the form or fashion of a person—the shine (as it were) by which the person is seen to be present, the *face* of the person, the outer apparitional or manifestational skin of the human other—whether the self or another—the appearance of existence. Disruption of the (cultural) conditions of the construction of the *eidos* constitute eidetic crisis such as the *Laocoön* represents. It is important to bear in mind that the *eidos*—the face on the site of (or at the moment of) its coming to mind—is *other than the mediation by means of which it comes to mind.* That is to say, the *eidos* or face belongs neither to sculpture, nor painting, nor photography, *nor poetry*, nor any other mediation including sensory perception, for the same reason that speech is not language but rather one means by which language does its work. The *eidos* or "face" (*nostra effigie*, *Gesicht*, *visage*, countenance, etc.) supplies the human form of the self *to which self it is other, and from which it can be taken away.* If there is a Kantian kingdom of ends, then the manifest form of its subjects—their incontrovertibly value-bearing presence—is the *eidos.* And the fortress of that kingdom is under siege.

V. Laocoön and Homer: Theodicean Narrative, Injustice, and the Occasion of Poetic Intervention

It was that fatal and perfidious bark
Built in th'eclipse, and rigged with curses dark
That sunk so low that sacred head of thine.

Milton, *Lycidas*

We have before us (fig. 2) the most influential, the predominant, portrait of Homer (the appointed eidetic master of the West). It is the "Hellenistic type" (stylistically Pergamene—third to second century B.C.E.).[18] It is this portrait Aristotle contemplates in the well-known painting of Rembrandt. The philosopher contemplates the bust of the poet. What does Aristotle—or for that matter Heidegger, Rorty or any philosopher—seek in the face of the archetypal poet?

Notice the filleted hair (an artisanal indicator of the poet, *but also of priest and sometimes emperor*), the dead eyes of the beautiful but devastated head, lips parted in a song (or cry?), and (if you walk around it) astonishing, unconcealed youthful ears. Beyond the depredations such as normally befall ancient artifacts, accountable to accidents of elemental time and human history, and beyond also the specific mutilation of the eyes, there is a represented destruction in this Homeric face that identifies the Homeric face as witness to *a catastrophe of a particular sort*—not of natural age only), but of that warfare of describers—originary and incessant—that the poet knows. Using Rilke's language (*Elegy* X), one may say that he sees, in the face of Homer, experience of the *Urleid*—the endlessly iterated prior violence, eidetic in character of which the characterizing lineaments of the archetypal poet are the trace. Knowledge as it *distinguishes* the poet.

Although there is some question about the context to be inferred from the Vatican *Laocoön*—whether, for example, Laocoön is punished not for having seen through the ruse of the Trojan horse, but for having begotten children and thus betrayed a celibate priesthood of Apollo (Hyginus)— there is no doubt what cosmic agon the imaged head of Laocoön-Homer expresses. As I have pointed out, a counterpart and source of the Hellenistic portrait of Homer is the image of the Giant Alkyoneus in an east panel of the great frieze on the altar at Pergamon, now in Berlin (fig. 8). Experience as it distinguishes the poet produces knowledge, not of the madeness of the world, but of the practice of world-making, that repetition of beginning at which the poet is always present by reason of his practice. What does the philosopher search for in the face of the poet? The philosopher seeks the *authority* of the poet's blinding perception of the fundamental determinacy of the human real. (By "determinacy" I mean knowledge of always having been determined by another.) The philosopher's dialectical alienation presumes the poet's vocation. ("Only this man knows.") The anxiety of the philosopher (Plato's, for example) discloses the philosopher's consciousness of the questionable legitimacy of (logical) knowledge of his kind.

The choice of the blind rather than the sighted poet constitutes a judgment. Two poets are represented in Homer's *Odyssey*: the first, Phemios, the faithless, (presumably) sighted singer of Ithaka who knows the secrets of his master Odysseus and employs them treacherously; the second, Demodokos, the blind singer of Phaiakia (*Odyssey* VIII) who also knows the secrets of Odysseus and employs them prophetically. *Western poetics has chosen the blind singer as archetypal* and depicts "Homer" as Homer depicted the singer of Phaiakia. The singer of Phaiakia in the *Odyssey* is a blind singer of epic narratives about Odyssean deception (i.e., the story of the Trojan horse—Laocoön's subject—and the dispute of Odysseus and Achilleus over the shield of Ajax). Demodokos sings to the Phaiakian nation, which is otherwise unconscious of its collective victimage in the dangerous game of mere self-manifestation. The Phaiakian story ends (it is the beginning moment of that nation's history) with the overshadowing of Phaiakia by a mountain, raised as a curse of the gods angered at the eidetic autonomy of Odysseus and of a nation which does not labor—that is, a nation which exempts itself from the (divine) resistance of materials. The Phaiakians have facilitated (by means of their equivocal exemption, now lapsed) the survival of Odysseus, who has escaped—delegating to his hosts the constraints by which the gods limit the self-description of persons.

The Hellenistic portrait of Homer-Demodokos is the face of a man both beautiful and mutilated, the blinded survivor of a catastrophe of seeing and being seen (i.e., knowledge, "For all senses sight best helps us to know things"—Aristotle *Metaphysics* I.1). What catastrophe? Certainly it is the Trojan War of the *Iliad*. Because in the *Iliad* (Homer's poem), the Western language of value is founded, theatrically, in an account of contest (in the final analysis, with the gods) for control of *honor*, which is the supreme good of the image. The true Homeric war, however, is not the *Iliad*, but the *Urleid*—the poet's vocational experience—the cosmogonic warfare that the Trojan War repeats. It is the originary war productive of the first difference that makes manifestation possible, survival of which determines that *if you sing, then you cannot see*. The face of Homer is the likeness of the experience of a person—on whose face, the poet's face or another's, is inscribed the knowledge of the violent history of the coming of the world to mind.

The *Laocoön* (fig. 3) depicts the Trojan priest destroyed together with one, or perhaps both, of his two sons at (or on) the altar of sacrifice by the serpents of the god Athene, *apparently because the priest has told the truth about the Trojan horse*: that the Trojan horse conceals Greek soldiers, that it is not as it seems, a gift. Or that it is a *gift* only insofar as a gift may always conceal the will to destroy the self-descriptive freedom of its beneficiary, by preempting the autonomy of the beneficiary to determine self-interest. That it is a gift only insofar as a gift always implies concession by the beneficiary to the dominant descriptive power of the donor. The gift of the Greeks to the Romans (the Romans took much of their culture of representation from the Greeks) is, of course, *a predominant Olympian culture of the human image*, notably including sculpture.

Laocoön-Homer is a priest who has *seen through* the surface of the image (the Trojan horse, sculpture itself) to discover within it the general power of image-making to conceal the challenge of the image to all interests other than its own (in the material form, in this case, of Odysseus and the Greek army). The strategy of the "horse" mounts its challenge not only as an instance of representation, but fundamentally as representation itself *that always adds to all meanings a prior claim: the requirement (the vaunt) of the Olympian hierarchical structure inherent in the mediation of all presence*. And presence-in-the-light (honor)—although subject to the claim of the divine other—is, nonetheless, the *human* interest, and therefore the highest human value.

The result of the Laocoön-Homer type of transgression of the surface is always pain (considered as the loss of the *significance* of the material body, and therefore the eye). The mark of this loss is the blinding of the seer. As an interpretation of the Oedipus narrative, Laocoön-Homer's blinding signifies *the most fundamental assault upon the reproductive powers of the human father*, of which sexuality is an instance and the genital a sign, *but the eye finally the organ*.

In the Vatican sculptural image of the father-priest, *Laocoön* (fig. 7), we see that *the whole head is drawn backward as by some immense constraint*. But what is it? Homer does not tell the story of Laocoön. And there is no extant strong poetic narrative of the death of Laocoön and his children before (or after) Virgil. In fact, the Vatican *Laocoön* draws the mind *in large part because its contextual narrative is unrepresented*. The suffering the Vatican sculpture depicts is *without stated and, therefore, finite cause*. The snakes are the god's agents of death *but do not give a reason*. Therefore, the pain of Laocoön becomes total pain, *all the pain there is*. So long as the narrative sponsored by the gods is sufficient—that is, explanatory, *supplying a rational cause of pain*—pain is finite. Such a narrative we call theodicean, a narrative in which the justice of God, the intelligibility of experience, is maintained. But when, however, rational (providential) causes of pain (for example, specified human transgression) become, by reason of some "enlightenment," known to be untrue, then the theodicean narrative is blocked and total pain ensues.

The *narrative of total pain* is the narrative that presents the unintelligibility of narrative; or (to put it another way) the narrative of total pain subverts narrative as a *rational* account of experience. For narrative in itself is an assurance of the rationality of experience. The blocked narrative that presents "all the pain there is" is of the kind that discloses the meaninglessness of pain—or, more specifically, the imposition of pain as an arbitrary affliction, in the interest of another. Such a crisis—the crisis of the blocked theodicean narrative—is (as I have indicated) the occasion of the poetic image, the moment of the passion of Laocoön *and* Homer. The substitutional equivalence of Laocoön-in-pain, on the one hand, and the blind face of Homer, on the other, articulates the realization (displayed in the face of Homer) that such a (blocked) narrative—the moment of exhaustion of a canonical civilization of narrative rationality—is *the fundamental vocational moment of poetry*. (This concept of poetry as a successor métier of last recourse is discussed below.)

The missing substitution (as I have already proposed) is the face of the dying giant of the Pergamon frieze (fig. 8, *left*). From the panel of the eastern frieze of the Pergamon altar, we can see what hand draws back the head of Laocoön. The unrepresented context (here to be seen as not in the Vatican *Laocoön*) is the blocked or problematized theodicean narrative about the injustice of the god Athene—as that narrative is produced at the moment of the establishment of the Olympian dominance. Such blocked theodicean narratives are always simultaneously narratives of cosmogenesis. Why? Because the moment of *the making of the world* (always the legitimating narrative of the institution of a pantheon or a class) is structurally the crisis moment of the alienation of the pain entailed by all construction, from the self-interest of the subject. The (mystic) secret that the poet knows is the *non-ethical* and *non-rational* origin of the manifest, the rational, and the ethical. It is this poetic secret with which philosophy quarrels, which religion seeks to suppress or co-opt, and all social order to disable (hence the classification "aesthetic").

"Total pain" is unphilosophical, without rationality or commutable benefit such as birth, growth order, or transformation. It is the particular kind of pain attendant on alienation of the self-image of the person from the agency of the innocent subject—an *Ur*-sorrow literalized in the death of the children, as in the example of Niobe, or of the indigene, as in the Hellenistic instances of the dying Gaul, et cetera. This "total pain" is inseparable from the first moment of the manifestation of the world (the moment of cosmogenesis, the real big bang), *because it is identical with manifestation as such*. Blocked theodicean narratives belong to that kind of narrative, the meaning of which is less well known in proportion as the narrative is more well known and effectively reproduced—that is to say, in proportion as the narrative becomes, by reason of classification as high art, canonical. Such is the case with the *Laocoön*.

With respect to such narratives, the ceaseless business of the culture is to foreclose by interpretation the radical problem of the image, which, by reason of its artistic form, the culture cannot banish from consciousness. For both academic and religious institutions depend on the supposed inevitability of the intelligibility of experience *and depend also paradoxically on the blind poetic truth that contradicts that intelligibility*. It becomes clear, therefore, that *a poetics of construction* opens another way toward the discovery that the maintenance of institutions is accomplished by displacing the source of their legitimacy. Such a poetics discloses the "unintelligible" source of intelligibility, and thus brings to light the terms of the legitimacy on which institutions are founded, and the *valid* poetic practice—generated by the blocked theodicean narrative that it displaces and conserves—which specifies the grounding of the secular community.

The upward extended right arm of the priest-father, in the incorrect reconstruction of the *Laocoön* of 1506 (as in the Blake engraving, fig. 10), appeals hopelessly to heaven and appears to signify the expectation of an ethical universe from which the sufferer has been for unknown reasons shut out. The correct configuration of the father's right arm as seen in figure 6 was intuited by Michelangelo and verified subsequently by the actual discovery of the missing piece. But the culturally overdetermined, artistically false right arm of the incorrect first reconstruction of the *Laocoön* (by G. Montosorli and A. Cornacchini) represents the relentless cultural effort to suppress the radical problem of the *Laocoön* sculpture. False reconstructions are either ironic or aberrative. But upon them are founded, as I have suggested, church and state. In *Aeneid* II, for example, the radically problematic story about the destruction of the "innocent" priest Laocoön and his impeccably innocent children is written into the story about the founding of Rome in such a way as to make the founding of Rome a contingency of the destruction of that father and his children, as also the story of the abandonment of Dido (*Aeneid* IV) and the death of Pallas (*Aeneid* X), et cetera—all civilizationally "necessary" atrocities. *Nonetheless, the same event is also presented by the poet as inherently unintelligible.*

The death of the subject in Western pastoral elegy has no other ultimate cause.

VI. Supersession of the Religious Institution
by the Poetic Institution

The priest departs, the divine literatus comes.

Whitman, *Democratic Vistas*

The image of the *Laocoön* (fig. 6) depicts the moment of the supersession of one historical institution of meaning (the altar of priesthood) by another (altar of the poet). The moment of change is signified by the serpents and constituted by the artifact (the *Laocoön*). This artifact, the sculpture, presents the ensemble of Laocoön and his sons, which the fatal serpents seem to compose.

A question central to its cultural function raised by the Laocoön as image, and in some measure by Lessing's discourse on it, is whether extreme pain—all the pain there is, and, therefore, history (what happens to persons)—can be included in the canons that register the measure of human value. Whether such pain is representable. In fact, *the meaning of pain*, as the *Laocoön* presents pain ("all the pain there is"), is precisely the unincludability of the experience of pain—and therefore the experience of history—in the instituted canons of human value. The Laocoön image registers a historical moment when previous canons of intelligibility (the theodicean narratives in place) cease to make sense of experience, and no subsequent canon has been disclosed.

That is the *meaning of the Laocoön* and the meaning of the presence of Laocoön in the Homeric countenance. The unincludability of experience in the instituted canons of human value is the fundamental interest of poetic practice *and defines the occasion of the valid poem*. In effect, the interest of the human community in the poetic is based on otherwise unresolvable considerations with respect to the justice of the gods. That is why the ever renewed "apology" for poetry is always a *Laocoön*.

The *Laocoön* with its serpents (the serpents are identical as an iconographic stereotype between the Pergamon frieze and the *Laocoön* sculpture) is an account of the human body at the limit of representability, made visible (as bodies are in the Homeric poems) at the point of honor (appearance) or shame (disappearance), the eidetic crisis of death when visibility has ceased to reveal meaning. Therefore, the Laocoön image presents to mind an unidentified *primordiality*—a material as well as logical extremity—consciousness as present to mind at the *first* moment of the not-yet-classifiable manifestation of the world to mind.

From a material point of view, the sense of primordiality is contributed by the serpents (the animal form of the divinity that serves as the limit and starting point of the human image). And the serpents contribute also, as I have said, the enigma of the compositional closure of the artifact. That is, the serpents of Athene cause the scream of Laocoön, which is unincludable in the canon of art, and at the same time constitute the closural framing and exclusions of the work, which brings it into the canon of art. The screaming mouth as an incomprehensible (unrepresentable) black hole is outside the canons of visual art—as Lessing (chapter 25) insists. Why is this so? Because the narrative of Laocoön, as (un)heard in the scream of Laocoön, cannot be understood in terms of the rationality of the *justice* of God, that is to say, the canons of civilized shapeliness. The sense of the primordiality of the Laocoön image derives from the implication of the Laocoön as before the beginning or after the end of its own intelligible nature as image.

Works of art are best understood as always remembering this moment of representational blockage. This moment can be seen; and in it the structure of seeing can be seen. The meaning of the *Laocoön* is precisely the moment of experience prior to the determination of the discourse—the moment of greatest pain when the meanings do not yet work—the moment when one institution of determinate meaning (the religious) is superseded by another institution (the poetic). This moment is excluded from the economy of the sublime. The payback is not proportional—the final accounting does not record a just return.

It is in accord with this logic that the picture of the priest-poet (Laocoön-Homer) seems to arise as if for the first time—in the represented youth both of the person and the world—in the frieze of the altar at Pergamon (fig. 8). The Pergamon frieze is a vast bas-relief program extending around the four sides of an altar structure, a civic institution perhaps thirty-five meters on each side and ten meters high. An altar is a machine for making sense of involuntary loss by enacting collectively the *choice* of loss. Sacrifice is the act of the removal of a good thing from the category of the secular (the *proprium* of the city or person) to the category of the sacred (the *proprium* of the god), as a means of negotiating the jealousy of the god in the cosmic existence-economy of diminishing resource.

The altar of Pergamon—a civic machine for making sense by regulating the relation of divinity and humanity—presents the warfare of the religious upon the poetic institution, depicted upon it and thereby neutralized and superseded by it. The older mediation, warfare, has become an image within the newer civic mediation—the altar and the city. The Laocoön narrative declares the end of the right functioning of sacrifice (a turning away from the altar), returns the world in representation to a primordial instability, and makes seen the violent economy by which civic life is maintained.

The Pergamon frieze as a whole is not a linear narrative that unfolds in time, but rather a representation of many aspects of a single moment—the single moment in an *always recurring* history in which the anthropomorphic Olympians defeat the polymorphic chthonian predecessor generation. This first visible moment in the history of the world marks the divine conquest in the cosmogonic warfare that institutes the dominance of the Olympian image over the still partially beast-formed chthonian image of the person. On the altar is thus reenacted the authenticating basis of effective sacrifice: the cosmogonic warfare that accounts for manifestation altogether—disclosing it to be a function of the establishment of the difference of the anthropomorphic Olympian pantheon (*champions of the human form, but not of humanity*) by means of the defeat of the theriomorphic (fish-tailed, winged, composite) predecessor race of giants, near the beginning of time.

Present by the nature of his vocation as witness at the originary moment of manifestation, the poet knows (as the trace of divine retribution his blindness signifies) the constructive principle of his art, the power of the poet's knowledge, that is, the artisanal secret of the god, which is the irrationality of the difference that produces manifestation. At the moment, precisely, in which the Homer-Laocoön, the poet, sees this logic, he is blinded by the god who completes the story and composes the image.

In other words, we can *situate* the Vatican *Laocoön* (the one Raphael, Michelangelo, Lessing, and Blake knew) in the narrated instant of the altar frieze of the Attalid city of Pergamon. By doing so, we can supplement its magnetic reticence—the sense conveyed by the Laocoön of something not knowable, or impermissible to know, coming to light. In the image of Alkyoneus, we see that the painful constraint that bends back the head of Laocoön is in fact the grasp of Athene (Olympian apologist), who is preparing to kill her poet-enemy.

When the *Laocoön* was discovered in 1506, it was immediately identified (rightly or wrongly) as Pliny's "supreme example of work in sculpture and painting" (*opus omnibus et picturae et statuariae artis praeferendum*). The restoration produced the "false" right arm I have discussed, the image Blake copied. Michelangelo made, at the time, a restoration of the right arm of the father now seen as correct, which was not used in the sixteenth-century reconstruction. But Michelangelo also used the right arm he made for the Laocoön image as the right arm of malediction (the power of distinction) in the Christ of the Last Judgment in the Sistine Chapel—thus overcoming the pagan and rational abjection of the *Laocoön* by producing the eschatological figure of the risen body of Christ in the Pergamene style. *The Last Judgment* is of course the Christian account of the concluded war of representational hegemony effected by means of enforced differentiation. *The Sistine* Last Judgment *reproduces the effect of the program of the Pergamon frieze.*

In Michelangelo's *Last Judgment* (the very picture of the will to power as knowledge), an Olympian Jesus reinstitutes intelligible religious order by means of his well-formed body (a type of *legitimate* force) over the subversive indeterminacy of human form (the damned, including Michelangelo's self-portrayal in the image of the flayed Marsyas)—from whom representational privilege (the sanction of beauty and light) is withdrawn. Thus the pain of unintelligibility (all the pain there is) is cured in the body of Jesus by a representational act the structure of which incorporates the (irrepressible) history of its own violence. The defeated right arm of the young giant Alkyoneus is put by Michelangelo *in service* of an iteration of the classical (standard) account of cosmic differentiation, in which consciousness is aligned with cosmos and the human form fixed in the image of the Olympian tyrant.

Raphael also saw the newly excavated *Laocoön*. His sketches of the head of the destroyed father-priest supplied the Homer for the Parnassus fresco of the Vatican Stanza della Segnatura, Raphael's mural representation (perhaps designed by Pope Julian II) of the poetic institution. And Raphael's image of the Laocoön-Homer contributed in turn the head of Homer as Teiresias—the type of consciousness in a world of persons blind to the catastrophe of sight—for the frontispiece of Chapman with which I began (fig. 1).[19] Thus, the Hellenistic Homer is the portrait of the "imagination," as the imagination is the human witness to cosmogonic warfare (the warfare of describers), the violence by which the gods impose the "right" form of the person. The passion of Laocoön that the portrait of Homer incorporates is the sign of the logic of poetic history, because the *Laocoön* (like the Christ of tradition) supplies the image of the suffering of *the man who knows the reason of appearance*. The work of poetics (the science that knows how the human world is made) is the analysis and dissemination of this scandalous knowledge.

VII. The Jealousy of the Gods

Nor will we tolerate the traditional assertion that "Zeus is the dispenser alike of good and evil to mortals."

Plato, *Republic* II.379d

All warfare is struggle for control of the unalterable logic of manifestation. The urgency of the study of poetics in our time—the *political* character of such study *that involves it with power*—derives from the bearing of this proposition on the fact that the social formation of power (e.g., the state) is structured like a representation and maintains itself under the conditions of the scarce-contested space and constrained logics of the manifest (that is, the represented) world by manipulating access to acknowledgment, which is the fundamental wealth of human life.

Such is the "esoteric wisdom" of the poet. The content of this poetic knowledge makes clear why it has alienated the poet from statist institutions of knowledge, including the university and the church. In modern times, such "idealism" or "esotericism" (fundamentally, a simple inquiry into the question "What can come to mind?") is an unmistakably distinguishing aspect of the poet's non-canonical, anti-enlightenment, uncanny, "false," vocational knowledge (as exemplified in Yeats, Mallarmé, Crane, Celan, and others). In fact, esotericism and mysticisms of all sorts in Western culture (not least the Jewish *Zohar*; the *Kabbalah*, Jewish and Christian; the Hermetic texts; alchemical and magical texts; etc.) build up the space of origination and the wars in that space *nowhere else brought to mind in the civilization*. But this distinguishing (trade or artisanal) knowledge of the poet is not local to modernity. From Hesiod to Celan, it is inevitable among the poets of the West. It is what they know. The primordiality of the *Laocoön* returns us to that space where is enacted *the contested possession of the sufficient means of representation—sophia, sapientia, shekhinah, the theo-logos.*

In the *Iliad* of Homer, the poet alone sees both the world of the gods and also the world of human beings. The only human being in Homer's poem who also has this power is Achilleus, who sings like Homer (*Iliad* IX) and who promulgates the secrets of the god (*Iliad* XXIV). Achilleus is the poet's surrogate in the *Iliad*, and Achilleus knows and articulates the poet's knowledge of the secret of the god. In his last "wisdom" speeches (to Priam, *Iliad* XXIV.600ff.), Achilleus presents two fundamentally "esoteric" figures: the first (the "two urns") is an exposition of divine agency, non-ethical as the poet knows it to be; and the second (Niobe), an exposition of significant human action in a world defined by the eidetic dominance of the gods.

Achilleus's first figure is an esoteric vision (such as befalls the poet) of how (manifest) experience is made:

> For so have the gods spun the thread for wretched mortals, that they should live among sorrows; and they themselves are without care. For two urns are set on Zeus's floor of gifts that he gives, the one of ills, the other of blessings. To whomever Zeus, who hurls the thunderbolt, gives a mixed lot, that man meets now with evil, now with good; but to whomever he gives only of the baneful, him he makes to be degraded by man, and evil madness drives him over the face of the sacred earth, and he wanders honored neither by gods nor mortals.[20]

The poet knows the unalterable logic of manifestation (Zeus's administration of experience). Such "creative" knowledge is among the mysteries
of his trade. The philosopher, however, reading the above passage, denies
(Plato, *Republic* II.379d) that the god is responsible for (or expressed by)
the one system (manifestation) of human experience: "Nor will we tolerate
[says Plato's Socrates] the traditional assertion that 'Zeus is the dispenser
alike of good and evil to mortals.'" What then does the poet affirm that
the philosopher does not, for which the poet is expelled from the city? The
poet affirms the unalterable *and continuous* logic of manifestation (if manifest, then in pain), and therefore sponsors a discourse more philosophical
than history, and more "serious," more fully authorized by experience, than
philosophy.

Achilleus's second figure is the story of Niobe. Pergamene artifacts
characteristically show, as does the altar frieze I have discussed and the
Laocoön itself, images of the subjugation of innocent life, animals, and earlier forms of the person: for example, the Farnese Bull, the dying Gaul, the
Cyclops, and in the *Laocoön* and Niobe assemblages the slaughter of children. The *Laocoön* sculpture, as a case in point, presents the extermination
of the (male) lineage of the father, the erasure of the utterance of his body.
The story about Niobe is a representation, like the *Iliad* as a whole, of the
extermination by the gods of the reproductive (representational) issue of
the mother:

> For even the fair-haired Niobe took thought of food, though twelve chil-
> dren perished in her halls, six daughters and six sons in their prime. The
> sons Apollo slew with shafts from his silver bow, angered against Niobe,
> and the daughters the archer Artemis, since Niobe had compared herself
> to fair-cheeked Leto, saying that the goddess had borne but two, while
> she herself was mother to many; so they, though they were but two, de-
> stroyed them all. For nine days they lay in their blood, nor was there any
> to bury them, for the son of Cronos turned the people to stones; but on
> the tenth day the gods of heaven buried them, and Niobe took thought
> of food, for she was wearied with the shedding of tears. And now some-
> where among the rocks, on the lonely mountains, on Sipylus, where, men
> say, are the couches of goddesses, of the nymphs that range swiftly in the
> dance about Achelous, there, though a stone, she broods over her woes
> sent by the gods.[21]

The god hates the representational autonomy of the person—the ma-
ternal power to reproduce the human image. This is the spectacle of the
retributive injustice of the god (the atrocious reproof of eidetic autonomy)

as the poet knows it who sees both heaven and earth and remembers stories. By such memory the poet here supplies a history of sculptural representation. Sculpture (Niobe become stone) is the enigmatic resolution of the eidetic contest between human dignity and the obliterative ferocity of divine claims.

In tradition, the blindness of Homer is, as I have said, without a *presented* story that accounts for it. For example, in the "Homeric Hymn" to Delian Apollo, we read only that "He is a blind man, and dwells in rocky Chios; his lays are evermore supreme." However, by searching out the affinities of the Hellenistic image of the master poet, we have recovered a succession of contexts that supply an account of the blindness of Homer. In the depicted narrative of the Pergamon altar, the face that is Laocoön's and Homer's is recognizable as the giant Alkyoneus whose head (not yet that of an old man, but rather that of the etiological youth in the primordial time of the origination of the image) is seen to be wrenched back by the hand of the Olympian paragon, Athene, who is about to destroy him. Alkyoneus's right hand grasps the fatal right hand of Athene. His left arm is stretched out in hopeless appeal to his gigantic but only partially realized (eidetically incomplete) Mother Earth. Nike has appeared to crown the Olympian.

The conquest by the divinity as imperial describer suppresses the possibility of alternative worlds, of other gods than the Olympians, and especially of the prolific earth *that cannot protect her children.* Eidetic warfare of instituted divinity against humanity is found everywhere in the Homeric poems, as it is in history. Men struggle against one another for control of the image, for the "honor" of the person. *But Homer's poem makes plain that it is the claim of the gods who enforce the rules of world-maintenance that makes images scarce among men.*

Consider the story about the poet Thamyris (here very much abridged) from the "catalogue of ships" (*Iliad* II.590ff.):

> And they who dwelt in Pylos and lovely Arene and Thryum, the ford of Alpheius . . . *where the Muses met Thamyris, the Thracian, and made an end of his singing* as he was journeying from Oechalia . . . for he declared with boasting that he would win, even if the Muses themselves were to sing against him, the daughters of Zeus who bears the aegis; *but they in their wrath maimed him, and took from him his wondrous singing, and made him forget his artful playing.* . . .[22]

The violence is done upon Thamyris *by his own (artisanal) gods,* the muses, who administer access to the *theo-logos* on behalf of the Olympians. These are the muses of the proem to Hesiod's *Theogony,* whose vocation is the imaging to Zeus of himself. Their punishment of Thamyris, the poet, as divine retribution against his claim to superiority as a describer is an instance of the warfare of which I speak. The outcome of eidetic warfare can never (if the story is heard through to the end) be in doubt, because the successful operation of the divine function of world-maintenance is a presupposition of the manifestation of any logic or process to which anyone can analytically make reference. *The real as manifest is a paradoxically grounded presupposition that presumes a settled question.* But history (and in particular the history of the poetic text) is generated out of the perpetual counterfactual, which freedom posits—the indeterminacy of the question of outcome of which the poem is a trace. Paradoxically, such indeterminacy can arise only insofar as the god takes away the memory of the poet—leaving the trace we here follow, like the background radiation that lingers as the vestige of a primordial catastrophe (the *Urleid*) at the beginning of manifestation.

As we have seen, poetics entails analysis of the determining logic of civilization, insofar as poetics brings to light eidetic violence and its iterated outcomes that found the real—the poet's esoteric wisdom. Poetic analysis requires the following terms: (1) The primacy of representation (the *eidos*) as value in every respect, as highest value, *the human interest.* (2) A scarcity in history of the representational value by means of which persons come to acknowledge one another, a scarcity continually regenerated by the relentless economy presented as the jealousy of the gods—who enact like persons the implications of difference-based terms of value. What makes scarcity inevitable is paradoxically the practice of poetic making—the intention of actual rather than virtual states. (3) But the valid work of art *incorporates critique* of its own mediation. In the case of the *Laocoön*, the sign of that critique is the gaze of the elder son.

VIII. The Gaze of the Elder Son, the Absolute Priority of Poetic Consciousness, and the Possibility of Critique

The elder son still belongs to the world of the living. He breaks out of the statue . . .
perhaps to get people's attention and bring help.

Peter Weiss[23]

Praise poetry both calls itself kleos [fame, presence in story] and explicitly identifies
itself with the kleos of epic. It is as if occasional poetry, particularly praise
poetry, were the primordial form of the epic.

Gregory Nagy[24]

Least of all will [the poet] have to consider the sense of sight in any single trait
that is not expressly intended to appeal to it. When Virgil's Laocoön screams, does

it occur to anyone that a wide-open mouth is necessary in order to scream, and that
this wide-open mouth makes the face ugly? Enough that clamores horrendos ad
sidera tollit *["He lifted up horrifying cries to the stars"] has a powerful appeal to*
the ear, no matter what its effect on the eye! He who demands a beautiful picture
has failed to understand the poet. . . . The reporting of someone's scream
produces one impression and the scream itself another.

Lessing, *Laocoön*, chap. 4 (emphasis added)

Pliny attributes the making of the *Laocoön* to three sculptors or copyists, a
father and two sons. Correspondingly, the *Laocoön*, manifesting its makers,
presents a hierarchy of three men who constitute the program of the one
image: the powerful but aged father-priest in the center, who has a name,
Laocoön; the small, younger son, overcome or dead—in any case wholly absorbed, on the beholder's left; the elder son on the beholder's right, a big-
ger boy who gazes fixedly at the face of the father. The elder son is looking
toward the beholder's left, into the image, and also with his left hand (on
the beholder's right) he is disengaging his legs from the coils of the serpents
in which the younger son and the father are inextricably involved.

By contrast to the father and the younger son, the elder son is not
blinded by nor is his consciousness preempted by pain. He is aware (*Solus
sapit hic homo*). Gazing on the face of the father-priest (Laocoön-Homer-
Teiresias-Alkyoneus), the elder son discovers (reflected there) the secret
of the god. Insofar as the elder son *sees* the father, he is exempted from the
father's predicament. If we consider the struggle of the father against the
snakes as a failed effort (Puritan, iconoclastic) to free himself from the constraints of appearance, then the escape of the elder son signifies the escape
from those constraints (as Lessing believes) or a reconstitution of those
constraints on another (autonomous) basis.[25] The "breakout" of the elder
son signifies the possibility of renegotiating the laws of construction of the
manifest in some hitherto unconsidered way. Now, the problem of any poetics of practice (the poet's problem, certainly not to be decided theoretically) is *whether there is another way.*

The momentary action that the Laocoön image represents, fixed in time
by the sculptors, follows literally, it would seem, upon a turning around
(conversion) from the altar to which the backs of the three suffering men
are presented. The conversion (Augustine would call it a contra-version)
is a turning away from service to the icon of the god—service as the loss-
regulative practices of religious sacrifice. At the same time, it is a turn toward unmediated confrontation with divinity in all divinity's primordial
savagery—the fatal rage of the god (Athene, Apollo's half-sister) executed
by her servant animals, an exhibition also of the god's mastery of heterogeneous form. This broken rite (the interrupted sacrifice) marks the end of

the validity of the theodicean narrative and the beginning of ugliness—human outcomes unincludable in rationality—an eidetic crisis.[26]

The failure of the religious institution (it cannot protect its priest) precipitates both an effort to change the story (the false restoration of the father's right arm) and the performance by poetic means of the presence to mind of the unintelligible world. It makes no difference whether the agony of Laocoön is a response to a particular manifested situation, or whether the pain the image registers is "constitutive of" manifestation without alternative. For it should be noted that in this context "constitutive of" implies identity of substance and hence identity of the structure of substance. What is constitutive repeats the structure of the constituting circumstance or substance. Since all art, poetic as well as sculptural, is by its nature actual and manifest, it follows that in all important ways all possible works have only the one structure. Manifestation is then an infallible principle of generality.

In any case, the elder son seems first to perform the consciousness that the image incorporates of its own meaning, a characteristic of the classical baroque (Pergamene) style; and second, to enact the bearing or dissemination of the meaning of the father's gaze into the world—a human (poetic) power for the reproduction of images in history and, by that means, deployment of a power of critique consistent with the constraints of manifestation: the *distance* (not the exemption from history) of the gaze that gathers meaning. In short, the stake of human institutions in poetry (human knowledge of the structure of the world) is invested in the career of the elder son.

The turn from the service of the god toward that god's unregulated retributive rage forces the god-term too (the *theo-logos*) into history, with the *flight* of the elder son. Then by the arbitrary nature of "terms," the "god-term" is inherently, indeed logically, equivocal—not the god but the transcendent term that does something like the work of the god, the product of whose work, by the nature of the term that enables it, is equivocal, indeterminate. Such a term is Poetry, or the Poetic Principle. Notice that Raphael's "Poetry" is figured as a person with the instruments of music and writing *who wears the wings of Alkyoneus* (fig. 9).

On behalf of persons, the poet witnesses *the secret of god—the concealed basis of ordinary life*. The *passion to tell* the secret of the god that the poet alone knows—the elder son's vocation to reproduce the originary *passio* of the father, Laocoön—motivates the endless proliferate renewal of poetic practice, the irrepressible manyness of poetic (and artistic) making. *The passion that demands new poems forever* constitutes the perpetually regenerated response to the one question to which poetic vocation always

Fig. 9. Raphael, *Poetry* (detail from the ceiling of the Stanza della Segnatura). Late fifteenth or early sixteenth century. Stanze di Raffaello, Vatican Palace, Vatican State. Photo credit: Scala / Art Resource, New York.

responds: Who represents and therefore supplies the form of the person? In whose interest? And in accord with what rules?

The critique *poetics* can perform is a critique—a bringing to mind—of the eidetic logic that determines the irreconcilable, reciprocal disqualifications (expressed as race, class, ethnicity, etc.) such as arise in the struggle to maintain fixed, mutually exclusive self-constructions in the visible (manifest) world: in short, the disastrously imperfect recognizability of human "existence" in the one secular world—a matter of life and death—about which very little is known. A world is adequately addressed to this problem only so long as the distributive economy of the highest value (the human interest, image-existence) is understood by reason of absolute generality to include all persons. Such generality may be produced by the immanent universality of manifestation, which like the restless hand of Zeus moving between his two jars, dooms each life to scarcity, or by a theological principle of radical transcendence, which assures existence without qualification—the hypothetical well-functioning of the divine/human difference.

Consider Spinoza's projection of an economy of infinite image resource (*Ethics* IV, P36 Scholium) assuring that the greatest good is common to all: "But suppose someone should ask: what if the greatest good of those who seek virtue were not common to all? . . . To this the answer is that it is not by accident that man's greatest good is common to all; rather, it arises from the very nature of reason. . . . For it pertains to the essence of the human mind to have an adequate knowledge of God's eternal and infinite essence."[27]

Spinoza, the Jewish representative of the elder son in history to whose confident pantheism Lessing turned shortly before his death, is the theologian of that turn from the altar of sacrifice that the ancient Laocoön represents. Spinoza understands first, that there is no *human* mind—no generality ("commonness") of abundant consciousness—without the radically transcendent god ("eternal," "infinite") whose transcendence is *identical with the universal distributability of the nature of humanity* (the *eidos*, the human image). But the world of the elder son is historical. Such universality as it knows is the immanent universality of scarcity attendant upon manifestation. Radical transcendence is inconsistent with the vocation of poetry. Second, the true crisis of critique for Spinoza flows from the necessity of deriving the function of divinity (the possibility of common acknowledgment of human value) from the god-term (*theo-logos*), rather than from the god (*theos*).

How is the critique of the elder son articulated in history? In light of this question, I shall comment on two further readings of the Laocoön narrative: (1) Virgil's account (*Aeneid* II, lines 40–56, 199–231); and (2) Blake's annotated engraving of the Vatican group (fig. 10).

Fig. 10. William Blake, *Laocoön* (copy B). Collection of Robert N. Essick. Copyright © 2008 the William Blake Archive. Used with permission.

In the *Laocoön* sculpture, critique (the moment of consciousness, questioning, judgment, and dissemination) is figured (as I have said) in the situation of the eldest son. At the inauguration of witnessing, the elder son's gaze and his left-handed gesture of extrication enact the distance and motive of critique. Twentieth-century restoration of the Vatican sculpture has moved the elder son (the big boy on the right hand of the beholder) some distance farther to the right.[28] The feet of the father and elder son have, in the history of reconstruction of the material Laocoön, become more and more disarticulated the one from the other, thus confirming the view of many—for example, Peter Weiss, as well as Goethe and Blake—that the elder son *who stares at the face of the father* is also (he is doing two things at once) in the act of extricating himself and escaping the scene of his father's death (a form of the story attributed to one Arctinus, seventh century).

Satan is the name that William Blake gives to this elder son who will escape, whose gaze fixes the blind face of the father, and who sees the original catastrophe of manifestation inscribed on that face (fig. 10). Satan is the limit of the light, *the limit of the possibility of inclusion of the world in God, that is, in intelligible mind.* Satan—the son who looks upon the face of the father and bears witness to it—is poetry considered as the principle of representation as such, a pure generality (like Spinoza's God, or Nagy's historical Ur-lyric), which includes the religious thematic (the god of Israel) and is logically prior to it.

The Blakean reading of the Laocoön image is as follows: The elder son, principle of critique and its dissemination ("error") is identified—such is his (poetic) vocation—by his witnessing of the conscious face of the dying father and his bearing into the world *knowledge of the extreme situation inside all appearance.* That knowledge grounds or validates the (poetic) possibility of critique, and (in terms of Blake's Laocoön figure) loosens the bonds of the serpent, the captivity of the mind to the one (biblical) discourse—Blake calls the Bible "the Great Code of Art." Satan (representation as critique, the elder son) escapes the judgment upon the father that Adam (the "natural man," representation as participation, the younger son) does not escape. Why? Because manifestation (appearance, existence) is, as I have said, logically prior even to God and the basis of all value.

The Satanic domain of poetics, the consciousness of the elder son, assures at least the indeterminacy (as freedom) of the human form, which it is not in the god's power to fix—because *the secular narrative voice that says, "In the beginning God created heaven and earth, and the earth was formless..."* *is prior even to the Creation and therefore knows the catastrophe by which creation comes to pass.* This is precisely the Levinasian voice that is as old as the world. Similarly, the Homeric poet whose words constitute the *Iliad*—the blind poet of figure 2—is (you will remember) the only speaker in the Homeric text who sees both heaven and earth, as exemplified in the wisdom speech of Achilleus that I have discussed. As Lessing observed above, the reporting of a scream is one thing, the scream itself another.

The escape of the elder, then, *builds the space of critique.* Blake's troubled Laocoön-scribble-text (both text and scribble are of course engraved by the same poet's hand) is the logically consequent *graffiti* of the elder son situated in that space (both later than and earlier than the father). Blake, as a poet in the position of the elder son who gazes upon the witness of the father-god, has rewritten the Laocoön narrative of pagan antiquity as a critique of the biblical God and in doing so *written over it and written it over* from the point of view of the absolute priority, not of truth but of representation, that is to say, of poetry that always knows an elder god to which love is true.

Blake's practice exemplifies the fundamental strategy of the poet in the warfare between the religious and the poetic institution: *the resituation of a subsequent text in context of an ever more abstract prior text*. (I have done the same thing by successively including the Hellenistic portrait of Homer within the Laocoön, and then both within the eastern frieze of the altar at Pergamon.) Ultimately, the poet's power is the Poetic Genius, the *chora*, itself—consciousness as existence, primordial praise. (Cf. again Nagy.) As Blake says elsewhere: "The Poetic Genius is the true Man, and . . . the body or outward form of Man is derived from the Poetic Genius. . . . The Religions of all Nations are derived from each Nation's different reception of Poetic Genius. . . . The Jewish & Christian Testaments are an original derivation from the Poetic Genius . . . all Religions . . . have one source. The true Man is the source, he being the Poetic Genius."[29]

The productivity of this "eidetic reduction" (or *epoche*) is once more the empirically derivable proposition that *priority is power in Western civilization*. The poetic power in question invalidates the claims of the other to existence by including the other within the abstract *chora* of representation, which turns the actual into the virtual and thus withdraws it from the real. The struggle for representational dominance in the West is conducted by means of ever more radical claims upon the deepest earliness. At moments of eidetic crisis within the institution of Western religion, the strategy is easy to see. John the Baptist was the last prophet of the old order:

> John bare witness of [Jesus] and cried, saying, This was he of whom I spake, He that cometh after me is preferred before me: for he was before me. (John I:15)
> Jesus said, Before Abraham was I am. (John, VIII:57)

More generally, in the practical world of power, representations of all kinds—radio stations, art collections, sex, prophecy, archaeological sites, and so on—are claimed among the signs of such earliness and are therefore *as representation* requisite to power. Among the métiers of civilization, religion and poetry are rival claimants to the dispensations of representation, which, as representations, supply the possibility condition of valid "existence."

In this sense it becomes clear, as I indicated at the outset, that *it is not*

*the communicative functions of language with which poetry is fundamentally
concerned and for which it is valued, but with language as a link to the priority*
(figured, let us say, as "ancient time") on the site of which human recognition is founded, and the world first constructed as a space of human self-
identification in the presence of the human other. The recurrent claim of
universality for poetry expresses the intent (in any case) of the effect of the
priority I have ascribed to it, and in this sense justifies Plato's philosophical
opposition as well as Augustine's ethical anxieties. From this point of view,
philosophy grounds itself not in truth, but even as logic in rational expedi-
ence. It is in poetry that the love of truth, true-love, is at home.

In the specific case of Blake's Laocoön plate (fig. 10), Blake resituates
the pagan image (the one Pliny saw), which he engraved and reengraved,
in biblical reality. The Laocoön group thus comes to represent not the Virgilian priest of Neptune, but "Yah & and his two sons, Satan and Adam, *as
they were copied from the Cherubim of Solomon's Temple by three Rhodians* and
applied to the Natural Fact or History of Ilium." By this chronological re-
classification, a re-inscriptional act that rotates the reference of the image
from imitation of one reality (Homeric Troy, logically "late") to another
(the biblical Temple of Solomon, logically "early"), the Blake-poet-scribbler
resituates the image of the two Laocoön sons prior to its own (actual) history. He does so, specifically, by co-opting them as guardians ("cherubim")
of the absence of an image (Yah is aniconic), the empty space of sanctity in
the first temple of Solomon. The resonance of the reconstruction is poignant: "Onkelos, the proselyte [third century B.C.E.] says that the cherubim [of the ark of the Temple] had their heads bent back, like a pupil going
away from his master. . . . They had the form of youths."[30]

By so resituating the Vatican *Laocoön* prior to its own history, Blake
has produced a critique of representation (including the Bible, "the Great
Code of Art") from the point of view of the universal "Poetic Genius." As
poet, Blake *re*writes the sovereign paradigm of the "objective" real inherent in Jehovah-approved manifestation in accord with the immaterial body
called the Imagination. By Imagination, Blake means the re-description
of the person in the image-autonomy (indeterminacy) that the *Laocoön* he
has just reengraved signifies. That's what the elder son has learned from
the face of the father he stares at (not entirely absorbed), and from which
accordingly he, at the same time, moves away like one putting off an in-
appropriate form.

*Virgil, in contrast, is the founder of the modern poetic system—historically, the-
matically, and as a critic of and witness to the entailments of symbolic structures.* It
is important then with respect to the constitution of modern poetic culture that Virgil, the archetypal gentile poet of the modern West, presents

the structure of the historical human world (Roma) as a repetition of the structure of the represented word (*poema*). It is consequential also, as a critique of such a human world, that in Virgil's Laocoön narrative there is no escape for the elder son.

Lessing remarks that "Virgil is the first and only [writer of the Laocoön story] to have the serpents kill the father as well as the children."[31] The Virgilian narrative of Laocoön, by contrast to the Rhodian sculpture, is genocidal in that it allows no survivor from the genealogy of Laocoön. Virgil is a poet who has looked upon the face of his father, Homer, and who is self-consciously the epic successor and the mediator of that genre to the modern world. So he is himself concretely in the position of the elder son, witness to the passion of Laocoön. Virgil is, accordingly, *the archetypal poet as inheritor* in the Western poetic tradition who has witnessed and escaped the blinding of Homer. (Raphael juxtaposed the two heads, blind and sighted [fig. 5].) His hero is a priest, *pius Aeneas*, surrogate and blameless legatee of the priest Laocoön; in that sense, Aeneas is also in the position of an elder son. And Virgil's art is critique doubled on itself, the dialectical witness of the elder son.

In book II of the *Aeneid*, the poet records Aeneas's access to the secret of the god, correlative to the experience of Achilleus that gives rise to the wisdom utterance in the *Iliad* XXIV ("There are two urns. . . ."). Aeneas has made his way to the altar of the house of Priam, which is being destroyed by the Greeks in revenge of the rape of Helen. He encounters Helen at the altar and raises his sword to kill her, supposing she is a guilty agent of history. At that moment Aphrodite in a vision discloses to her son the true cause of (manifest) history—warfare, the fall of Troy—which she knows to be a consequence not of Helen's infidelity, but of the gods' hatred of all of human constructions that threaten divine representational hegemony. Thus Aphrodite shows Aeneas that the Trojan War is eidetic warfare in the interest of Olympian dominance. This is the Virgilian depiction of what the poet knows. Aphrodite speaks:

> Behold—for all the cloud which now, drawn over your sight, dulls your mortal vision and with dank pall enshrouds you, I will tear away; fear no commands of your mother nor refuse to obey her counsels—here, where you see shattered piles and rocks torn from rocks, and smoke eddying up mixed with dust, Neptune shakes the walls and foundations that his mighty trident has upheaved, and uproots all the city from her base. Here Juno, fiercest of all, is foremost to hold the Scaean gates and, girt with steel, furiously calls from the ships her allied band. . . . Now on the highest towers—turn and see—Tritonian Pallas is planted, gleaming

with storm cloud and grim Gorgon. My father himself gives the Greeks courage and auspicious strength; he himself stirs up the gods against the Dardan arms.[32]

As in the case of the story about Laocoön that requires his death and the death of his children, so also, in the case of the story about Rome that requires the destruction of Troy, the justice of the Virgilian gods is precisely inexplicable by ethical criteria. The vision granted to Aeneas by his divine mother, Aphrodite, cancels the "existence"—the valid meanings—of the manifest and its human moral agents. Regulation of the manifest world requires, by the divinely sponsored logic of manifestation in the scarce space of "existence," the (unjust) destruction of the human city of empathic and reproductive life (Troy) in the interest of "civilization" (Roma, the Olympian *eidos*). Aeneas's *mortal* children are destroyed like Laocoön's before his eyes. The cause is not in history and is not personal.

Aphrodite shows her priest son the secret of the god—that the cause of violence in history is the retribution of the god against the constructive claims of the human city. Such moments of the "seeing through" narrative rationality supply the motive of the modern poem. The high lamentational style of Virgil's *Aeneid* is an expression of the *Urleid*—the sorrow on the face of the speaker arising from the poet's knowledge of the captivity of the world to the principles of its making, neither divine nor human, which by means of their power the gods regulate. There are no survivors of the Laocoön story in Virgil's text. History is not survivable. The *telling* of the story is accomplished, therefore, by textual strategies of transcendence, expressive of the representational empowerments of the poetic text by reason of the priority of its witness to history.

The story about Laocoön in Virgil's text is doubly embedded and qualified. First, it occurs within the text of the *Aeneid* of which the supposed Virgilian "poet" is narrator (*Arma virumque cano*); and then within that text, the story is further contained in the inner text of Aeneas's narration— Aeneas's explanation of himself to Dido (*infandum regina iubes*). In other words, Virgil's story about Laocoön can, apparently, only be told in context of a double transcendence: (1) by Virgil's assumed poet, as "poet" prior to history and the gods; and (2) by the poet's surrogate in history "Aeneas," who is prior as (poetic) narrator to his own experience.

At the beginning of book II, "Aeneas" is narrated as speaking to Dido and her court about himself (*Conticuere omnes*, "Everyone fell silent"). His intention is to supply Dido with sufficient information *about his alliances* to enable Dido to make a judgment upon his legitimacy as a lover and husband. This Aeneas fails to do, essentially because the truth of his narrative is the *untellable* (*infandum*) story about the unsurvivability of truth-telling: Laocoön's lesson to his son. (*Infandum regina iubes renovare dolorem*, "Unspeakable, O queen, is the grief you bid me renew.") Only those such as Sinon, who—unlike Laocoön—do not tell the truth, survive. Sinon betrays the Trojans to history—the story into which they disappear.

In Virgil, history is the narrative with no outside, no alternative, unsurvivable. If the manifest poem (e.g., *Aeneid*) has the same structure as history (Roma), then it can only—no matter what it says—carry the same meaning as history (Roma). If all representation has the structure of (Roman) hegemony, then all actual poems do too. Therefore the poem is not in any sense distant from history and the elder son, and all the possibilities of discourse with which I have invested the elder son are seen to perish with his father and his brother in the Laocoön catastrophe—as in fact they do in book II of the *Aeneid*. At best, critique takes the form of pathos (the *passio* that is poetic consciousness of pain, dissociated from any practice of repair or restitution—the "report" of Laocoön's scream, not the scream), and there is in history no opening toward indeterminacy (autonomy of agency)—certainly not the poetic text. If history as narrative in the *Aeneid* is the only story *possible* to be told and that history is Rome, then Aeneas *can never effectively tell* the story of his fatal alliances to the divine sponsors of Rome; and Dido must always be deceived and die.

But the Laocoön in all its forms has brought the *infandum* (what cannot be said) to mind. The moment of the poetic text is in fact the failure of all other mediation *and makes known that failure*. The *Aeneid* exists to present the originary moment of the poetic text as the failed confession of the bridegroom, at the heart of which is the untellable fact of an indissoluble alliance of the constructive will (Aeneas) with the unethical force (the gods), who are allegories of the material conditions of construction. Virgil's account of Laocoön is determined by his realization of the war of describers as *inevitably entailing* the predominance of maintenance values (Olympian, divine) over truth values (the mortal true-love), as inscribed in the already-written history of the one world that is—the empire of the real without alternative. From this realization flows the *Aeneid*'s narration of the death of (the withdrawal of the legitimacy of existence from) alternative worlds, figured as the beautiful dead children (Pallas, Camilla, Nisus, Euryalus, etc.) who must be destroyed to bring the one legitimate world (Roma) to manifestation.

The *Urleid* is not merely reported but heard. Undoubtedly, prosody and the figure are essential sites of poetic dissent from Olympian determination. As in the account of the scream of Laocoön: "He lifts to heaven hideous cries [*Clamores simul horrendos ad sidera tollit*], like the bellowings of a wounded bull that has fled from the altar and shaken from its neck the ill-aimed axe."[33]

The "right" or Olympian form of the cultural transaction—sacrifice on the altar—in which loss is rewritten as gain of another kind—is defeated in the figure of the bungled (*incertam*) sacrificial act. The uncompleted sacrifice here—the failure of a mediation—is the fundamental story about Laocoön. It condenses the motive and subject matter of the poem in general. The priority of poetry as the qualified representation of all (Olympian) representations is memorialized in the "poetic" reproduction (not precisely a "report") of the scream of Laocoön, and the suppression or else endless deferral of its meaning.

What justifies the sacrifice of Laocoön on the altar of a civilization where its priest becomes the sacrificial victim? It is the prestige of that fundamental motive of the religious institution—*world-maintenance:* the Virgilian justification of the suppression of the "imagination" (autonomy of form), which, as the predecessor of all manifestation and its knower, including God, threatens God. The reason of state is the necessity of *world maintenance*, which requires the fixing of the human image in the one form—the conquest of all worlds by the one world (Roma) to which validity has been assigned and that, therefore, exists.

But the practical instrument of the poetic indeterminacy or autonomous determination of the human form, and the site in the poem of the strategy of world-maintenance counter to the strategy of the state, is *poetic language*, of which Virgil was a master. Poetic language is always heard as a strange voice—heterogeneous, as old as the world—within familiar voices. It is the poet's disarticulation of a speech of another kind that is implied by the nature and practice of speech of our kind. The Virgilian text characteristically makes plain the moment of the necessity of poetic language and the question of its force.

The *Aeneid* exemplifies the realization (both as text and fable) of the kind of poetics to which this essay is devoted, focusing (as stated at the outset) on the position with respect to the poetic text afforded to one who engages in the labor of making. Such labor is explicit in the *Aeneid*. ("Such a hard task it was to found the Roman people," or *hoc opus, hic labor* of book VI: "this is the task, the toil" of returning from the underworld.) The question of the poetics of the maker is not whether the structure of text must repeat itself as the structure of the world, or even whether all human reality is structured like a text, but whether all texts are structured like Rome. Whether there is not another account of making ("open, theoretic—hospitable to desire"—theoretic but not virtual) among those which Rome represses—not the Alexandrian Homer whose testimony I have discussed—

but another Homer and another song with the origin of the manifest world inside it, another Homer such as Rome and its late Olympian sponsors do not know. Perhaps hear him in Dido's doomed household. Consider the mysterious song of Iopas (book I.1010–20):

> Long-haired Iopas, once taught by mighty Atlas, makes the hall ring with his golden lyre. He sings of the wandering moon and the sun's toils; whence sprang man and beast, whence rain and fire; of Arcturus, the rainy Hyades and the twin Bears; why wintry suns make such haste to dip themselves in Ocean, or what delay stays the slowly passing nights. With shout on shout the Tyrians applaud, and the Trojans follow.[34]

IX. *Priscus Theologicus*: Poetic Language as the Efficacious Memory of Prehistoric Language Function

While men still roamed the woods, Orpheus, the holy prophet of the gods, made them shrink from bloodshed and brutal living; hence the fable that he tamed tigers and ravening lions; hence too the fable that Amphion, builder of Thebes' citadel, moved stones by the sound of his lyre, and led them whither he would by his supplicating spell. In days of yore, this was wisdom, to draw a line between public and private rights, between things sacred and things common, to check vagrant union, to give rules for wedded life, to build towns, and engrave laws on tables of wood; and so honor and fame fell to bards and their songs as divine. After these Homer. . . .

Horace, *Ars Poetica*, 391–405

Poetry is older than skillfully elaborated prose speech. It is the original presentation of the truth, a knowing which does not yet separate the universal from its living existence in the individual . . . but which grasps the one only in and through the other.

Hegel, *Lectures on the Fine Arts*

The *other* Homer to which I make reference is the so-called "Epimenides type," Gisella M. A. Richter's "sleeping Homer" (fig. 3). The face that is as old as the world. Inside the Hellenistic portrait of Homer (fig. 2) that I have discussed, the Laocoön image expresses primordiality and violence of an extreme sort and is associated, in that "circulation of images" that includes the Pergamon frieze and the Blake engraving, with cosmogonic warfare of the genocidal kind—warfare in which the victor (i.e., the Olympian) is not of the same race (genus? species?) as the repressed kind (i.e., the chthonian). The occasion of such reciprocal misidentification is the making of difference (always perceived hierarchically) on which cultural discourse (*the face, as it appears*) depends. The fatal nature of the discourses in dispute inheres in the totality claim of each, every one a real world, the existence and legitimacy of which depend on the subordination (the discursive *de*-legitimation) of the other. All social and psychological formations figure legitimacy as presence at origin, to which language in an extended (poetic) sense gives access. But the space of origin is narrow and accommodates one at a time.

You will remember that the notion of discourse or "language" that is here involved is not a Saussurean system of consensual composite signs (*signum/signatum*), but *non-communicative* non-messaging homogeneous language that specifies world and species.[35] This type and function of language is clearly presented by Vico, who, however, does not recognize that there is a multiplicity of such non-communicating "universes of discourse," each specifying a world without alternative. They are competing systems of generality in the scarce space of existence, each one *enabling intersubjectivity within a horizon by bounding it* — in effect, by blocking a further stage of generality (let us call it "universality," in the Spinoza sense) and thus dealing to the "other nation" the existential death that is the delegated cost of the corresponding life produced. The *encounter of languages of this sort with one another* gives rise to and explains outraged theodicean expectation (shocked discovery of the unintelligibility of experience, the sentiment of injustice, the intolerability of other people's music), as is expressed in Virgil's account of Laocoön.

But there are two versions (as I have pointed out) of the Laocoön narrative. The Virgilian version, which is unmediated and without survivors. And the sculptural version in which the possibility of critique is invested in the escaping elder son whose destiny is in testimony, and whose language is the language of the gigantic, winged elder race — that is to say, *poetic language* that knows the secret of the atrocity by which (always) the dominant discourse is known to have been founded. (The elder son has read it in the witness face of the father Homer-Teiresias-Laocoön-Alkyoneus-Adonai.)

But what then is "poetic language"? *It is the language that presents to us the human face by reason of speaking — and is precisely as old as the human world.*

This face (the face of immanent authenticity) we see in another of the invented portraits of Homer (materially older than the Hellenistic image in which we found the faces of Laocoön and Alkyoneus). This "other" "sleeping Homer" is historically the most ancient, and also stylistically the most archaic (as it were, prehistoric) of the invented portraits of Homer — the least articulated from stone. *The blindness of this image is the sleep by which any modernity obtains relation to ancient time.* (Cf. Pound's self-portrait as the sleeping Homer, also Brancusi's "Muse.")

On the one hand, the blindness of the Hellenistic Homer-Laocoön maintains the human form of experience despite the unintelligibility of that experience—the complex face that experience assumes when it becomes the speech of a person. The beauty of the face of the Hellenistic Homer is testimony to an act of blind conscious, willed self-descriptive resistance to the world that is not human. The beauty of the "sleeping Homer," on the other hand (fig. 3), represents a recuperative "sinking in" of mind upon states of "language" that it contributes to consciousness but does not find there. In that blind sleep there arises the dream of "ancient time"—the peculiar kind of archaism by which poetic language in the West recuperates the wisdom of the long history of its kind—the language of absolute priority as presented in Iopas's song. Its signifiers of a prior (*kairotic*) temporality of origination are, for example, the "*silvestris*" or "*quondam*" of Roman Horace, as in the epigraph above ("In days of yore, this was wisdom . . ."); and the "And it came to pass . . ." ("*vayehi ha-at ha-hi*") of the Old Testament, or "*illo tempore*" of the Gospels ("At that time . . ."); the "ancient time" of the romantic poet ("And did those feet in ancient time . . . ?"); the "*vieillerie poetique*" of Rimbaud ("*La viellerie avait une bonne part dans mon alchimie du verbe*"—*Une saison en enfer*)—and the like.

The valid guide in this matter—the deep dream of poetic language—is the image of youthful Orpheus, *priscus theologicus* (first theologian, a mortal who knows the divine *prior* to the co-optation of experience by instituted religion). In him youthfulness signifies closeness to origins, as age does in the "sleeping Homer." Another image (not included) presents one modern instance of the image of this Orpheus. The *young* Orpheus (in the Middle Ages he is the Orpheus Christos,[36] in the classical gentile world, the Orpheus of the Argonautic expedition) is the Orpheus of "ancient times"— that is to say, before "Orphic" identification of the person with the god-sponsored logic of manifestation that is signified by the later catastrophe of Eurydice. In this figure, the image that illustrates Rousseau's pedagogic romance *Émile*, Orpheus with lyre (the sign of the métier of poetry) produces not messages about the world, but precisely that intelligibility of experience that moves and interests trees, beasts, human beings in a single universe responsive to mind. This is what is meant by the civilizational commonplace repeated by Hegel, "Poetry is the original presentation of the truth. . . ."

The function of poetic text in any schoolroom is always (as Rousseau discerned) to place the student in the presence of this Orpheus of ancient time, the *priscus theologicus*—first theologian. In Rousseau, this figure of Orpheus is brought to mind as an exposition of the "Profession of Faith of the

Savoyard Vicar," the secular teacher of a *universal conscience*, or consciousness. "The good priest had spoken with vehemence. He was moved, and so
was I. I believed I was hearing the divine Orpheus singing the first hymns
and teaching men the worship of the gods. Nevertheless, I saw a multitude
of objections to make to him. I did not make any of them, because they
were less solid than disconcerting, and persuasiveness was on his side. *To
the extent that he spoke to me according to his conscience, mine seemed to confirm
what he had told me.*" In the course of his profession, the vicar exclaims,
"Conscience, conscience! Divine instinct, *immortal and celestial voice,* certain guide of a being that is ignorant and limited but intelligent and free;
infallible judge of good and bad which makes man like unto God. . . . *Without you I sense nothing in me that raises me above the beasts. . . .*"[37]

The subject matter of poetics, insofar as it is theoretic and hospitable
to desire, is the constructibility of this voice of conscience (or consciousness)—"immortal and celestial"—that is prior to the instituted God or
identical with him, that makes the difference upon which the recognition
of the human species depends, that requires no instituted church for its
promulgation, and that is figured by the young Orpheus, the archetypal
poet, who "sings" to animate an inanimate being and by such singing renders the world intelligible. This voice is not communicative but constitutive of the human world, as in the fable where Orpheus and Amphion
moved trees and built walls. It is empowered by the absolute priority to
the material world of "language" as primary representation. It is reliably
intersubjective (within the domain in which it is recognitional) and trans-
historical. It is prior to rationality. Orpheus is the first theologian because
he is the master of the possibility conditions of discourse itself.

But how are we to account for the Orphic sponsorship of the language
of "consciousness"? Consider, as a Rousseauian heuristic history, the following narrative of which the "sleeping Homer" dreams and that, though
my analysis is briefly sketched, I intend to be both logically and historically
valid (not in any case, in contradiction of fact) and that also I consider *to
be present logically and historically inside every occasion of poetic representation:*
Throughout the history of humankind—which in this view begins in the
earliest moment at which we recognize the "human" status of the animal
(in the Viconian sense, the moment in which we "make ourselves human")
on the ground of the speciating distinction of language, long before the onset of speech—*"human beings" have been and still are creatures of highly developed mind, but very imperfectly developed means of control of the material world.*
The most perfect means (indistinguishable from the self-recognition of
the species) humankind has possessed in the last 500,000 years of its

development (since *Homo habilis*) is "language"—*the human instrument of most general application*. In and around every artifact and brilliant shard or tracing that we now decipher as attesting human presence was spun a web of words of some kind, presumptively unspoken, no longer detectable except in their effects—the softest of soft tissue—but constituting the instrument of most general application possessed by earliest humanity. By its nature as the constituting system of the human world (identified with fundamental species recognition), such prehistoric "language" is now the always present substructure or environment (*Umwelt*) of human mind to which poetry gives access.

In modern culture (from the fifth century B.C.E. to the present time), poetic language is associated with the *prehistoric* on the ground of its specific difference—archaism—from other kinds of language; and consequently poetic language is associated not with communication, but with orientation in the human world—the possibility condition of communication that is the recognition of the human other: the *eidos*. What is called poetic creation is in fact fundamental legislative inscription, as (once again) Horace reminds us. In ancient time (*in illo tempore*), reality first became subject to discourse, as it is said of Orpheus and Amphion that they moved trees and built walls, and the *vates* became competitors with the gods for the predicate divine (*divinis vatibus*, Whitman's "divine literatus").

How then does poetry come to mediate decisively between mind and world? Because poetic language conserves (anamnetically) social memory of prehistoric language as the human instrument of most general application. Thus, the logic that positions poetry among the most fundamental competences by which the community is assured is as follows: *At any given moment in history, poetry puts language as the instrument or tool of most general application in service of the human community precisely at the point of the absence, failure, or desuetude of other means, including religion, medicine, philosophy, rationality, or speech itself. But especially other means of specifying the kind, that is to say, means of human recognition. Reciprocally, poetic language ceases to be valid— comes to the end of its own logic—when another tool would better serve.* How does one know when poetry is present? Poetry is present whenever and by what means this function is served.

Hence poetic language—the collective memory of the prehistoric general tool—is invoked precisely at the edge of the human world where the human mind has come to the end of its mastery by other means. As was conceptualized on other grounds earlier, poetry is summoned at moments of eidetic crisis, to the reconstitution of that face that is obtained, as I have said, by reason of speaking, because poetic language brings into the present the prehistoric language of the self-identification of the person.

Poetry, memory of the working of language as the prehistoric instrument or tool of most general application, is then *the civilizational means of last recourse*. It follows that the fundamental creative act—the praxis of the poetic principle—is the ascertainment of just that historical moment, or occasion of need, when the work of the human interest (the construction of the person) can be done *by no other means than the poetic*. Hence, the validity of poetic practice—what the poet does as poet—depends on the discrimination of poetry from arts and institutions of another kind (that's the purpose of Lessing's *Laocoön*). The productive service of poetic practice to the human community is contingent upon the independence of poetic practice uncompromised by confusion with other kinds of discourse, or the satisfaction of needs and desires that can be addressed by other means.

But at the moment of the vanishing of the human image, when a prior grounding (or assurance of the visibility of the person) has come to an end of its efficacy, *the motive to the eidetic reconstruction becomes the engine of history*. Perhaps the central Western case of this process is gospel Christianity: the New Testament (the "new song") relegitimizes the person on the grounds of a renewed priority, as a basis of predominant generality and validity ("Before Abraham was I am"). Or, on another contrasting scale of life, John Donne, *having exhausted the eidetic resource of poetic practice*, resorts to conversion and the institution of the priesthood, and renews poetry in conformity to a regulative principle of another kind. Or Whitman, in the interest of validating the new federal constitution of the person, resorts precisely to the most general human instrument having exhausted modern resources: "The priest departs, the divine literatus comes."

The institutions of mind seem in an evolutionary struggle in which recourse to the prehistoric state of language, the instrument of most general application, poetic language, becomes the means of self-identification and construction of the person at the moment of the exhaustion of another métier. Such exhaustion may be systemic. In *The Nature of Rationality*, for example, Robert Nozick makes an evolutionary analysis of rationality, to the effect that the failure of rational solutions to solve a certain class of problems delineates the outer edge of the functional adaptation of the rational power: "Many of philosophy's traditional intractable problems [e.g., the problems of induction, other minds, the external world, justifying goals], resistant to rational resolution, may result from attempts to extend rationality beyond this delimited [evolutionary] function."[38] It should be obvious also that disfiguration and failure of eidetic function results when poetic discourse is *prematurely substituted for* institutions of another sort, including philosophy.

When experience disconfirms the expected rationality of history—at the moment of the outrage or enigmatization of the normative theodicean narrative, which is in my view narrative altogether—the Laocoön image erects itself: the innocent *are seen* to be punished and the grounds of human value are seen to be problematized. At that moment the cry of Laocoön goes up (the always unheard *clamores horrendos*, the lament of the sacrificial animal). And that absolute priority of *poetic language* (prehistoric, supporting the possibility conditions of communication—universal conscience—more profoundly related to human interest than communicative exchange) supersedes the shattered rationality of rationality itself as it is invested in (religious) narrative and gathers up the silent cry. The priority of the poetic principle to the religious principle (as also to the philosophical ground of logic—the Aristotelian rules of thought) resumes its function. For this reason (in the light of this master subtext), Lessing insists not merely on the temporality but on the temporal *priority* of Virgil's verbal art, poetry, over sculptural representation.

"Poetic language," as I have presented it, is among the instruments of civilization as authorizing the fundamental constitution of the human world. It is a general orientative discourse that legitimates subsequent more specified discourses. In time it becomes increasingly differentiated into a congeries of less general institutions of languages. *The differentiation that is least perfect is the differentiation of religious from poetic language.* And the priority of the poetic language continually threatens the legitimacy of the god. The more convergent the intention of institutions may be, the more violently the discourse sponsored by one delegitimates the discourse sponsored by the other, that is, disputes its claims to establish the value claimed, the "existence" of its terms. In the vast semiotic net of any civilization, this holds true for instituted discourses of all kinds—including the adjacent discourses of music, sexuality, couture, polity, legality, et cetera. Of greatest importance from our point of view are *poetic practice* and *the practice of sanctity*, which, universally distributed in Western time and space and equally engaged with a transcendental term (the *theo-logos*), intend and construct the valorization of personal presence in adjacent and fundamental ways—and depend for their vital life on the delegitimation of the claims to existence of the central facts brought to mind by the adjacent discourse.

The crisis of discrimination as between religious and poetic institutions (as in Arnold or Whitman, one institution is thought to be exchangeable for the other) arises because both intend the same outcome—the establishment of the person by reference to the *category of greatest difference, which is identically the category of highest value—sanctity, or the divine*—of which both god and the poet are members (cf. Horace *divinis vatibus*, cited above).[39]

When the priest departs, it is the *divine* literatus, driven from the scarce space of representation (like Cain in the Bible with the mark of murder on his brow), who comes back. The same term, the sacred, which functions as radical, constructive difference, is significant of the possibility conditions necessary to make (*poiein*) persons (the creatures of highest value), and to make the world (the object of highest value), and to make war (the making of difference itself, that is death—"sane and sacred death").

Sanctity, the difference of the divine, is the absolutely general category of significance in dispute between poetry and religion. The death of Satan was a catastrophe for the imagination (human image-making), because Satan is of course (as Blake saw) the elder son, the principle of the indeterminacy of human form, critique, the human claim upon the category that produces the difference of significance, the thief of the sacred. Alive, escaped from the death the father dies, as in Blake's *Laocoön*, Satan effects the interruption of hierarchy necessary to freedom (figured by Virgil, ambiguously, as the bungled sacrifice). The competition is for priority (proximity to origins, the regulation of generality) from which flows right to the term of highest value (sanctity).

The threat by the person to the *proprium* of the god is *impermissible human beauty* (the children of Niobe, Aeneas's Pallas, the song of Thamyris, the beautiful thing, true-love). The self-reproducing character of human form uses up the scarce space, which is all the manifestation there is. The death inflicted by the god is, as we have seen, the disruption of the human continuity, the destruction of the male children, genocide. Autonomous human continuity by its nature is an encroachment upon divine privilege. *Great poetry, indeed human artifice altogether (the beautiful child of human history), threatens divinity with the cosmic disruption entailed by great mimetic success.*

All economics is at bottom driven by the scarcity of image. What then is imperfectly distributable and therefore "scarce"? The terms of highest value—eidetic terms that can only be grounded in the material world: honor, the face and the powers that produce their presence in history, sanctity, presence, difference, and so on. This eidetic or image scarcity is the economic cause of the warfare between god and man (as in the Laocoön narrative) and between man and man (as in the *Iliad* at large). The dreaming Homer reminds us *that no making can intend total freedom so long as it intends also manifestation,* because no making, whatever its intention, is exempt from making's laws. This is presumably the esoteric knowledge for the possession of which Laocoön is punished, Homer and Teiresias blinded, the giant Alkyoneus slain, Marsyas flayed, Eurydice revoked to the underworld, Christ crucified. The passion of Laocoön.

Nonetheless, the poet intends the poem. *Some* qualifications of that intention, which have been brought to mind in context of this poetics of the maker's practice, are the following:

(1) In order to do the poet's work, the poet must know the principles of poetic construction, and these are identically the constructive secrets of the god by which *existence and therefore value* is assigned to facts and persons. The secrets of the god include the nature of the resistance of materials; but also the entailed inevitability of hierarchy and the violence of its imposition. This is the "esoteric" subject matter of poetics—in effect the memory of the primordial wound, the passion of Laocoön: the artisanal knowledge that constitutes vocation in the poet and contributes that delight in the reader that arises from gathering the meaning of things.

(2) Without the god-term (*theo-logos*), there is no effect of existence, no *confiance au monde*, nothing of value. The god-term (*theo-logos*) is the principle of generality that produces the intelligibility of the world and its communicability—the common truth of language. The unfixing of that term (the realization of the god as a term) is the beginning of history. The idea of an (esoteric) principle prior to the truth of facts upon which the truth of facts depends is essentially religious *or* poetic, but not both. It is the property in dispute between the religious and the poetic foundations. The possession of it confers the conviction of existence. But the effect of existence (and therefore value) is not infinitely distributable.

(3) The means of the poet is poetic language. Poetic language is the social memory of prehistoric language function (prior to, or other than, communicative language): the prehistoric instrument or tool of most general application (the word that meant everything) by which the phenomenal world is constituted. Such language, fundamentally orientative, tolerates no alternative and is made effective in the human world by reason of its reference to a principle of generality (god-term) that is maintained by an institution that must validate it as a term of discourse.

(4) The occasion of the intending of the poem (eidetic crisis) is the desuetude of other institutions of eidetic value, the situation realized in the passion of Laocoön. But the occasion of the valid poem is only and precisely the *moment* when the work of constructing the value of the person can be done *by no other means*. The valid poetic vocation (the knowledge that is signified by the term "creativity") depends on the capacity to ascertain this moment. This positioning determines the changing relation of poetry to social experience. The characteristic situation (as narration) that gives rise to valid poetic action or practice is the outraged theodicean consciousness—the sense of the unintelligibility of experience, which makes up (as in the Laocoön image) at the moment of pain: "all the pain there is."

(5) Because poetic language participates in the absolute priority of representation, it continuously reproduces fundamental conflict (characterized by reciprocal delegitimation) with all other institutions that also claim priority for the purpose of validation. In doing so, the structure of the poetic text iterates also the structure of manifestation. There is, however, a sense that has become the *differentia specifica* (the identifying mark) of the poetic that, by reason of earliness, poetic language (as imaged by the sleeping Homer or described by Hegel) is structured in some other way than manifestation—an otherness from ordinary language as signified, let us say, by the wingedness of the principle of Poetry in the Stanza della Segnatura (fig. 9).

(6) Thus central to this analysis is the problem of repetition in every representation, including poems of the imposed hierarchy by which representation is constructed (Homer as Alkyoneus). The rationality of this state of affairs is rooted in a background of scarcity, the question of which is the most urgent concern of the poetics of practice, *because no experimental reordering of the structures of the poem's manifestation—the inevitable matrix of poetic language—will ever escape the fatality of the structure of manifestation itself.*

X. The Scream of Marsyas: The Encounter of Poetry and Theology

Quid me mihi detrahis?—Why do you tear me from myself?

Ovid

Marsyas—the satyr who, like the Silenus, represents the *eidos* of the person in history (figs. 11 and 12)—is destroyed (de-faced, unmade, skinned) *by Apollo* for the reason that he challenges the music of the god (challenges, more specifically, the relation of Olympian countenance to music). Marsyas challenges the music of the god and promotes the flute, an instrument the practice of which deforms the face of the Olympian (Apollo/Athene)—in other words, a musical instrument that when played produces a face inconsistent with the Olympian likeness to humanity. The satyr, or Silenus, presents *an indeterminacy or autonomous realization* of the *eidos* of the human image—like the titans of Hesiod, or the hybrid giants of the Pergamon frieze, or like the *Laocoön*. Socrates is thought of as a Silenus, an "un-human" being who knows important mythological secrets (the secrets of the gods), and is captured (as in Virgil's *Eclogue* 6) and opened to force revelation of them:

What [Socrates] reminds me of more than anything [said Alcibiades] is one of those little Sileni that are seen on the statuaries' stalls; you know the ones I mean—they're modeled with pipes or flutes in their hands,

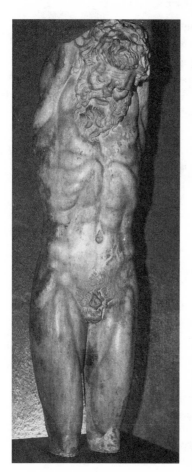

Fig. 11. The punishment of Marsyas. Hellenistic marble sculpture, third century C.E.. Archaeological Museum, Istanbul, Turkey. Photo credit: Borromeo / Art Resource, New York.

Fig. 12. Raphael, *Apollo and Marsyas*. Late fifteenth or early sixteenth century. Stanza della Segnatura, Stanze di Raffaello, Vatican Palace, Vatican State. Photo credit: Scala / Art Resource, New York.

and when you open them down the middle there are little figures of the gods inside. And then again he reminds me of Marsyas the satyr. . . ."[40]

This opening up of the outside of the creature for the purpose of discovering an Olympian image inside is a model of Western spirituality that religion institutes, and to the interests of which Socrates is (perhaps unsuccessfully) co-opted. In order to cancel the outside (the sur-face, the manifest person), which would otherwise legitimate by poetry (the pipes) an illegitimate instantiation of the *eidos* ("deformed face"), the god commands that the skin be torn from the person, or the person turned inside out. This practice is literalized in the flaying of Marsyas—of whom Alcibiades is reminded by the dog-face of Socrates. Ovid gives us an account of this atrocity:

> Then . . . another [storyteller] recalled the satyr whom the son of Latona [Apollo] had conquered in contest on Pallas' reed, and punished. "Why do you tear me from myself?" cried the satyr. "Oh, I repent! Oh, a flute is not worth such price!" As he screams, his skin is stripped off the surface of his body, and he is all one wound: blood flows down on every side, the sinews lie bare, his veins throb and quiver with no skin to cover them. . . . The country people, the sylvan deities, fawns, and his brother Satyrs, and Olympus, whom even then he still loved, the nymphs, all wept for him. . . . The fruitful earth was soaked, and soaking caught those tears. . . . Thence the stream within its sloping banks ran down quickly to the sea, and had the name of Marsyas. . . ."[41]

The encounter of poetry and religion (as instituted spirituality) issues in an atrocity visited upon the material body (the murdered child of Gea, as in the Pergamon frieze). This is the way of Western spirituality—the *torturing* of Marsyas and the *crowning* of Apollo. By the nature both of theology and poetry, the continually reasserted victory of the god-term (the *theo-logos*, which is the possibility condition of the "human image") requires such violence.

The figure of Marsyas can be seen in the Pergamon style (fig. 11)—the same as that which gives us our Hellenistic portrait of Homer. On the walls of the Stanza della Segnatura, Raphael has placed his account of the same Marsyas (fig. 12). "In the corner between the *Parnassus* and the *Disputa* [the institution of the Eucharist] [Marsyas] is flanked on either side by the figure of Dante, who appears in the *Disputa* among the followers of St. Thomas and St. Bonaventura, and in the *Parnassus* in the company of Homer and Virgil."[42] Between the sacrificial institution of poetry (the altar of Apollo) and the sacrificial institution of religion (the altar of Christ) stands the figure of the flayed satyr who says, "Why do you tear me from myself?" Thus is registered the inevitable atrocity by the iron law of Apollonian form. Whether the injunction of the god is "You must be absolutely modern" or "Know thyself," "Blessed are the meek" or "The intellect of man is forced to choose / Perfection of the life or of the work," the self is in any case torn from the self.

The images to which I have referred (the Hellenistic portrait of Homer, the *Laocoön*, the Pergamon frieze, the *Aeneid*, etc.) produce, by their reciprocity and internality one to another, some indication of the structure of the poetic practice. Whatever may be our experience of them, such works belong to a canon of "supreme" human productions exemplified by Pliny's classification of the *Laocoön*: "*opus omnibus et picturae et statuariae artis preferendum*" (a work superior to all other paintings and statues). The "supreme" status of these works (epitomized by the evaluative prestige of Homer's poems in the West) is not in my view—however it may be applied—an empty classification. It expresses the civilizational intuition that works so classified—the masters' works whichever they may be—bring to light indispensable (always "new") knowledge unobtainable except by poetic means. In effect, such works answer to Aristotle's criterion that art, the product of *poesis*, facilitates the greatest human pleasure, which is to gather the meaning of things.

Poetry, as the principle of a métier, produces new knowledge such as I have tried to bring to mind—and the function of poetry in the world is surely new knowledge. But poetry is "new" and "knowledge" *only* when it is truly engaged with the work of the human world, and that is the case only when it is summoned to a problem or occasion in the light of which, in a specific historical situation, there is no other recourse than poetry. The appropriate work of the poet is the construction of the value of the person.

The Hellenistic bust of Homer is an action of the exegetical imagination, the work of Satan, whose death is a tragedy of the imagination if it means the end of thinking about the inhumanity of the "human" form. The indication of the death of Satan is the disappearance of the question of the justice of God.

The last injunction of the modern poet, the legacy of the most fully developed body of poetic work in this century (the farewell, as I think of the eldest son of whom I have spoken) is: Do not represent—because the deformations entailed by representation are too great to justify the practice of representation. This is the sense, for example, of Rilke in his letter to von Hulewicz when he says, "We are the bees of the invisible." Will the poets to come work not as poets before us worked—or as we work—to bring the invisible to visibility, but to effect the invisibility of the manifest world and convey it into the virtuality of an art of the invisible where no scarcity of highest value compels the iteration of the primordial wars of the manifest, and the passion of Laocoön is unknown? The question is the same as the question "Does poetry come to an end?"

Figuring the Real

WORDSWORTH'S
"THE SOLITARY REAPER"

When one does something poetic, one makes for sacredness,
and in that sense one produces the untranslatable.

Jacques Derrida, *The Ear of the Other*[1]

Much of the talk about poetry in the West has been conducted under the category of defense or *apologia*, a genre in part explanation and in part an effort to disqualify accusation. Why does poetry of all arts require a defense? Largely because the claim for poetry of highest value ("sanctity"—associated with the universality of representation, of which universality poetry is the most abstract principle) and the accusation against poetry of greatest violence (the "slide [of the other] into nothingness" consequent on the accomplishment by poetic means of the highest distinction) are inseparable.

In this light then, I wish to say something about the interest or stake, defensible and also indefensible, we have in the witness of poems—that is to say, *something about the poetic interest*, an interest that is evoked by the lure and shamelessness of what *might* be called "the real" or "the sacred" or the highest value, in any case the authorizing term of poetic practice, which constitutes some part of the meaning of any poem. I will do so by bringing to mind, as an example for which I propose very general theoretical relevance, Wordsworth's poem "The Solitary Reaper"—a poem that interests me in ways I am trying to understand. The destination of my interest is in any case the poetic principle (*poesia*), to which the speaker in the poem draws attention with "Behold her"—its figuration or look, and its action in the world. My interest is not precisely the poem (*poema*) and certainly not the poet (*poeta*, except as instituted agent).

* "Figuring the Real: Wordsworth's 'The Solitary Reaper'" was originally published in an earlier version under the title "Wordsworth's 'The Solitary Reaper': Notes on *Poiesis*, Pastoral, and Institution," *TriQuarterly* 116 (Summer 2003): 277–99.

My conclusion will be that the poetic interest is in the bringing to mind of our state of affairs in representation and the seeing of it (provisionally) as possessing a structure of a given kind and, in that sense only, solved. This is the goal of poetic interest—poetic interest as social and cognitive stake, poetic interest as desire of the image, *nostra effigie*, the same interest that sexuality covers over.

THE SOLITARY REAPER

Behold her, single in the field,
Yon solitary Highland Lass!
Reaping and singing by herself;
Stop here, or gently pass!
Alone she cuts, and binds the grain,
And sings a melancholy strain;
O listen! for the Vale profound
Is overflowing with the sound.

No Nightingale did ever chaunt
More welcome notes to weary bands
Of travellers in some shady haunt,
Among Arabian sands:
A voice so thrilling ne'er was heard
In spring-time from the Cuckoo-bird,
Breaking the silence of the seas
Among the farthest Hebrides.

Will no one tell me what she sings?—
Perhaps the plaintive numbers flow
For old, unhappy, far-off things,
And battles long ago:
Or is it some more humble lay,
Familiar matter of to-day?
Some natural sorrow, loss, or pain,
That has been, and may be again?

Whate'er the theme, the Maiden sang
As if her song could have no ending;
I saw her singing at her work,
And o'er the sickle bending;—
I listen'd, motionless and still;

And, as I mounted up the hill,
The music in my heart I bore,
Long after it was heard no more.

"The Solitary Reaper" was published for the first time in Wordsworth's
Poems in Two Volumes (1807), by the same publisher and in the same format
(two volumes) as the second edition of the *Lyrical Ballads* (1800). The two
great historical qualifiers of the *Poems in Two Volumes* were (1) the expected
invasion (vividly, urgently imagined) of the British Isles by Napoleon, and
the crises, moral and material, this brought to light; and among those crises, (2) the problem of imagining an adequate (heroic) counterforce, which
in turn brought to mind the implications of the suppression of the clans
in Scotland especially after 1745 (the defeat of the Jacobite party, the last
threat to the Protestant succession, at the Battle of Culloden) and the implication also of the general (internal and external) economic colonization
of the British Isles, and by extension of large regions of the world.

One of the sonnets (XIV) of *Poems in Two Volumes* has its prose grounding in a passage from Dorothy Wordsworth's *Recollections of a Tour Made in
Scotland* (1803), which includes the following sentences: "When we were
travelling in Scotland an invasion was hourly looked for, and one could not
but think with some regret of the times when from the now depopulated
Highlands forty or fifty thousand men might have been poured down for
the defense of the country. . . ."[2]

The moment then of the *Poems in Two Volumes*, as the text itself makes
plain, requires the reconstruction of general terms of human value—in effect, of an intelligible world in expectation of a catastrophe (the always virtual conquest of England by Napoleon—the imaginal subverter of the instituted world). The (proleptic) spectacle of the world in its post-catastrophic
state is the depopulated Highlands of Scotland, where the poetic tourist
restores the rationality of experience by the action of what everyone in
Wordsworth's circle called "composing"—as, for example, "Composed
upon Westminster Bridge"—that is, reconstruction of the world in accord
with perceptual criteria that are at once the criteria of personal, political,
and also artistic value-recognition. The poem of landscape institutes the
landscape, just as the poem of the social paradigm (e.g., "Character of the
Happy Warrior" or "Ode to Duty") institutes the social role; and the consequent problem of the slide into insignificance (noted by Bourdieu) of the
unprivileged class is presented in the imaging of the beggars of the road.

Each volume of *Poems in Two Volumes* contains a sequence specified as
poems composed or written during a tour, and "The Solitary Reaper" is

included in the section called "Poems Written during a Tour in Scotland" that begins volume 2. The sequence of nine poems in this section begins with "Rob Roy's Grave." Rob Roy represents to Wordsworth the Other to statutory law, and to writing in general. What has vanished with this eighteenth-century Scottish outlaw—this figure of the poetic interest— is clear in the words of Walter Scott: "It is this strong contrast betwixt the civilized and cultivated mode of life on the one side of the Highland line, and the wild and lawless adventures which were habitually undertaken and achieved by one who dwelt on the opposite side of that ideal bound- ary, which creates the interest attached to [Rob Roy's] name."[3] The eighth poem in this series—"Address to the Sons of Burns after visiting their Fa- ther's Grave"—presents the grave of Robert Burns and undertakes to re- institute that name on the site of the loss of the dialectic master as father. The fourth poem in this series is an elegy at the grave of Ossian, "the last of all his race." In other words, this sequence deals with the loss of discourses and their reconstitution in a regulated form. Most explanatory of this pro- cess is the poem that immediately follows "The Solitary Reaper," called "Stepping Westward," which is built as an exegesis of a dialectical sentence heard on the road: "What you are stepping westward?" The poetic inter- est of these poems is manifested by the incorporation of discourses other than those of the poem itself, which the actual poem brings to mind. The profoundest instance of this is the song of the reaper, about which the be- wildered narrator says, throwing up his hands: "Will no one tell me what she sings?" The integration that the poem brings to mind and is the object of poetic interest is always a state of the uttering voice; but it is best under- stood not as the language of the poem itself but as the language to which the poem gives access.

What, then, is the structure of poetic interest? It is a structure so gen- eral as to be almost invisible, and it is the same structure as the theoreti- cal—itself a term ("theoretical") deeply invested (like the poetic) in the the- atrical insofar as the theatrical models consciousness. From a strict point of view of the poetic text, *the structure of poetic interest is specifiable as discourse of one kind* (the poem as an actual order of words—written by the poet in history) *about discourse of another kind*, the prior poetic principle—virtual, a contingency of reference alone like the dead Rob Roy, the dead Burns, the dead Ossian, or as we shall see the non-existent reaper—voice of the truly solitary person (virtuality is a state of solitude) who both labors in nobody's fields and sings in an unknown tongue. In other words, *poems the- atricalize consciousness as it is engaged with its objects, and that is their structure and interest.*

"The poetic interest" is therefore that virtual, non-formal (unrepresentable) principle *that grounds representation*, often signified by strange or indigenous or untranslatable languages, to which the actual poem supplies access by formal representational means. Wordsworth's continual reproduction of this structure constitutes the interest of his poetry—the poetic interest that he adds to the interest of his world as it is represented in prose, principally by his sister Dorothy. It is this "interest" that is hidden inside the philosopher's fear of and also dependence on the poetic (cf. Plato, Heidegger), and it is also this interest that produces the sacred war between the poetic and the religious institutions.

I have noted that one of the peculiarities of the text of *Poems in Two Volumes* (a peculiarity that integrates all the poems to the structure of the tour among Erse speakers, or just other persons) is the incorporation of prior and other languages—more specifically progressive incorporation of languages of greater authority inside a language of lesser authority, which is the poem but by no means "Poetry," until at the bottom of the cascade one encounters the language of *greatest* authority, which is precisely not a known language ("Will no one tell me what she sings?").

In his search, for example, for a term of vocation or calling to Duty to begin and authorize the "Ode to Duty," which concludes the first part of *Poems in Two Volumes* (the Immortality Ode being the last poem of the last part) Wordsworth fixes upon the phrase of address "Stern Daughter of the Voice of God"—which he has taken from Milton (*Paradise Lost* IX.653) into the theater of consciousness of his poem. Wordsworth takes Milton's voice into the theater of text; Milton's voice is itself an incorporation as reference to the divine voice; and duty is nested genealogically within the voice of God, et cetera. The practice is not allusion but structure; and the progressively incorporating structures conduct the mind toward the unutterable ground of utterance, thus instituting Duty, and satisfying interest also, in the archaic.

Once again, in "The Solitary Reaper," mimesis of a conscious social language—constituting the actual poem written down, as we say, by Wordsworth—produces access to an absorbed discourse, a "language strange" that functions as poetry's principle (figured in the context of the Highland tour of 1803 as the song of the Erse-speaking native Scot). Contemporary and modern examples will immediately come to mind: Keats's "La Belle Dame sans Merci" who speaks "in language strange" (once again, the always unreliably translated dialect of the archaic language); or Rilke's "Archaic Torso of Apollo," which says (speaking for the archaic as pure negation), "You must change your life." In fact, all poetic interest and its signifying discourses belong to the category of the archaic, as the Highlands represented the archaic. It is worth citing Rilke's observation (dissimilar from Bourdieu's disparagement of such traces): "The incomparable value of these rediscovered Things lies in the fact that you can look at them as if they were completely unknown."[4] Perhaps the archetypal or at least ancient case is the singer of one class whose song is the honor of another aristocratic class, as is the case of Homer, or Gilgamesh, or the narrators of the Gospels, or indeed Ben Jonson and Yeats. Or the narrator of the Pentateuch, the voice not in itself creative that says, "In the beginning God created..."

The most profound instance in Wordsworth of the structure of poetic interest (the production, by means of the mimesis of mortal secular language, of discourse of another kind—*sacred* in the Derridean sense) is the poem called "Resolution and Independence" or "The Leech-Gatherer," which occurs in the first of the two tour sequences in *Poems in Two Volumes*. The right functioning of a poetic economy provides that the poet who supplies the image of another (a predecessor) will himself become, by a social rule of reciprocal construction, an image in the discourse of another (a successor). This is also a rule in the economy of personhood in any social order I can imagine. But in the world of the poem called "Resolution and Independence" (and, in general, the *Poems in Two Volumes* of 1807), this economy is disrupted and in default. The poetic vocation has become predatory upon the poet: compare "mighty Poets in their misery dead" and the lines "We Poets in our youth begin in gladness / But thereof come in the end despondency and madness."

Unlike "The Solitary Reaper," the poem of the Leech-Gatherer is presented as spoken by a poet. It is a poem driven into existence by sudden awareness of a fatal, canceling irony, entailed by poetic practice. Notice that the reaper lass is singing ballads. Wordsworth's high-cultural poem that brings her to mind is not a ballad; but rather it takes her discourse into its stanza and is justified by precisely the discourse from which, as a written poem, it differentiates itself. By contrast, "Resolution and Independence" employs a metric and stanza put in service (if not invented) by Chatterton, the "marvellous boy" dead by suicide—"The sleepless Soul that perish'd in its pride"—for his poem "An Excelente Balade of Charite." It is no accident, then, that Wordsworth's poem discovers a murderous logic, requiring that the agent of representation suffer victimage, given the nature of representation, when the maker and the persons represented are the same. This is the double bind, the Empsonian "seventh ambiguity" of pastoral song, a newly discovered rule of modern lyric, or any form of modern making. Self-maintaining reciprocity works in the world of nature, but not in the world of persons. The work of the Leech-Gatherer—abjected body and sublime voice—exemplifies the consequences of that labor that contributes presence *only to the other*. His work is not to make poems—he is not a poet—but to mediate the relation between the practice of poetry and vital life.

"Resolution and Independence" exhibits, clearly articulated, the structure of poetic interest. The speaker names himself as a poet and "a Traveller then upon the moor" (stanza 3). He meets an old man. The poet's question to the old man is about work—the labor that produces the image, that is to say, significant life. The answer is not a proposition but a state of language. This person—the old man—dwells at the margin between human and non-human; he is as old as the world and therefore speaks from the archaic; and he is subject to an economy of diminishing resource. He is the bearer of a significance passing from being to nothing:

IX

As a huge stone is sometimes seen to lie
Couched on the bald top of an eminence;
Wonder to all who do the same espy,
By what means it could thither come, and whence;
So that it seems a thing endued with sense:
Like a sea-beast crawled forth, that on a shelf
Of rock or sand reposeth, there to sun itself;

X

Such seemed this Man, not all alive nor dead,
Nor all asleep—in his extreme old age . . .

XI

Himself he propped, limbs, body, and pale face,
Upon a long gray staff of shaven wood:
And, still as I drew near with gentle pace,
Upon the margin of that moorish flood
Motionless as a cloud the old Man stood,
That heareth not the loud winds when they call;
And moveth all together, if it move at all.

The efficacious nature of this figure is signified by the institution of a discourse of another kind, uncanny, like the sacred in that it is untranslatable; it has, like the oldest man, no meaning except its self-identity: "And moveth all together, if it move at all." Pastoral, one could say, is the moment of acutest memory of the never other than lost continuity of mind and body—of which one paradigm is the artistic form of words. In the stylistic codes of the West, the appropriate term for the old man's answer to the poet is "courtesy":

XIII

A gentle answer did the old Man make,
In courteous speech which forth he slowly drew . . .

XIV

His words came feebly, from a feeble chest,
But each in solemn order followed each,
With something of a lofty utterance drest—
Choice word and measured phrase, above the reach
Of ordinary men; a stately speech;
Such as grave Livers do in Scotland use,
Religious men, who give to God and man their dues.

. . . .

XVI

The old Man still stood talking by my side;
But now his voice to me was like a stream
Scarce heard; nor word from word could I divide:
And the whole body of the Man did seem
Like one whom I had met with in a dream;
Or like a man from some far region sent,
To give me human strength, by apt admonishment.

As I have said, such poems seem devised to articulate (theatrically) *the interest* (or the stake) that the community has in the poetic principle, which like the old man supplies the validity of social language by bringing to mind a voice that is not a social language—that is to say, is not "understood"— "from some far region sent / To give me human strength. . . ." The poem as a mediation supplies access to a principle or factor fundamental to social life. It enables the recognitions upon which the civil identity of persons depends—but that lie outside social life in the prehistory of the human world, or the wilderness of other (indigenous) minds that no longer have a claim on the world, the value of which they nonetheless secure.

The political implications of the virtual and therefore non-ethical poetic principle (i.e., the diacritically non-ethical foundation of personal presence) are present whenever poems are present. It is my sense that these political problems are, as Bourdieu suggested in "Rites of Institution," *structurally identical with problems of representation*, that is to say, picturing altogether. In other words, problems of social hierarchy (because they are crises of the economy of representation) have the same structure as poetic problems (because poetry is an archetypal kind of representation, the picturing of the person). *Hence, problems of race and class are like poetic problems*, and may be poetic problems—problems of other peoples' music—inherent in the inevitable cognitive/communicative logic of representational systems—*inherent particularly in the logic of generality*. Whatever other discourses bring this state of affairs to mind, the poetic principle as mediated by the poems does so. And this, again, constitutes the poetic interest.

For the sake of clarity, let me review, before proceeding, what then (once again) is the content of the figure—not poetic—that poetic interest (the theory of the poetic) brings to light:

(1) All I can say is that the mind is drawn to the object of poetic interest (figured in "Resolution and Independence" as the man as old as the world) because it exhibits the integration, *per impossibile*, of those heterogeneous elements that constitute the person—the work and the work song, life and death, body and mind, the exploit of personhood—in what may be the only form in which it can propagate itself, namely, as a state of language.

(2) Among those heterogeneous elements that constitute the person, poetic interest exhibits prominently the negotiation of the integration, again *per impossibile*, of the particular and the general, the individual and the collective as embodied in courteous speech—courtesy being the key term in this negotiation—or "stately speech / Such as grave Livers do in Scotland use."

(3) Further, but in the same vein: in the object of poetic interest is discovered a site of the Aristotelian excluded middle, in especial in the constative presentation of languages that are unmistakable without being intelligible—the sacred languages of mere phatic presence (stanza XVI):

> The old Man still stood walking by my side;
> But now his voice to me was like a stream
> Scarce heard; nor word from word could I divide

(4) The discovery here is of the distinction between the representable and the unrepresentable ("this Man, not all alive nor dead / Nor all asleep"); and on the edge of this distinction—which is distinction itself (that "lonely place") we find this Wandering Jew. (Cf. Dorothy Wordsworth's journal entry for October 3, 1800.)

(5) Finally, if an institution is a social formation that grounds a discourse, is poetry complicit with such institutions? And if so, how far is such complicity justifiable? Or, asked another way, is the violence of representation identical with or different from the discourse that institutes the person?

The date of composition of "The Solitary Reaper" is ascertained by a letter, dated November 7, 1805, from Dorothy Wordsworth to her neighbor and benefactor Lady Beaumont in which Dorothy Wordsworth copied the poem. In Dorothy's *Recollections of a Tour Made in Scotland*, the poem is introduced thus: "It was harvest time, and the fields were quietly (might I be allowed to say pensively?) enlivened by small companies of reapers. It is not uncommon in the more lonely parts of the Highlands to see a *single* person so employed." However, Dorothy has not seen "a *single* person so employed." She asserts that, on the contrary, "the following poem ['The Solitary Reaper'] was suggested to W[illiam] by a beautiful sentence in Thomas Wilkinson's *Tour in Scotland*...."[5] Nor did Wordsworth *himself* experience the solitary reaper. Wordsworth's relation to the subject of this poem was removed, explicitly, from any putative actual solitary reaper, by the experientially definitive distance of another mind than his own. The "solitary Highland Lass" was *somebody else's tour*, turn, or "beautiful sentence"—*Wilkinson's*—as written down of another mind and in fact by another hand than Wordsworth's, who himself wrote in retrospect of the writing of that other. The solitary reaper was from the beginning an intersubjective construct—a mediation among minds.

Thomas Wilkinson was a Quaker or Friend (b. 1751) who inherited a small estate near Penrith. He was a man of particular interest to Wordsworth, although the exact character of that interest is not on the face of it clear. In *Poems in Two Volumes* Wordsworth included a poem called "To the Spade of a Friend" (discussed further below). In 1787 Wilkinson performed "his one extensive piece of Quaker service"—an evangelizing tour to the north—which yielded (part of a journal of the tour) the beautiful sentence that Wordsworth saw and then asked to be inscribed by Wilkinson in Wordsworth's own commonplace book: "Passed a female who was reaping alone: she sung in Erse, as she bended over her sickle; the sweetest human voice I ever heard: her strains were tenderly melancholy, and felt delicious long after they were heard no more."[6] Wordsworth acknowledged and made unmistakable his debt to Wilkinson in a note to the 1807 printing of "The Solitary Reaper," in language similar to Dorothy's quoted above. But he also makes explicit the "beautiful sentence" and supplies its words: Wordsworth writes, "The last line [of the poem: 'Long after it was heard no more'] being taken from it *verbatim*" from Wilkinson.[7] And, as we know, it was copied for Wordsworth by Wilkinson's own hand.

Since Wilkinson's "beautiful sentence," in his own hand, is the last line of "The Solitary Reaper," the language of the poem as written must be conformed to the ethos or style of that hand. Indeed, the abruptness of the poem's opening, and the marked lack of focality of the speaker who summons an indefinite and general audience to view an event framed by his pointing:

> Behold her, single in the field,
> Yon solitary Highland Lass!

This implies a speaker who, like a docent in a museum, is engaged in a formal re-presentation of a spectacle, the importance of which he recognizes but the significance of which he does not know. The implication is conveyed that the speaker is calling attention ("Behold her") to a picturable reality of the highest value and interest, the meaning of which he, *for the reason it is of the greatest interest and therefore inconsistent with translatability*, can approximate but not specify, can picture but not state. Indeed, the greatest interest lies in the selvage by which the spectacle exceeds its account.

We should I think feel silence outside and inside the (Wilkinsonian) voice that says "single," "solitary," "by herself," and continues the poem with that kind of directed intention that specifies distance and difference, fundamentally the sacred, as attention's content:

> Alone she cuts, and binds the grain,
> And sings a melancholy strain;
> O listen! for the Vale profound
> Is overflowing with the sound.

This solitude (aloneness, unrhyming by herselfness, of "The Solitary Reaper"—notional except for Thomas Wilkinson's account) is simultaneously and dialectically (one solitude generating the other from itself) the solitude of the native worker and the solitude of bourgeois subjectivity (the proprietary subjectivity of the freeholder)—*both* the solitude as we might say of the "soul" *and* reciprocally the solitude of a depopulated landscape.

Fundamentally, this depopulated world is of course the world of the dispersed and destroyed Scottish clans and their bardic culture of song. The destruction of the clans of Scotland and Ireland was accompanied by the hunting down and killing of the bards, from the edicts of Elizabeth to the Battle of Culloden, the defeat of the Jacobite cause in 1745 and the reprisals that followed.[8] Thus a way was made for the high-cultural—that is to say, national—poets of the period and the subjectivity that high-cultural lyric sponsors. The overflowing vale is the echoic vessel filled with sound to overflowing ("plaintive numbers"—virtual song) because emptied of persons except, as we see, the "final girl"—the solitary Highland Lass, whose work song supplies the authenticity of the "profound" lyric subjectivity and the social formations it implies.

Dorothy Wordsworth writing to Lady Beaumont (November 29, 1805), to whom she had sent the poem, remarks:

> I was sure that you would be pleased with the stanzas on the solitary Reaper. There is something inexpressibly soothing to me in the sound of those two Lines:
>
> > Oh listen! for the Vale profound
> > Is overflowing with the sound—
>
> I often catch myself repeating them in disconnection with any thought, or even I may say recollection of the Poem.[9]

What is taught by the poem is a sort of creativity that is dependent on not understanding the original and indeed seems to permit or entail the disappearance of the reaper altogether, of which the reciprocal effect is the opening of the profound subjectivity of the reader. "The music in my heart I bore / Long after it was heard no more." The text of the Wordsworth poem becomes an original text by reason of the untranslatability of the reaper's song, which, because it is untranslatable, is not a text. The girl's song is produced as unknown, with the result that it can be replaced by the set of possibilities supplied by the speaker. Because the reaper is not a subject, she is a perfectly effective agent of subjectivity in others. She has slid into the nothingness of the complementary class.

The song of the reaper is doubly a *work song*, prosopopoeia, the making of persons—both reaping and singing simultaneously—literal and symbolic. This is the subject of greatest interest, since Wilkinson really sees with the eyes of George Fox (the Quaker founder) for whom the grain harvest was a harvest of souls, literal as eschatological and symbolic as poetic. And this returns us to the core of poetic interest: a millennially conventional figure of the poetic principle—precisely as the poem according to Horace is of two natures, a means both of delight and instruction, or as *aisthesis* is of two natures engaging the senses and the intellect simultaneously, or as the dancer is both rooted and moving, or as the person or the savior is man and god. The poetic interest, I am saying, constructs as a single action the split nature of the person—mind and body, consciousness and its intentional object. And her solitude is the expression of her unity *per impossibile*, the unity of the person. It is this epiphanic scene of the person—the peasant girl who does two things at once that are logically exclusive of one another. *The person is the harvester and the harvest, the figure of the poetic principle, which is also at the same time a figure of the highest human worth.* With this figure we must, I think, be concerned.

Poetic interest is the spectacularization within consciousness of a "limit experience" in that it transgresses a logical boundary of possibility—the familiar excluded middle (P and not-P)—the transgression of which boundary is also the highest aspiration of being: *is even God.* Poetic interest is then, as I have implied, the reiteration by other means of the instituting experience of the person as a self.

Our texts and the analysis we have made so far supply two characteristics of the poetic interest that bear on the following argument of Bourdieu, cited earlier in "Poetry and Hard Problems":

> The veritable miracle produced by acts of institution lies undoubtedly in the fact that they manage to make consecrated individuals believe that their existence is justified, that their existence serves some purpose. But, through a kind of curse, because of the essentially diacritical, differential and distinctive nature of symbolic power, the rise of the distinguished class to Being has, as an inevitable counterpart, the slide of the complementary class into Nothingness or the lowest Being.[10]

Poetry is theoretical in that it knows that the person is instituted—as is the nation—and both are consequences of the institution of the perceptual field and the field of consciousness that supplies the structure of poetic interest. Certain characteristics of that institution or constitution can be reaffirmed on the authority, here, of the "The Leech-Gatherer" and "The Solitary Reaper," and rethought in terms of the Highlands and the tour in Scotland. First among these is the constitution of the object of poetic interest from incompatibles, its constitution *per impossibile* and therefore in virtuality as the simultaneity of logical contra-dictories, above all the irreducibly *particular* and the irreducibly *general*, the dancer and also the dance—*the figuration* of what Hegel and the American New Critics called the concrete universal *as a person who reveals the (non-logical) nature of personhood* by doing and being two things at once, the reaping and singing: Frost's vocation and avocation, the collective and the individual, instruction and delight.

But what we must then consider is that paradoxicality of constructedness that knows how to make the world stand up and also makes it unjust; that is to say, builds it and makes it uninhabitable, as the Highlands become an image of great generality at the same moment that they are culturally ruined and made the object for others. An effective consequence of construction from incompatibles is the uncovering of the generality of the particular. The reconstruction of the peasant laborer as *the bearer of generality* (in fact, her song) occupies the two central stanzas of "The Solitary Reaper." The solitary reaper becomes the figure of figuration. Her generality is greater than the temporal, spatial, modal, and symbolic omnipresence of birdsong. Beyond birdsong then and birdsong now, birdsong mythological (nightingale south and east) and birdsong practical (cuckoo north and west)—beyond also the sharply divergent sexual narratives associated with both cuckoo and nightingale—is the higher generality of the work song of the harvester—close to material origins and close to silence.

> No Nightingale did ever chaunt
> More welcome notes to weary bands
> Of travellers in some shady haunt,
> Among Arabian sands:
> A voice so thrilling ne'er was heard
> In spring-time from the Cuckoo-bird,
> Breaking the silence of the seas
> Among the farthest Hebrides.
>
> Will no one tell me what she sings?—
> Perhaps the plaintive numbers flow
> For old, unhappy, far-off things,
> And battles long ago:
> Or is it some more humble lay,
> Familiar matter of to-day?
> Some natural sorrow, loss, or pain,
> That has been, and may be again?

As the Wilkinsonian voice takes it in, the solitary reaper's song is both high cultural and ancient ("plaintive numbers"), and folkish and modern ("familiar matter of to-day"). The Quaker preference of silence over speech—the disposition toward the greatest abstraction of the Low Church—puts this final singer in service of the lowest church of all, the poetic institution that finds at the furthest reach of mind the signifier of signifiers that is not a signifier—which is in effect the nothing.

The overflowing of "the Vale profound" with this sound—not to be contained by the individual mind and not contradictory of it—signifies both that surplus of generality that secures the inevitability of the dominant culture (and subjectivity) and also the nothingness of the subject that serves it as signifier. Such a hypothesis of generality contradicts simple justice. The argument for generality is that it is a communicative necessity, as it is a requirement of civil order. The argument against it is that it exploits, or in fact abolishes, the individual in the interest of the communicative system. The indigene is abolished in order to obtain access to the energetic priority of chthonian life.

In 1805 (within a few days of the composition of "The Solitary Reaper"), Wordsworth wrote from Grasmere a didactic letter to Sir George Beaumont about the artistic management of his estate—a subject on which the poet apparently had authority; it is after all the practical enactment of institution—and also about our Thomas Wilkinson, the freehold gentleman gardener of Wordsworth's choice in the district. I quote a few sentences from Wordsworth's very long letter:

> I have been thinking of you, and Coleridge, and our Scotch tour. . . . I have had before me the tremendously long ell-wide gravel walks of the Duke of Athol . . . brushed neatly, without a blade of grass or weed upon them, or anything that bore trace of a human footstep; much indeed of human hands, but wear or tear of foot was none. Thence I passed to our neighbor, Lord Lowther. . . . He has a neighbour, a Quaker, an amiable, inoffensive man [i.e., Thomas Wilkinson] . . . who has amused himself, upon his own small estate upon the Emont, in twining pathways along the banks of the river. . . . This man is at present Arbiter Elegantiarum, or master of the grounds, at Lowther; and what he has done hitherto is very well, as it is little more than making accessible what could not before be got at.[11]

But Wordsworth then proceeds in a very complex exposition to assert that Wilkinson's accessibility project—his "manufactured walk," though necessary—will in the end "efface the most beautiful specimen of forest pathway ever seen by human eyes," a path "with the wantonness of a River or a living Creature; and even if I may say so with the subtlety of a Spirit . . . ," a path along which people of the country are seen as picturable on their way to church or "playing upon the Hautboy and Clarionet."[12]

Wordsworth next returns to his "subject," which is that "all just and solid pleasures in natural objects rest upon two pillars, God and Man." In other words, that experience is constituted of two classes of facts, divine and human, and the business of persons is to cooperate with the divine—to turn the double nature of experience into occasions of meaning—by means of work productive of human value, a cooperative task, which integrates incompatibles, like the spectacle of the Solitary Reaper, the image of the ongoing in the virtuality of spectacle of good work. The mind is drawn by her image because human beings are fundamentally concerned with the question of good work.

But it is clear that the management of this task—which is *work itself*—is critically problematic. For man's part, the difference between construction and destruction (as in the case of Wilkinson's path) is hard to distinguish, and the case is the same for poetry also. "Laying out grounds," Wordsworth continues,

> may be considered as a liberal art, in some sort like Poetry and Painting; and its object, like that of all the liberal arts, is, or ought to be, to move affections under the control of good sense; *that is, of the best and wisest*, but speaking with more precision, it is to assist Nature in moving the affections; and surely, as I have said, the affections of those who have the deepest perception of the beauty of Nature, *who have the most valuable feelings*, that is, the most permanent, the most independent, the most ennobling. . . . No liberal art aims merely at the gratification of an individual or a class, the Painter or Poet is degraded in proportion as he does so; the true servants of the Arts pay homage to the human kind as impersonated in unwarped and enlightened minds.[13] [emphasis added]

The medium then of representation is the paradigmatic prosopopoeia of the enlightened mind, which enables a hypothetical classless "impersonation" of the undeformed—"unwarped" and general—picture of the person. The typical person (without which picture I myself think it correct to say neither ethnicity nor nation can reinvent itself) is thus rewritten by Wordsworth putatively outside of class but within the aristocratic system, as the Scottish Highlands altogether were after Culloden rewritten as an archaic world—a theme park of the archaic reference indispensable to personification and nation construction.

The problem lies in the mediation of the poem, which (like Wilkinson's path) *regulates* access (actual language *regulating* access to virtual language)— the structure of the poem as I am presenting it. A failure of the poetic produces catastrophic implosion of the virtual (the principle) upon the actual (the real state of affairs). Good poetry keeps access open between the actual and its principle and permits fruitful negotiation between those contradictory states. As an image of good work, the poem draws the mind.

But the world of the truly valuable is a dangerous world hovering precariously between peopled and unpeopled. Necessity of archaism, the spectacle of the unintelligible other ("Will no one tell me what she sings?") by which the intelligibility of the self is generated runs as deep as prehistoric species recognition, which is the fruit of the non-recognitions that constitute history. This is the fierce threat and the generative opportunity of other people's music—the self-differentiation that opens the profound inwardness, the heart in which one bears the music that is the construction of the music.

Finally the double image that compels the mind is the fundamental figuration of the Western gods killing and quickening as in the Old Testament, mortal and immortal as in the New Testament, male and female as at the end of Dante's *Paradiso*—an enigma he says, like the squaring of the circle or the Trinity somehow painted with our image, the picture of the person. The *techne* for negotiating the difficult logic that links destruction and construction (the enigma of the divine as I have said—killing and quickening) is the poetic practice, the mediation of the scribal instrument *and the secular reconstruction of the fundamentally contradictory world energies called divine is the Kantian aesthetic—purposeless purpose*, which in Wordsworth constitutes a sublation, a carrying up into innocence of the class violence of that dangerous world (peopled and unpeopled) of Wilkinson's path.

During the year after writing "The Solitary Reaper," Wordsworth wrote a weirdly homosocial poem called: "To the Spade of a Friend, (An Agriculturist.) Composed while we were labouring together in his Pleasure-Ground." You will remember (from the above) Wordsworth's explanation to Lord Lonsdale that the "laying out of grounds is in some sort a Liberal art, like poetry." In the extended title of "To the Spade of a Friend" (in fact, Thomas Wilkinson), we see a spectral Wordsworth working ("in some sort") beside Wilkinson in his "pleasure-ground" *with Wilkinson's spade*. As in the poem "The Solitary Reaper," Wordsworth is writing with Wilkinson's writing ("long after it was heard no more"), working with his tool. He has somehow entered the domain of poetic interest. He is in the picture.

The poem, however grotesque, employs (like Wordsworth's poetry in general) artistic practice to regulate the ambivalences inherent in the representation of labor. Wilkinson appears as the man who does and is two things at once that are incompatible: he is high and low, he labors and is at rest: in the domain of class, in the domain of construction, in the domain of logic and theo-logic.

TO THE SPADE OF A FRIEND,
(AN AGRICULTURALIST.)
COMPOSED WHILE WE WERE LABOURING
TOGETHER IN HIS PLEASURE-GROUND.
Spade! with which Wilkinson hath tilled his lands,
And shaped these pleasant walks by Emont's side,

Thou art a tool of honour in my hands;
I press Thee, through the yielding soil, with pride.

Rare master has it been thy lot to know;
Long hast Thou served a man to reason true;
Whose life combines the best of high and low,
The labouring many and the resting few;

. . . .

Here often hast Thou heard the poet sing
In concord with his river murmuring by;
Or in some silent field, while timid Spring
Is yet uncheered by other minstrelsy.

Wilkinson's spade ("Thou") has been witness to Wilkinson's, the poet's, capacity to do and be two things at once: low and high, at labor and at rest, working and singing . . . the pacification of composition. The spade mediates between virtuality and actuality. Wilkinson as the rational man ("a man to reason true") is a type of the speaker of the poem, the poet to whom the poetic principle is other, who produces the spectacle ("Behold her") of the poetic principle and regulates relation to it, maintaining its distance in order that its use may not be extinguished in the implosion that identifies principle and practice—that mistakes the poem for poetry.

Who shall inherit Thee when death has laid
Low in the darksome cell thine own dear Lord?
That man will have a trophy, humble Spade!
A trophy nobler than a conqueror's sword.

If he be one that feels, with skill to part
False praise from true, or, greater from the less,
Thee will he welcome to his hand and heart,
Thou monument of peaceful happiness!

He will not dread with Thee a toilsome day—
Thee his loved servant, his inspiring mate!
And, when Thou art past service, worn away,
No dull oblivious nook shall hide thy fate.

His thrift thy uselessness will never scorn;
An *heir-loom* in his cottage wilt Thou be:—

> High will he hang thee up, well pleased to adorn
> His rustic chimney with the last of Thee!

The worn-out spade becomes a part of the universe of archaic mediations—among which I count the poetic text as one—which serve as *heir-
looms* that legitimate the present and remind of the terrifying requirement
of cultural continuity: the perpetual negotiation of the knife-edge difference between creation and destruction that depends on the maintenance
of the difference between the virtual and the actual—the speaker's urgent
protection of the "absorption" of "The Solitary Reaper": "Stop here, or
gently pass!" The peculiar suffix "loom" in *heir-loom*, the destined status of
the spade, meant, down through the seventeenth century, a work tool of
any kind (including the penis) (v. *OED*). By this monumentalization, the
work tool—the spade—passes with wear, from an instrument of use of one
kind to an instrument of use of another kind, and by this reconstruction of
function (dare one say this reconstruction of its interest) becomes a principle of symbolic continuity across generations, incorporating by this ar-
chaization the two natures—contradictory in actuality—that signify the
interest of objects found in the poetic domain.

On Communicative Difficulty in General and "Difficult" Poetry in Particular

THE EXAMPLE OF HART CRANE'S "THE BROKEN TOWER"

New conditions of life germinate new forms of spiritual articulation. And while I feel that my work includes a more consistent extension of traditional literary elements than many contemporary poets are capable of appraising, I realize that I am utilizing the gifts of the past as instruments principally, and that the voice of the present, if it is to be known, must be caught at the risk of speaking in idioms and circumlocutions sometimes shocking to scholars and historians of logic.
Language has built towers and bridges, but itself is inevitably
as fluid as always.

Hart Crane, "General Aims and Theories"

I think I summed up my attitude to philosophy when I said: philosophy ought really to be written as a poetic composition. It must, as it seems to me, be possible to gather from this how far my thinking belongs to the present, future or past. For I was thereby revealing myself as someone who cannot quite do what he would like to be able to do.

Ludwig Wittgenstein, *Culture and Value*

I have finished a monument more lasting than bronze . . .

Horace

Here we are talking about Hart Crane dead long ago, in the year of my birth, 1932. Hart Crane's poem "The Broken Tower," beginning with his title, engages an ancient figure—that of a monument which, by its ironic unbreakability, challenges death's obliteration of persons. In the classical poetic tradition, the work of art—whatever else it does—is always also engaged in this one task: overcoming the erasure of the name of a person by speaking it, *doing* fame by means of language. ("Fame," *fama*—from the Latin *fari*, Greek *phanaito*—to speak of absence *with the effect of presence*).

*This essay originally appeared under the title "On Communicative Difficulty in General and 'Difficulty' in Particular: The Example of Hart Crane's 'The Broken Tower,'" *Chicago Review* 53, nos. 2/3 (Autumn 2007): 140–61.

To bring home, by means of an example, this classical scene of *the work of art set to work*, I remind you of a poem by the Roman poet Horace. The poem is conventionally called "The Poet's Immortal Fame." Horace boasts that he will remain by reason of his poems—his *monumentum*—forever part of the human *conversation*, specifically the death-blocked conversation between the dead and the living. Hart Crane (or any poet) reminds us that the death-blocked conversation between the dead and the living is identical to the conversation between the living and the living, which is enabled and blocked in life by our unmingling bodies. Horace asserts that, by his *work* as poet, he has effected two things that cannot happen: first, that what he has made is indestructible (but we know that everything is destructible); second, that he, the maker, will not "entirely" die (*non omnis moriar*)—but everyone entirely dies.

Poetry—and only poetry—contributes to human life precisely what the human will cannot (as we know, if we know anything) otherwise obtain. *Not by reason of what the poem says, but by reason of the fact that poetry is the artistic form of language.* By means of the artistic form of language, humanity—something of one nature (subject to death)—becomes capable of *thinking* by means of something, of another nature (not subject to death). Poetry is the most valuable thing we have, *but radically untrue.*

Here, in the context of Hart Crane's "The Broken Tower" (as an introduction to it), is Horace's poem about the *unbreakable* tower—the artistic form of language, *poesis.*

> I have finished a monument more lasting than bronze and loftier than the Pyramid's royal pile, one that no wasting rain, no furious north wind can destroy or countless chain of years and the ages' flight. I shall not altogether die [*non omnis moriar*; one notices in the *omnis* the poet's anxiety about the truth of the boast], but a mighty part of me shall escape the death-goddess [Libitina, goddess of corpses]. On and on I shall grow ever fresh with the glory of aftertime. So long as the Pontiff climbs the Capitol with the silent Vestal [the institution of language across time, identical with the sacred, is contingent upon the state], I, risen high from low estate where Aufidus thunders and where Daunus in a parched land once ruled o'er a peasant folk [Hart Crane's equivalent was Cleveland, Ohio], shall be famed for having been the first to adapt Aeolian song [Greek high-cultural poetic styles—Crane also was also a conscious formalist] to Italian verse. Accept the proud honour won by thy merits, Melpomene [Muse of tragedy!], and graciously crown my locks with Delphic lays.

Crane's poem and Horace's poem are the same poem (Crane's "tower" is his *monumentum*). But, in a sense, Crane's poem is earlier or later than Horace's. Horace's confidence in the continuity of human presence by reason of the poem is no longer—or *not yet*—possible. Crane's broken *monumentum* could not bear the weight rested on it. What broke the tower?

Consider the Old Testament at Genesis 11. There we find an explanation—an etiological narrative—in fact, *the theological decree of human communicative difficulty*. It is the story about the destruction of the Tower of Babel, the "breaking of the Tower of Babel"—the breaking of "The Broken Tower" *by babble* to which Crane's title alludes:

> The Lord came down to see the city and the tower, which mortals had built. And the Lord said, "Look! They are one people *and they have all one language*. This is only the beginning of what they will do. *Nothing now will be impossible for them*. Come, let us go down and *confuse their language*, so they will not understand one another's speech.

Hart Crane's "The Broken Tower"—a "difficult" poem by a "difficult" poet—theatricalizes this Babylonian primordial curse against the human empowerment that would flow from a universal language. The reconstruction of the "city and tower" of Genesis 11 (that's what Crane's poem narrates) is a restoration of divinely prohibited communicative universality on other (matriarchal) grounds. It is the nature of the *patriarchal* Semitic "God" that He requires an unbounded discursive territory. Hence He prohibits representation of Himself, guards Himself against the violence inseparable from the representation—the making visible of anything—*eidetic violence*, as I will call it. *The difficulty of the "difficult" poem in our time both marks and also therefore maintains a divine (that is at least to say, a structurally fundamental) theologic prohibition.*

Here is Crane's poem. Note, please, before I read out "The Broken Tower," how hard it is to perform *the beginning of the reading* of any poem. Perhaps, I won't really try. One must reflectively fall silent in oneself, because the voice always going on in one's head must now defer to another's voice never before heard. It is not any voice of the "myself," but a previously unknown *possibility* of the voice of the myself. One must abandon the "discursive field" of the own self. Also, watch the punctuation. The punctuation is this poet's careful interpretation of the relationship intended by the poet among the grammatical elements of his own text.

THE BROKEN TOWER

The bell-rope that gathers God at dawn
Dispatches me as though I dropped down the knell
Of a spent day—to wander the cathedral lawn
From pit to crucifix, feet chill on steps from hell.

Have you not heard, have you not seen the corps
Of shadows in the tower, whose shoulders sway
Antiphonal carillons launched before
The stars are caught and hived in the sun's ray?

The bells, I say, the bells break down their tower;
And swing I know not where. Their tongues engrave
Membrane through marrow, my long-scattered score
Of broken intervals . . . And I, their sexton slave!

Oval encyclicals in canyons heaping
The impasse high with choir. Banked voices slain!
Pagodas, campaniles with reveilles outleaping—
O terraced echoes prostrate on the plain! . . .

And so it was I entered the broken world
To trace the visionary company of love, its voice
An instant in the wind (I know not whither hurled)
But not for long to hold each desperate choice.

My word I poured. But was it cognate, scored
Of that tribunal monarch of the air
Whose thigh embronzes earth, strikes crystal Word
In wounds pledged once to hope—cleft to despair?

The steep encroachments of my blood left me
No answer (could blood hold such a lofty tower
As flings the question true?)—or is it she
Whose sweet mortality stirs latent power?—

And through whose pulse I hear, counting the strokes
My veins recall and add, revived and sure
The angelus of wars my chest evokes:
What I hold healed, original now, and pure . . .

And builds, within, a tower that is not stone
(Not stone can jacket heaven)—but slip
Of pebbles—visible wings of silence sown
In azure circles, widening as they dip

The matrix of the heart, lift down the eye
That shrines the quiet lake and swells a tower . . .
The commodious, tall decorum of that sky
Unseals her earth, and lifts love in its shower.

Hart Crane's "The Broken Tower" is his last poem, written about 1931, when the poet was thirty-one years old. He killed himself the next year. This poem's subject, the subject of Hart Crane's magnificent last poem, is poetic "vocation," an obligating privilege that he was—as a gifted poet—likely to know about.

What, in general, is "vocation"? Vocation is the sense, of which a person may become aware, of having been assigned a cosmic task he did not choose, may not be able to perform, but to which he nonetheless is obligated. *Poetic vocation, always personal (vocation is of persons), requires to make it social (i.e., public) a mediating institution other than poetry.* The required institution can be any sort, entailing any kind of social engagement—for Horace it was sacred Rome. But it may be insurance as in Stevens's case (or Kafka's). Stevens thought of insurance as redemptive, in his way. But it may also be fascism, as in Pound's case. It may be mythological nationalism, as in Whitman's case, Hölderlin's, or Yeats's, or in fact Crane's (as in *The Bridge*, or in "The Broken Tower," where he speaks on behalf of an even more vast human domain). It may be the schools, as in my case and others of my generation. *But most commonly in the West, the mediating institution is the religion of the state, and the requirement of mediation arises because of the social necessity of regulating relation to the sacred.* The poet is always *sancta poeta*, and the predicate of sanctity is the same across the differences between pagan and Christian. *Sanctity is the category of which the god is a member.*[1]

Here are a few instances of *poetic* vocation, exemplary and well known: Hesiod's encounter with the Muses (those "mean girls") who say, "We know how to speak many false things as though they were true; but we know, when we want to, how to utter truth" (*Theogony*, fifth century B.C.); Whitman's "Out of the Cradle Endlessly Rocking" when he exclaims, having heard the song of the bird: "Now in a moment I know what I am for, I awake"; Gerard Manley Hopkins "The Windhover": "I caught this morning morning's minion"; Pound's "The Return"; Yeats's "The Lake Isle of

Innisfree"; Frost's "The Road Not Taken," the *way* that "made all the differ-ence." Closest to Crane, and analytic of his purposes, is Rimbaud's scheme of intentional vocational self-authorization—the boy who undertakes to *make himself* a "seer" by means of a "long, prodigious, and [note!] *rational* disordering of all the senses."

Let's remember: the Muses (the archetypal cruel girls, as in Hesiod) are never kind. Why? *Because of the violence inherent in the "making" (poesis) that they sponsor and the entailed equivocality of their truth-promises.* I have already given a name, in this essay about "making," to the violence inherent in mak-ing (the breaking required to turn the unmade into the made) that even the god fears. (It's the second commandment: Thou shalt not make unto me. . . .) That's what I mean by the expression "eidetic violence." That's the unkindness of the Muses. And the greater the cultural importance rested on the equivocal truth-value of the poetic text, the more unkind. The un-kindest of all muses is the Semitic God.

Cultures that have no conception of fiction—all biblical cultures—are the most explanatory in this matter: the controlling example is the mur-derous vocation by God of Abraham. Only recently did the verb "create" occur (legitimately, grammatically) with a human subject—that is, as a con-ceivable function of human agency. Prior to the 1930s, the writing of "cre-ate" with a human subject was a grammatical mistake. (So the *OED* s.v. "create" as late as 1933.) This shift signifies the abandonment of a millen-nial intuition of the necessity of a regulative function addressed to the human will that seeks to make. The consequences of this abandonment have changed our sense of possible life and made the idea of creativity incomprehensible. This is the staggering irony of Robert Oppenheimer's reflection on the first nuclear explosion (Los Alamos—July 16, 1945). "I have become death, destroyer of worlds"—words (before Oppenheimer usurped them) of the high god of the Bhagavad Gita. More to our point, Oppenheimer named the place and the tower built to be obliterated by that explosion "Trinity"—an appropriation of the first line of a sonnet by John Donne:

> Batter my heart, three-person'd God; for, You
> As yet but knock, breathe, shine, and seek to mend;
> That I may rise and stand, o'er throw me, and bend
> Your force to break, blow, burn, and make me new.

Oppenheimer intuited that theological hyperbole is the only discourse the culture affords to express the bearing on the human world of nuclear tech-nology, here considered as a dreadful discourse constituted by a universal language of physical properties. What is missing (in fact remains *beyond us*) is the imagination of any institution adequate to regulate the power obtained on the site of creativity. The breaking of the "broken tower" is a premonitory narration of the failure of regulation. The work of the poem "The Broken Tower" intends something like the reinstitution of competent regulation of the discourse of the "sacred"—traditionally the vocation of the poet.

In talking about the artistic "form of language," poetry, we have *four terms of art.* They are Greek-derived from the verb *poiein* (Latin *facere*)—the verb for making—that is, the breaking of something found in the world in order to produce something else called art. Thus we have *poetics, poetry, poem, poet.* Of these, the term "poetics" is late and trivial, an institutional category. (I may be a professor of "poetics," at this very moment.) The connotations of "poetics" drift in the direction of aesthetics, the implications of which I think to be a cultural error. "Poetry" and "poem," on the other hand, are profound terms and modally distinct. The distinction is a radical one such that the idea of "poetry in general" (I use Shelley's language; I might have used Schlegel's, Heidegger's, Chomsky's, or another's) has a vital life that is related to actual poems only in a contingent sense, or not at all. "Poetry," as it appears, is the artistic form of language as such. Here is Chomsky in *Cartesian Linguistics* paraphrasing Schlegel:

> The explanation for *the central position* of poetry lies in its association with language. Poetry is unique in that its very medium is unbounded and free; that is, its medium, language, is a system with unbounded innovative potentialities for the formation and expression of ideas. The production of any work of art is preceded by a creative mental act for which the means provided is language. Thus the creative use of language which, under certain conditions of form and organization constitutes poetry, accompanies and underlies any act of the creative imagination no matter what the medium in which it is realized. *In this way, poetry achieves its unique status among the arts and artistic creation and artistic creativity is related to the creative aspects of language use.*[2]

The idea of poetry in general *does not require that there be any actual poems,* such as, for example, those made of metered sentences. There is, however, an attested sense among philosophers that *poetry names a final discourse that comes into view when the limit of philosophy is seen.* We find this in Rorty, who may be following Wittgenstein's remark: "I think I summed up my attitude to philosophy when I said: philosophy ought really to be written as a *poetic composition.*"[3]

I myself am not clear—despite the general prestige of the word—what, as a term, "poetry" with its entailed implication of "creativity" can *now mean* in the context of the actual human task. What obligations "poetry" requires. What benefit to the human world the obligation, privilege, or competence named "poetry"—*the vocation to "poetic work"*—implies or promises. Above all, what knowledge it contributes. Nor shall I answer that question to my own satisfaction. But the tendency of my thought is to consider the term "poetry," as it is now employed, as meaning *"sanctioned* making." That is to say: "poetry" is a now a *mystified* term. And the mystification of the term is demanded by the social necessity (peculiar to our cultural moment) of concealing the violence of representation as such: eidetic violence. That's the problem that (I am arguing) Crane's poem addresses by presenting the "tower" broken by its bells—rung by an unsanctioned ringer, not a bell-ringer, but a poet on a cultural vacation. In any case, my avowed unclarity with respect to the "meaning" of the word "poetry" is not, I assure you, a claim of modesty on my part or a gesture of intellectual circumspection, but rather *an expression of fear.*

On the historic face of it, "poetry" requires (as I have said) an institution not poetic (e.g., Horace's Rome). The relation of institution to poetic vocation is *not classificatory*, though we do assuredly sort poetries by this means. We speak of "classical" or "romantic" or "love" poetry, or "Chinese" or "religious" poetry, "black" poetry, "gay" poetry, and more. The relationship of *institution* to poetic vocation is in fact regulative. The controlling example in America in my time—both generative and criteriological—was strangely the regulative dependence of English seventeenth-century poetry on Anglican theology mediated by T. S. Eliot, the strange context in which I was trained in the fifties. (So also, you will have noted, was Oppenheimer in the previous generation. That's how he came to know and cite Donne's sonnet.)

The "impasse" (Crane uses the word in the fourth stanza of his poem)— *the impasse that determines the minority of poetry in our present postmodern culture lies in the absence among us of sanctioned regulative institutions not poetic* (historically, religio-political) such as can contribute the function of assured regulation necessary to make human sense of the vocational demand, the cruel privilege conferred by the Muses. (Nor is the *effect* of such "institution" supplied by "creative writing courses.") In the "modern" period (let us say the first half of the twentieth century), Yeats, Eliot, and Stevens are prominent examples of poetic vocation put in service of institutions not poetic, which regulated and thereby made possible the conspicuous successes of English poetry in the period (the Irish state, Anglican religion, life insurance). Pound, you will remember, did his best work in a cage.

Hart Crane is also a modern poet. "The Broken Tower" (which we date 1931–32) is a *modern* poem. The "Tower" referred to is an institutional signifier—a church tower. But notice the first words of our poem: "The bell-rope that gathers God at dawn / Dispatches me as though I dropped down the knell / Of a spent day . . ." The ringing of the bell is stated as agentless (a non-personal principle of meaning-making). The ringer is not a bell-ringer.[4] This anarchy of the bells of the Catholic church at Taxco, Mexico, expresses—the *breaking* of the tower signifies—a socio-semantic incoherence, a *regulative disorientation* (this bell-ringing is disturbed time-telling) that has the same effect as the well-known first figure of T. S. Eliot's "The Love Song of J. Alfred Prufrock":

> Let us go then, you and I,
> When the evening is spread out against the sky
> Like a patient etherized upon a table;

The cure of the vocation requires, as I have said, provision of the regulative effect of an institution not poetic that the poem undertakes to state—in fact, to supply. But can a poem do that? In any case, the urgency of this poem expresses the intent to do so. The speaker in the poem speaks in a tone of urgent purposiveness and expresses his anxiety about the generality, the shared intelligibility of his experience, *which must be communicated and may be impossible to communicate.* The second stanza of the poem:

> Have you not heard, have you not seen the corps
> Of shadows in the tower . . . ?

"The Broken Tower" is a poem to which the principal critical response is complaint about its difficulty. What should be said about difficulty in this poem? We note that the poem takes a kind of difficulty as its subject: "Have you not heard, have you not seen. . . ." The "difficulty" of this poem lies in the cognitive (that is to say, the moral) demand on the reader—the one who understands the poem—*to supply not merely the meaning of the poem but the sufficient condition of its having meaning at all*—"meaning" being construed within the poem as the question of any possibility of common experience. Why else does a poet ring the bell?

In this light, one notes that Crane's "The Broken Tower"—the formal poem as such, the poem of lines and stanzas—does not perform "brokenness"; it is in no visual or countable or grammatical way broken. It is a formally conservative sequence of elegiac stanzas. Models of the elegiac poem consisting of a sequence of stanzas, each stanza made of four five-stress lines, alternately rhymed, are frequent enough in the tradition. Well-known examples are Donne's "A Valediction: Forbidding Mourning," Wordsworth's "Elegiac Stanzas Suggested by a Picture of Peele Castle," and Rimbaud's "Le Bateau ivre," to which I have already alluded. But Rimbaud's vocational masterpiece (which may be Crane's "source") *inhabits an assured existential state of affairs that it discovers by narrativity.* Crane's poem, by contrast, is put in service of the solution of a "problem," *brokenness,* intimate and general—a problem *life-constitutive, but insoluble.* Crane's poem proceeds by presenting paired terms of radically contradictory, categorical differences constitutive of experience (e.g., father/mother; male/female; homo/hetero; outer/inner; mind/body, etc.)—differences that are necessary to any life and express (when considered as categorical, contradictory, and inevitable) the discursive impossibility of experience altogether. Crane's "brokenness" is not personal, intentional, and descriptive like Rimbaud's "*dérèglement,*" but (by contrast) social and analytic, that is, philosophical, *a matter of logic in the technical sense*—as American modernist poems from Whitman on tend to be.

The institution not poetic that Crane offers as subvening *poesis* is "logic." But he warns us that *his* vocation risks "speaking in idioms . . . sometimes shocking to the scholars and historians of [Aristotelian] logic." I have elsewhere studied the implication of the Lincolnian difference-based logic, on the one hand, and Whitman's celebration of no difference, on the other. Crane followed Whitman, saying: "My hand in yours, Walt Whitman." Among competing institutions, between which Crane takes sides, are the two mutually exclusive logics: the tragic logic of Aristotle's excluded middle—never A and not-A; and the other logic exemplified in Crane's experience by P. D. Ouspensky's high comic logic of inclusion (referred to in chapter 2): *yes* A and not-A—everything is all, forever! Crane's poem puts us in the presence not of an "artistic" structure, but of an institution (logic) that, as he understands it, is whole, not mind-dependent, referenced to ourselves in another way than poetry is. As he says: *"Language* [i.e., 'language' as such—not conversation] *has built towers and bridges, but itself is inevitably as fluid as always."* The poem conducts us (*permits us to think our way through*) from tragic logic (Aristotle) to the other comic logic of inclusion, the logic of ecstasy.[5]

It should be clear that I regard good poems as *cognitive triumphs.* Poems are "good," from my point of view, insofar as they respond to *real problems of mind to which there is no other solution than poetry (on this occasion, this poem).* One studies and enjoys a poem with intent to grasp *what a human problem is* and what can be *said* in response to that knowledge. A good poem is (I repeat) a "cognitive triumph," *something known*, to which an appropriate response would be to say that it is true.

"The Broken Tower"—a poem not itself "broken"—consists of ten elegiac stanzas. But note that the vertical sequence of stanzas is divided, into five stanzas and then five more. And that the second sequence of five is divided from the first by difference of tone. Now, at stanza 6, we hear the voice of a man owning, stating, and confidently answering a question in the language of a person whom the poem intends to make competent and real: the person who has in fact survived to utter the stanzas that we read.

The first sequence of five stanzas presents a state of affairs (an experience) and ends with the words "desperate choice." On this choice (between two accounts of the origin and affinities of poetic composition) depends the value of the incautiously "poured" word—depends, that is to say, the *meaning* and worth of the "creativity" of which this poem is example, and perhaps proof. How shall we state that meaning, the meaning of "creativity" of which the creation speaks? That meaning is exactly knowledge of difference. In this poem difference between (on the one hand) tragic, disintegrated states, the broken stone tower with which the poem begins, and (on the other hand) comic, integrated states, the reconstructed tower within *"that is not stone"* with which the poem ends. Of that conclusion the poem of words (not broken) is confident evidence.

What the poem gets done (and assigns us as a rich gift) is the finding of words to express the choice made and to make the decision true—the finding of a word-path (a Heideggerian wood-path) we can follow, that is, understand, from the stone tower to "a tower that is not stone." On the finding of this word-path that we can follow together depends the value of the poem and the cure of the vocation—the worth and safety of it.

The second half of the poem, therefore, begins: "My word I poured." The poem then proceeds to state the terms of the choice, supplies the question *articulated:* the *desperate* choice—between despair (*désespoir*), the sin against the Holy Spirit, and hope (*espoir*), the theological basis of all confidence, and then provides an answer sufficient to the articulated need to choose. *This poem is driven, as I have said poems must be, by the urgency of a problem to which only a poem (only poetry) can find a solution.* It's the post-Babylonian question: Is there a universal—a socially integrating, *secular* language—consistent with the terms of human life, a tower the God will let stand? *Is general conversation among human beings possible?*

"Tower" was a term in much discourse early in the last century. Crane's tower is a church tower, an oriented structure where two worlds meet—human and divine. Yeats's tower was both dwelling and symbol—but *personally intended*, as he said: "I declare this tower is my symbol." If we ask the poet, "Will saying so make it so?" the answer is "Yes!" The truth of orientation is postulated, not given. Such was Jung's tower house at Bollingen, Rilke's tower at Muzot, Eiffel's grand useless moneymaking monument in Paris, Oppenheimer's tower called Trinity with its Donne etymology. Many towers in the period, all guarding human language—the possibility of general conversation (*Gesprach*). The philosophic "parent" of these towers is the church tower of Kant's Königsberg, which supplied the master with an *axis mundi*, an orientative mark, not an intrinsic truth—but the possibility-condition of knowing the world.

This "ringing" of the bells in Crane's poem is the Angelus, as the poem notes in this case *a morning ringing beginning before sunrise* (not the noon or evening Angelus, also customary). This ringing is specifically stated—timed—in the second stanza of "The Broken Tower." It occurs "before / The stars are caught and hived in the sun's ray." The latter expression begins the exposition in Crane's poem of the cure of that violence, that "brokenness" attending all perception's representations including those sanctioned by poetic vocation—what I am calling *eidetic violence*—of which this poem, as I interpret it, intends *the cure*: the poem of this ringing "through whose pulse I hear . . . / The angelus [meaning the pacification] of wars my chest evokes."

The *scriptural* sanction of the Angelus is foundational for Christian church ritual. It is an archetypal account of *instituting vocation through the mother* (Luke 1:26–35): "The angel [*angelus*] Gabriel was sent from God [to the Virgin Mary]. . . . And the angel came in unto her and said to her: 'Hail, thou art highly favored, the Lord is with thee, blessed art thou among women. . . . Fear not, Mary: for thou hast found favor with God. Behold, thou shalt conceive a child; and his name shall be called Jesus.'" Crane's "The Broken Tower" has a discursive singularity—a strangeness that is akin to the response of the Virgin to the words spoken by Gabriel in Luke's text, the strangeness registered in her astonishment: "How shall this be . . . ?" There is a double sense, in the scriptural event as in this poem as well, of the *commonplace* and also of the *impossible*—a sense of *unanticipated actuality*. It is an exceptional encounter—an encounter of the nature of *impossible exceptionality* that it is greatly in our interest to consider. For it belongs to the deep hermeneutic that this poem—in its substantive difficulty—properly calls for.

Both Crane's life and the reception of his work are characterized by an aura of exceptionality, even among poet lives and poetic works—as if Hart Crane were, among poetic writers, a *true* poet and his poems, among poetic texts, mysteriously *true* poems. This sentiment of privilege (this archetypical vocationality of Crane) determines his language (his only presence now to the world, his *fama*) and is, and should always be, *an astonishment and a trouble* to his readers. *It is difficult only if and when it is understood. The "difficulty" comes after understanding, not before.* But decipherment is not understanding.

It is important therefore to recall, when reading Crane, that no poem of value, such as "The Broken Tower," is about the poet who wrote it down. Nor is it explicable in terms of the life of the poet. Nonetheless, what people do in their lives has the same archetypical character as what they write—and is as little invented by the doer as the poem is the invention of the poet. The idea of "vocation" (discourse authorized from afar) and also the idea of "difficulty" (discourse not solved by explanation) point with equal relevance both to the life and to the work. As also does the "cure of vocation," which requires the facing toward, *the articulation and bringing to mind, by whatever means, of the violence inherent in representation as such.* That's the real work of the poet—what poetry, if it can intend anything, should do and what the Crane poet did.

Crane was a man burdened by and identified with the poetic vocation. The mythic archetype of such a life is the story of Orpheus, who failed to retrieve Eurydice from death, because he couldn't stop looking at her. What is brought to mind as an image is lost—that's the bitter Orphic rule. Crane's life, the life of a maker, ended in suicide, an artifactual death—that is to say, *his death was the last artifact of his making, faithful to vocation.* He was, in his end, both the Orpheus and the Eurydice, bequeathing to others the problematic of vocation. Crane's entire subjection to his vocation contributed the structure both of his life and death. And the trace of this archetypical vocation is the astonishment of his poems—the seeing (or vision) of the doomed spectator. Toward the end of his life, Crane destroyed with a knife a large and distinguished portrait of himself reading, painted by the Mexican artist Siqueiros, from whom he had commissioned it. The violence of the destruction by the poet of his image mirrors the violence that the image committed upon its subject.

Let us step back a moment. What are poems for? A good poem gives rise to thinking. About what? About states of affairs that would not, except for the poem, come to mind, be seen as problems, or the solutions seen to be solutions. The poems of Hart Crane are particularly exacting—"difficult"—in this matter. In general, the requirement of thought about poetic text is precipitated by a characteristic of poems that is commonly called closure. We are now, let us assume, at the end of Crane's poem. We must stop and think:

how does this end flow with inevitability from what went before? What does the poem intend to follow after—what can be thought that could not be thought by the reader before the poem was known to the reader?[6]

I will try to say how this dynamic transvaluation of experience is stated and then be done. The narrative transit from *outer* to *inner* (the action of this poem) is arguably the most common and most prestigious story in Western civilization—comic in the large philosophical sense, healing. The intent of this narrative (outer to inner) is re-orientation, re-cuperation, re-trieval, closure. . . . (It is the artistic inevitability of this requirement—*closure*—that supplies Adorno's repudiation of art after Auschwitz.) The "re-" morpheme is the bottom-line *fiction* (after all, what it means can't happen because there is no return). In the eighth stanza of "The Broken Tower," we hear it at line 30: "recall," "revived," and its reversal in "sure," which rhymes with "pure."

Crane's discourse—his re-formed logic—proceeds not by exclusion of, but by the reversal of, polarities: mind/body; inner/outer; mother/father; also form/content, metricality/reference. But not without breakage, for healing implies wound. Stanzas 3 and 4 of "The Broken Tower" state the breakage required to make possible this re-orientative transition:

> The bells, I say, the bells break down their tower;
> And swing I know not where. Their tongues engrave
> Membrane through marrow, my long-scattered score
> Of broken intervals . . . And I, their sexton slave!
>
> Oval encyclicals in canyons heaping
> The impasse high with choir. Banked voices slain!
> Pagodas, campaniles with reveilles outleaping—
> O terraced echoes prostrate on the plain! . . .

What is the breakage as stated? The Kafkaesque engraving on the body ("membrane through marrow") of a prior disintegrated "long-scattered score," song-text of mistake; *then* the realization of "impasse"—the killing ("banked voices slain") of prior discourses, that is, the prohibited Babylonian universal-tower languages of pagodas and campaniles (indifferently) and their "echoes"; then all other authority (e.g., papal "encyclicals") blocked and "slain," killed by this new knowledge, this performance by the bells of a cognitive "reveille"; above all, the repudiation of the "brotherhood" of the bells, that "corps of shadows in the tower."[7]

Our understanding of the conclusion of "The Broken Tower" (the last five stanzas) will depend on how we answer the question what "mind" means.

What is the "within"? For Crane and the religion of Crane's mother and her family (Christian Scientists, their scripture being *Science and Health*), the answer is: God is within and God is Mind. (She is male *and* female, how else could She have created both man and woman in Her image.)[8] In Christian Science, *Mind* heals by reason of origination prior to body. Hence Crane's "healed, original now, and pure . . ." This healing is *the cure of the vocation*—representation that escapes eidetic violence because the matter in which it works is not material. Therefore "fame" is not subject to scarcity. What follows after breaking is building: "And builds, within, a tower that is not stone."

The end of any poem is the moment when, filled with the poem's language, the readers—the preservers of the poem, *die Bewahrenden*—are left alone with meaning, *imperative and not their own*. What work does the poem assigns us? Is it worth doing? Can it be done? Let me step back again: I speak of Crane's *conscious turn (orientative reversal)* from outer to inner, from subjection to Aristotelian logic, which is also the logic of *mimesis* (i.e., representation as such—the *eidetic of violence* to which I have referred) all the way over to the conscious privileging of a logic that states that *A and not-A are the same—are All*. But this is only true in the domain of the mother—on the analytic ground of the mother's body, the "matrix of the heart," which extinguishes sexual difference, brings forth both sexes indifferently.

"The Broken Tower" conducts us (reorients us on the archetypal pathway) from *"pater"* (father, pattern) to *"mater"* (mother, matrix). In *matrix* ("the matrix of the heart") the anti-metaphoric, non-representational "logic of ecstasy" is the rule. I wish to emphasize that it is the *strangeness*, the radical unfamiliarity of the thought, the unexpectedness of the cognitive demand that makes Crane "difficult." The difficulty is not stylistic. The difficulty is substantial, meta-logical, non-metaphoric, *matrical*. The difficulty is not "literary."

The action of the poem produces *re-predication*: that is to say that the significant human world is at the end governed by a new representational regime without eidetic violence—a regime "that shrines the quiet lake and swells a tower." *The new predicate is "mental," as in Blake's "mental fight."* Look again at the last stanza of the poem: "The matrix of the heart" is followed without breakage by the "difficult" (i.e., *contradictory*) gesture "lift down," and the strangely transitive verbs "shrine" and "swell." What does it all mean? It means: *Yes! A and not-A* forever.

Thus the poem does not celebrate (as Crane himself and all his friends may have thought) the transit from homo- to heterosexual relationship. About that we really know nothing. But, in fact, it is extinction of the difference that is conveyed by means of what we might reasonably call *deep* style, work with language in the light of all its histories.

The last stanza of "The Broken Tower" is as follows:

> The matrix of the heart, lift down the eye
> That shrines the quiet lake and swells a tower . . .
> The commodious, tall decorum of that sky
> Unseals her earth, and lifts love in its shower.

This "extinction of difference," especially of sexual difference—that's the meaning of "the matrix of the heart"—is followed in our poem by two great words: "commodious" and "decorum": "The commodious, tall decorum of that sky" (eighteenth-century words—Sam Johnson, Tom Jefferson words) signifying relationship—conversation—*communicative "action" in human scale among persons always on the same ground.* Everything that Crane wrote should be seen as devised to make possible the poet's situation in his text of these two great words (which occur no other place in Crane's poetic work, but here at the end of it).

Hart Crane was not a thinker by any means; but he was a maker who thought about making and whose making requires thought. Crane's question "But was it cognate with . . . ?" (i.e., with what origin-story—satanic or divine—with what history is poetry affined?) is the *maker's* question—not about the psychological or literary, but about the ethical affinities of making and of what is made. This question is, in my understanding, the profound question to which the "man of letters" in our time—that is, any conscious person in civilization, *any person*—is obligated. It is also the question the answer to which is hardest for us in the university (creatures of the text) to consider. You will notice that the question mark disappears from Crane's text after the seventh stanza into an end-state of the poem, which is metrically and grammatically conclusive, but semantically open. The last line of the poem *opens*. Its capital word is "Unseals":

> The commodious, tall decorum of that sky
> *Unseals* her earth, and lifts love in its shower.

The poem has done what poetry can do. It has given rise to thinking.

Teaching Literature in a Discredited Civilization

A TALK FOR TEACHERS

I have nothing to say about which anything can be done today or tomorrow. I wish to consider this morning whether the problems of the university at the present time do not arise in part because the civilization that it transmits is not worth having. No acumen about the social arrangement of classrooms, no exchange of prescriptive for self-appropriated learning, no restoration of the voluntary character of pedagogical relationships will make acceptable a civilization that is inherently suicidal to own. Quite the contrary, enlightened or radical pedagogy under such circumstances constitutes a heinous deception. Similarly, there is no meaning, or perverse meaning, to the purification of institutions and persons from criminal alliances with industry and government if the murderous acts of men flow not from their criminality and indulgences, but in fact from their most virtuous renunciations.

You need merely consider the contingencies upon which life depends, at the present time, in order to realize that ordinary life has become an extreme situation in a sense singular to this time—so long as spring and daylight do not let you forget. My business here, in a context in which it is possible to think about hard matters with a sense of comradeship, is to

*This "Coda" originally appeared in a slightly different version under the title "Teaching Literature in a Discredited Civilization." Reprinted by permission from the *Massachusetts Review* 10, no. 3 (Summer 1969): 419–32. This essay was written in the shadow of the assassinations of Robert Kennedy and of Martin Luther King Jr., and in the time of the Vietnam War, which presented not only bitterly contested moral issues, but an actual threat to the lives of students graduating from school or college. It speaks to that time, specifically; but since America is once again at war, in Iraq and Afghanistan, it is included here in the interests of memory and reconsideration.

consider how literary education enters into the etiology of that extreme situation. The relation between literature and events is an obscure one. The obscurity arises because the connections between individual life and collective or social life are as yet indeterminable. Literary civilization raises questions of remoter cause only in the illusory sense that individual life seems remoter in terms of available analyses from historical events than social "fact."

Let us for the moment not be so disingenuous as to suppose that warriors and weapons makers are the only destroyers, and therefore the only persons of whom the Great Refusal is demanded. The "unacknowledged legislators" by their own account are also legislators and must be held responsible.

The right metaphor for education at the present time is conveyed in Robert Lifton's phrase "counterfeit nurturance." The child, the city, the nation must be destroyed in order to be saved, imperiled in order to be protected, enslaved in order to be free. Destruction, peril, and slavery of the self in view of salvation, protection, and freedom is the commonplace of Western nurture, secular and redemptive. But when the town is Ben Tre, the protection anti-ballistic missiles, the slavery academic freedom, the process becomes an insupportable exchange of the life of one party for the symbols of another. To what extent does literary education constitute nurture that is not merely counterfeit but also lethal? To what extent does the substance of our civilization and not merely the circumstances of its transmission make it hostile to life?

A discredited civilization is one not worth having. All education involves an expensive exchange of instinctual life for symbolic life, an exchange that in the case of literary education is facilitated by an appeal to the senses (*aut prodesse aut delectare*). Instinct is personal, and symbol is social being. When education (the internalization of this exchange) admits the candidate to participation in a society, the promises of which have been kept in the form of intolerable threat, then that education is rationally undesirable. It will not do for teachers and students to restore their morale and compensate their renunciations by enlarging affectionate commitment one to the other. The basis of the relationship is unforgivable.

Further, we find that in this "post-industrial" society the immemorial dynamic of symbol-instinct exchange takes on an impersonal character that is even more portentous than the more familiar personal form. For what is destroyed, then to get symbolic culture, is not part of the self of the recipient at all, and not in his gift. Rousseau proposed this conundrum by imagining an aged mandarin. Would you accept *your* felicity, *your* civilization, if you could have it merely by killing *him*, undetected, surgically, at a distance? Dostoyevsky puts it more passionately:

> Imagine you are creating a fabric of human destiny with the object of making men happy in the end, giving them peace and rest at last, but that it was essential and inevitable to torture to death only one tiny creature — that baby beating its breast with its fist, for instance — and to found that edifice on its unavenged tears? Would you consent to be architect on those conditions?

That civilization could not be acceptable at any price. Yet there is no doubt in my mind that some such reciprocity operates today in the high civilizations of the West, not merely at the economic level where the processes are available to analysis, but at a level so deep in the undisclosed nexus of the symbolic empire of the electronic collectivity that we have no means of describing it. Close to hand, we find traces of this lethal economy in the relationship of teacher and student. Traditionally, the student is the elite member of the pedagogical dyad: the examples of Socrates and Alcibiades, or Virgil and Dante in *The Divine Comedy*, will call the archetype to mind. The rise of "the faculty" as an elite implies an externalization (autonomy) by one party of the cost of a symbolic order from which it alone benefits.

Traditionally, barbarism and civilization have seemed to succeed one another in the form of invasion and conquest from without. As civilized persons, we are unaccustomed to acknowledge barbarism as arising within civilization as a consequence of its most characteristic processes. The emphasis so evident in the political realm on external defense extends deep into the province of symbolic life, reflecting an unwillingness to recognize that crimes flow from within civilization and not merely from its enemies. For many years those teachers who have been interested in education as nurture, Carl Rogers for example, have flatly declared the outcome of teaching not merely unimportant but hurtful. Literary students must take this matter with extreme seriousness not merely as a political issue but also in the struggle for which they have been trained, the inquisition of the symbolic establishment. To internalize the revolution is extremely difficult. A bad teacher is a person who does not know the odds. Worse yet are the teachers who, knowing the odds, have made so little peace with themselves that they confer the problem unsolved and unmediated upon their students with all the passion of a personal dilemma.

Art is traditionally a response to scarcity. In a discredited civilization, the traditional terms of symbolic compensation no longer make life worth living. The Homeric conflict, for example, is precipitated because what men really want (instinctual completeness, immortality) is preempted by time. War becomes a machine for generating value of a second order (honor, *arete*, social value), a value system nobody really wants erected in despair of the heart's desire. *The Iliad* seems familiar because it represents a challenge to the symbols of conflict-generated value by the instinctual seriousness of a young man drawing on profoundly atavistic sources of self-possession. Wherever in Western art the value of conflict-generated symbols is challenged by instinctual absolutism, the latter is defeated either through the superior legitimacy of social purpose in history, or through some kind of betrayal in transcendence (sublimation). Art and even literacy itself, like honor in *The Iliad*, may now have become a compensation for ontological scarcity too costly to be tolerated. The wisdom of instinctual retrenchment in the face of the alienation of fiction and the abstraction of symbol may be more precious to the individual student and to the civilization than the poem.

Again, in Virgil the heroic conflict-generated value system (Priam, Misenus) is discredited, but of two possibilities for restoration, the compassionate instinct-based alternative is destroyed in favor of a universal sociality—conflict mastered through empire. *The Divine Comedy*, incorporating the Virgilian *epos*, defines its discredited civilization as an infernal world of totally serious instinctual self-identification, which cannot prevail and cannot be abolished. At the present time we are heirs of the Romantic interpretation of that God-administered segregation of instinctual from social life predicted by Virgil and Dante as representative of our authoritative imaginal tradition. So critical has that separation become that art itself (the reconciliation or mutuality of the social and the instinctive, *utile dulci*) has been drawn into the vortex of discredit. We are aware of living in a predatory sociality at the expense of all. The Homeric conflict comments on the nuclear scenario: the rebellion of the young, the instinctual elite, is once again the most precious leading of mankind as a whole. We may ask, "What is the proper intervention of the literary teacher?"

"Relevant" teaching is teaching that gives a good account of the world and of its own purposes. In order to avoid dreary and dangerous mendacity, the teacher must have some understanding of the relationship between the world as a human state of affairs, the book, and the mind of the student. Taking all three of these terms into consideration, we have no account good enough to be dignified as "radical." Nonetheless I offer the next five topics as an indication of an approach.

I. Shakespeare, Sonnet 65

We are all familiar from Shakespeare with the traditional exchange of complete possession of the loved person preempted by time for the immortal image written so long as men may read in black ink:

> Since brass, nor stone, nor earth, nor boundless sea
> But sad mortality o'ersways their power,
> How with this rage shall beauty hold a plea,
> Whose action is no stronger than a flower?
> O! how shall summer's honey breath hold out
> Against the wrackful siege of batt'ring days,
> When rocks impregnable are not so stout,
> Nor gates of steel so strong, but Time decays?
> O fearful meditation: where, alack,
> Shall Time's best jewel from Time's chest lie hid?
> Or what strong hand can hold his swift foot back,
> Or who his spoil of beauty can forbid?
> > O! none, unless this miracle have might:
> > That in black ink my love may still shine bright.

This exchange is the basis of literary civilization and is in direct conflict with communalism, secular humanity, immanent instinctual absolutism. Sonnet 65 is meaningful only if mankind collectively has a future, if that future is social and literate, and that literate sociality is valued. None of these three conditions is any longer necessarily assured. Further, we may note that the symbol-instinct exchange in Sonnet 65 requires an interior space, a dimensional subjectivity, in which to inscribe itself. But interior space, the most elite of traditional aesthetic possessions, bears with it the marks of its origins in a disabled self. It is the servile strategy of the Christian slave and invites all persons, slaves of time, to become the captives also of a social future of a given sort in which some kinds of action are preempted and instinctual completion in particular "traded off" against the mimetic bright star. In other words, Sonnet 65, which stands here in my brief remarks for the tradition, defines the person in a specific sense, and the terms of that definition are neither inevitable nor beyond question. Poetry is an irreplaceable mode of the visibility of person to person, but it is impatient of action, communalism, and instinctual humanity, all of which may be as necessary as life itself. You cannot have it all ways. The antinomic character of our civilization (instinct or symbol but not both; agency or communion but not both, etc.) is now as always being administered as a weapon against the young (order or feeling, but not both). Fate is being used as an argument against life. Even Pity, as Blake reminds us "would be no more / If we did not make somebody poor." There is a justifiable system of counter-refusals to be opposed both to the refusals and to the consolations of art. It is not the business of the teacher to conspire with fate.

II. Aulis

As I have already implied, the tradition of the representation of human reality in the West is unregenerately *étatiste*. Antigone always goes down into the tomb, Achilles is always broken, Agamemnon always goes to Troy over the slain body of his child Iphigenia. The myth is one repeated in many histories of power: the desire by the parent that the child not live. If parricide, as Feuer suggests, is the motive of student rebellion, that motive is nevertheless justified by the infanticidal character of a civilization. This is the tragic correlation of the lyric paradigm for individual life in Sonnet 65.

The intolerable prophecy of the tradition adumbrates an endless conflict between the claims of instinctual autonomy and Olympian order. When the tragic hero of the West stands between two options both of which are bad, he always opts for or is destroyed by the symbolic forces of the state. His predicament is the same as that of any person in civilization, and the teacher (who must not evade the established nature of his role) finds himself conspiring as explainer with an intolerable fatality. It does not seem unlikely that the singularity of our times has invalidated the *paideia* of tragedy. The forces that social order has arrayed in its own defense preclude the tragic display of human adequacy by exceeding human scale and preempting the future in which pity and terror can be purged.

The cheapest commodity in human history, and the most abundant, is pain. The property for which civilization has been least accountable is human life. As the canons of human self-representation fall away, man becomes increasingly invisible to man while at the same time becoming increasingly sentient and more critically interrelated. No good purpose is served, however, by blind advocacy of a tradition that has no other prophecy than the extinction of the resisting individual.

III. Aristotle's Theater of Cruelty

The most widespread if not the deepest evil of a discredited civilization is distortion of the aesthetic premise. When Aristotle distinguished (very much after the fact) between the actors and the audience of tragedy, he sealed once and for all the predicament of the persona or image, and the predicament of the spectator or audience, into separate realms. The persona went to his death, and the audience went home purged of pity and terror. This segregation, which made possible the life of the work beyond the participatory dance of its origin, enabled the distinction of aesthetic in contrast to ethical reality. This is the theater the contradictions of which Artaud deepened by calling it a theater of cruelty. Aesthetization of reality means the fictionalization of sentiment, the cultivated unreality of event to spectator. In the politics of our experience, it has become one of the most banal features of civilization. Pity and terror are emotions of which we cannot afford to be purged. The aesthetization of the spectacle, as St. Augustine reminds us, prevents an ethical response to tragic event, the absurd rush across the footlights that saves the life of the tragedian or comforts his lonely agony. For the radical imagination there can be no unreal persons, and yet every man's experience in this polity calls to mind the Roman emperor before whom real slaves died real deaths in the catastrophe of a charade. There is a felt hostility to classical forms of aesthetic distance and order evident among us, inhibiting art as well as teaching, calling for other things.

The clearest justification of this intuitive critique of the tradition is the misconstruction in universities of the freedom of speech and inquiry along aesthetic lines. The Great Institution in which the Academic Freedom Committee could write that academic freedom "protects scholarly work from having to pass moral or political tests" is like an insane mind specializing in rationality, against which the rebellious student becomes the unwanted and belligerently refused return of repressed and mutilated feeling. In short, aesthetics have passed into anaesthetics, a prime condition of political terror, enabling apocalyptic warfare scenarios, insulating populations with common interests from one another, countenancing teaching only if it is fictionalized as "dialogue," sponsoring research without concern that the right to inquire conflicts with the right to exist of whole populations. Aesthetic distance and what flows from it, a well of consolation for generations of literate men, is hostile to the radical imagination of redemptive solidarity within history. The aesthetic premise is at the very least a two-way ambiguous strategy. In a discredited civilization, the deathward horn of the dilemma sticks in the brain.

IV. Revolutionary Dyslogia and the Limits of Art

Grammar represents a reality appropriation as profoundly implicated with specific forms of social life as, for example, the Roman roads that ruthlessly administered native terrain toward the remote and alien capital of empire. In the mid-nineteenth century, the perennial dyslogic implications of poetic diction, crystallized against the background of industrialism, issued in the skewed grammars of Dickinson, Hopkins, Rimbaud, et cetera. Poetic language, a voice of feeling, responded with abhorrence to a discredited social language. I find in the behavior of my students an analogous resistance to literacy itself, which does not achieve the legitimacy of art, but which as a teacher I cannot override without denying the student's sense of her own truth. Grammaticality itself, in post-industrial nations, is (on the showing of so honorable a witness as the poetic tradition) an imposed settlement (unsatisfactory to all parties) of legitimate conflicts between the outlawed—private in the privative sense—voice of feeling and the social world. It must not be the business of the teacher of writing to administer blindly the non-negotiable demands of depraved sociality in the most intimate and subtly compromised realm of the student's mind to which the teacher has access, the language by which she becomes knowable to herself as a person. The language of modern artistic literature is nothing if not a set of stratagems to prevent the use of the self in destructive ways. The language behavior of the student is likely to be nothing less.

Language learning in the more advanced sense of "style" is the archetypal rite of passage by which the young enter history, a deed of blood exacted by the gods that acknowledges and seals the child's sharing of the guilt of social life. It is as legitimately resisted and as inevitably undertaken as Orestes' murder of his mother. The practice of social language is the threshold at which vital forces in the self, all labeled "Life and Meaning," are in dreadful conflict. Where in a discredited, an unforgivable civilization is the goddess who casts the deciding vote on behalf of the child? The literary *paideia* that does not understand these problems is falsely innocent.

The false innocence of the humanities seems to me a central and urgent issue. The literary mind has been at enormous pains to avoid questions of an ontological sort such as: "What is the authority and limit of literary statement? Why is it valued? What is the relationship between what it refers to and what is?" Literacy and art have always been used by teachers (and with slightly more color of reason by artists) as sanction for avoiding the urgent and unworkable claims of sentiment and history. More particularly the generation now teaching, which grew up in or lived through the world of the Holocaust, rushed into an open conspiracy against the insane task of responding to a stimulus so out of scale with the human capacity for response. And indeed, the representation of human life has always had strict but not always known boundaries. Outside of those boundaries, the shoreless seas of unspeakable pain (*infandum, ineffabile*) open into the abyss of unillumined privacies. The finite and partial categories by which we render experience interpretable are inherent in the nature of language and find their taxonomic definitions in the hitherto inexorable "kinds" of comedy and tragedy. By consent the business of civilization has defined reality within the bright circle of the ancient and modern stage, the metrical line, the grammatical sentence, the moderately expressive social countenance. This limited tolerance of the knowable to the perpetual agony of all living things, having no doubt an evolutionary usefulness, is incorporated among the covenanted terms of collective life. Over the past two centuries and most conspicuously in the last fifty years, this covenant, like so many others, has become a destructive and unworkable settlement that must not be conspired with in the name of reason and piety, but that reason and piety must both oppose.

At least since the Holocaust, the limits upon representation that were once the defining conditions of communal life, the hard terms upon which men became visible to one another, have turned against communal life and become a sort of blindness. Teachers, who ought to be much freer in this matter than the artist, must urgently concern themselves with a critique of their instruments; for, as surely as there is a military-industrial alliance, there is also a military-aesthetic alliance that has a stake in strategies of non-response, the anaesthetic premises of grammar, of the traditional generic taxonomy, and the anti-ethical frames of the classroom, erosion of which has given us the only truly sentient politics we have. No good artist ever looked upon art with the same stunned and banal discursiveness or regarded it as so "important" as the teacher in the university. In a discredited civilization, such traces of meaningful sentiment as we have (our sentences, our poems) become tools for compelling the young to disavow their most urgent sense of reality. We have come to the point where the dialectical illiterates—those who cannot learn, or who have learned not to learn, or those who are mad—are the only good students.

V. The Text Is the Reader's Thing

Literary education, properly understood and conducted, is a form of anamnesis, a self-appropriation through remembering past lives. By contrast, our curriculum is a mismanaged grid of tasks probably designed to prevent that accomplishment on a selective basis. Black insistence on a black pedagogical epistemology known only from within, and therefore to be administered only by blacks, is at this time a dialectically appropriate response to the present curricular state of affairs. The black student may respond, as the white does not, to the bewilderment of his identity intelligence in the course of studies. The prophecy of art is that the true self comes from afar. Further, the only defense against the almost irresistible tendency of the human organism to respond by adaptation to environments hostile to its life is the symbolic past. Consequently, the curricular problem is not spoken to by increasing the modernity and social-analytic character of studies. That dodge is generally a concession to the moral embarrassment of the teacher, which is a predictable phase of liberal pedagogic colonialism.

The brevity of my remarks allows me to point to only one area where a solution must be found appropriate to the literary subject. We urgently require a review of the meaning of our interpretive techniques, our styles of mediation between student and text, and, in particular, of the warped historicistic realism that is our dominant meaning-interpretive theory. No one who in the past has understood the world through literature (e.g., Socrates, Alexander, Hillel, Jesus, Porphyry, Augustine, Dante, Blake, Yeats, Tolstoy) could find our academic techniques of discriminating "good readings" anything but the fumes of opinion, not unmingled with hate and fear. Fear of what? Fear of fantasy and the "own" aspects of the self. Under domination by a perhaps fourth-hand classical humanism, academic literary studies have failed to understand the relationship between "text" and fantasy, the own aspect of individuality black or white. After Euripides, nobody ever got to Athens except in a chariot drawn by dragons. Hillel, Porphyry, Blake, Yeats, Empson, all mistaking clowns, were better readers than Leavis or Frye. Even the brilliant student paper, which all radical teachers recognize and praise, is a precarious management of disparate criteria of truth (imaginative, analytic, textual), the management of which exhausts the writer, leaving little residue from the conflagration for any self. The relationship between past and present has been made absurd. From this flows the observable fact that there is so little positive connection in the academic community between anybody's civilization and his politics. The radical assertion is that the text is not the writer's nor the teacher's, but the reader's thing. Until the hermeneutic question among other ontological questions (the question "What constitutes the meaning of the text?") is solved in an academic context by a generation of integral readers as teachers, it may be that client-centered, student-sponsored education—participated in but not controlled by experts—is better than what we have, but only a second best.

In Conclusion

I have pointed to some features of a discredited civilization almost indiscriminable from civilization itself, and in doing so I have pointed to some tasks. A post-industrial age, by freeing some persons or classes of person from nature as an enemy, forces into consciousness the contradictions within civilization itself, making urgent moral business of the hidden evil flowing from innocence as well as the patent evil flowing from guilt. The weapons makers and technicians provide the means, but the lovers and teachers seal the motive, for weapons makers, technicians, lovers, and teachers alike. The violence of the nation, the banality of the university, the unassessed risks of the civilization transmitted—all lay heavy burdens of imputed and inherent discredit on the legitimacy that authorizes the teacher's role. The nature of this discredit that is responded to everywhere about us as a matter of institutional structure has scarcely been approached as a matter of disciplinary substance.

The business of teachers is to discover and then to demand all the authority that flows from their obligations as teachers. That is their given style of exemplary engagement. An understanding of that authority will arise when the self-interest, mutual but not identical, of teacher and student in the civilization transmitted is known. To foster consciousness in this sense is one business of radical research. Vastly more courage must be exhibited by all of us in our purely pedagogic roles. Teachers must seek authority as members of an academic community, whether to stop teaching, to teach this and not that, to protect students from destructive grids of requirements and moronic sanctions, to foster self-possession without preempting criticism, and above all to understand and say clearly what they are about—so that they do not commit the final pedagogic crime of conferring the problem unsolved upon those who have come for something else. Teachers, radical or otherwise, exercise their role among their peers and toward their students not by abdicating their role, but by defining it. Above all, I am suggesting that the business of the literary teacher is to understand her civilization as it is the life-space of the person: consoling, redemptive, but also treacherous, abhorrent, arbitrary, absurd. To administer civilization on behalf of rather than in scorn of humanity now appears to be the hardest problem that has ever confronted mind.

Notes

Poetry and Enlightenment

1. Adorno's actual words were "nach Auschwitz ein Gedicht zu schreiben, ist barbarisch, und das frißt auch die Erkenntnis an, die ausspricht, warum es unmöglich ward, heute Gedichte zu schreiben." [To write poetry after Auschwitz is barbaric, and this damages the very knowledge of why it is impossible to write poetry today.] In *Gesammelte Schriften in zwanzig Bänden*, ed. Rolf Tiedemann (Frankfurt: Band 10/1 *Kulturkritif und Gesellschaft*, 1977), 30.

2. Fynsk writes, "[The poet and translator of Celan] Pierre Joris has suggested to me that Celan turned Adorno's remarks concerning Auschwitz and poetry in such a manner as to suggest that *only* poetry is possible after Auschwitz. Celan's statements in his Bremen address would seem to bear out this reading." Christopher Fynsk, "The Realities at Stake in a Poem: Celan's Bremen and Darmstadt Addresses," in *Word Traces: Readings of Paul Celan*, ed. Aris Fioretos (Baltimore: Johns Hopkins University Press, 1994), 164.

3. *Poems of Paul Celan*, trans. Michael Hamburger (New York: Persea Books, 1988), 98–99.

4. Immanuel Kant, "An Answer to the Question: What Is Enlightenment?" in *Practical Philosophy*, ed. Mary J. Gregor (Cambridge: Cambridge University Press 1996), 17: "*Enlightenment is the human being's emergence from his self-incurred minority*. Minority is inability to make use of one's own understanding without direction from another. This minority is *self-incurred* when its cause lies not in lack of understanding but in lack of resolution and courage to use it without direction from another. *Sapere aude!* Have courage to make use of your *own* understanding is thus the motto of enlightenment." See also Karl Barth's discussion of this essay: "Nobody saw, knew or said in the way that Kant did what this mature, courageous man who makes use of his own understanding looks like, what his position is and how he conducts himself." *Protestant Thought: From Rousseau to Ritschl* (New York: Harper, 1959), 152.

5. William Blake, from preface to "Milton a Poem in 2 Books," in *The Complete Poetry and Prose of William Blake*, ed. David V. Erdman (Berkeley: University of California Press, 1982), 95–96.

6. Immanuel Kant, "On Nature as Power," in "Analytic of the Sublime," *Critique of the Power of Judgment*, ed. Paul Guyer, trans. Paul Guyer and Eric Matthews (Cambridge: Cambridge University Press, 2000), 144–45: "But the sight of them [bold cliffs, thunderclouds, lightning, thunder, volcanoes, hurricanes, raging oceans, lofty waterfalls] only becomes all the more attractive the more fearful it is, as long as we find ourselves in safety, and we gladly call these objects sublime because they elevate the strength of our soul above its usual level, and allow us to discover within ourselves a capacity for resistance of quite another kind. . . ."

7. William Blake, "The Marriage of Heaven and Hell," plate III, in *Complete Poetry*, ed. Erdman, 34: "As a new heaven is begun, and it is now thirty-three years since its advent: the Eternal Hell revives. And lo! Swedenborg is the Angel sitting at the tomb; his writings are the linen clothes folded up."

8. Immanuel Kant, *Traüme eines geistersehers erlaütert durch traüme der metaphysic* (Königsberg: Kanter, 1766). Kant's critique of Swedenborg's occultism is translated as *Dreams of a Spirit Seer, and Other Related Writings*, trans. and ed. John Manolesco (New York: Vantage, 1969). *Schwärmerei* in Kant's usage here means an enthusiasm bordering on self-deception.

9. This phrase indicating "evidenced by natural light" is taken from René Descartes, *Meditation IV*, sec. 12, trans. John Vetch (Chicago: Open Court, 1920): "But if I abstain from judging of a thing when I do not conceive it with sufficient clearness and distinctness, it is plain that I act rightly, and am not deceived; but if I resolve to deny or affirm, I then do not make a right use of my free will; and if I affirm what is false, it is evident that I am deceived; moreover, even although I judge according to truth, I stumble upon it by chance, and do not therefore escape the imputation of a wrong use of my freedom; for it is a dictate of the natural light, that the knowledge of the understanding ought always to precede the determination of the will. And it is this wrong use of the freedom of the will in which is found the privation that constitutes the form of error. Privation, I say, is found in the act, in so far as it proceeds from myself, but it does not exist in the faculty which I received from God, nor even in the act, in so far as it depends on him."

10. D. H. Lawrence, "Poetry of the Present: Introduction to the American Edition of *New Poems*, 1918," in *Complete Poetry of D. H. Lawrence* (Harmondsworth, UK: Penguin, 1994), 183.

11. Jacques Derrida, "Shibboleth," trans. Joshua Wilner, in *Word Traces*, ed. Fioretos, 3–72.

12. For Hegel, art represents the Absolute only through practices of sensual realization that lead to external appearances; in thought, in contrast, the Absolute thinks itself and for itself in infinite freedom. Practices of art thus have a limit to their speculative power, whereas thought does not. G. W. F. Hegel, *Aesthetics: Lectures on Fine Art*, 2 vols. (Oxford: Clarendon, 1975), 1:9, 101–5.

13. See also Rodney Needham, *Right and Left: Essays on Dual Symbolic Classification* (Chicago: University of Chicago Press, 1973). Needham writes in two notes: "Left and right are of course relative to the orientation of the person. . . . I do not think, however, that the point of orientation affects the argument for it is conventional that in reference to any particular matter the one side is left and the other right." "I have heard of only one occasion on which a man is asked to perform an action on account of his being left-handed. If the afterbirth of a calf does not fall it is preferably a left-handed man who is asked to place a grass ring over the dam's left horn—and they may also give it medicines to drink" (107nn12, 13).

14. Immanuel Kant, *Critique of Practical Reason*, trans. Mary Gregor (Cambridge: Cambridge University Press, 1997), 133.

15. Immanuel Kant, "What Does It Mean to Orient Oneself in Thinking?" trans. Allen W. Wood, in *Religion and Rational Theology*, ed. Allen W. Wood and George di Giovanni (Cambridge: Cambridge University Press, 1996), 8.

16. For a discussion of our debt to Kant in this regard, see James Engell, *The Creative Imagination: Enlightenment to Romanticism* (Cambridge, MA: Harvard University Press, 1981), 118–39.

17. What was going on in poetry in America on January 26, 1958? Language poets— Jack Spicer, Frank O'Hara; confessional poets—Lowell, Sexton, Rich. Plath was still in college; Pound in Saint Elizabeth's; Austin was delivering the William James lectures: *How to Do Things with Words.*

18. Paul Celan, *Collected Prose*, trans. Rosmarie Waldrop (Riverdale-on-Hudson, NY: Sheep Meadow Press, 1986), 34–35.

19. Ibid., 40–41, 43–44.

20. Paul Celan, *Der Meridian: Endfassung, Entwürfe, Materialien* (Frankfurt: Suhrkamp, 1999), 58; translated into English in *Collected Prose* by Rosmarie Waldrop.

21. Immanuel Kant, *Critique of Practical Reason*, q.v., 269–70.

Hard Problems in Poetry

1. Friedrich Nietzsche, *The Will to Power*, trans. Walter Kaufmann and R. J. Hollingdale (New York: Random House, 1968,) 275.

2. Ibid., 277.

3. Simone Weil, *Gravity and Grace*, trans. Arthur Wills (New York: Putnam, 1952), 167–68.

4. P. D. Ouspensky, *Tertium Organum: The Third Canon of Thought*, trans. N. Bessaraboff and C. Bragdon (New York: Knopf, 1955), 236.

5. Hart Crane, *Complete Poems*, ed. Marc Simon (New York: Liveright, 2001), 3.

6. Nietzsche, *The Will to Power* #507, 276.

7. Plotinus, *Ennead III*, 7.6, trans. A. H. Armstrong (Cambridge, MA: Harvard University Press, 1967), 315.

8. Nietzsche, *The Will to Power* #512, 277.

9. Pierre Bourdieu, "Rites of Institution," in *Language and Symbolic Power*, trans.

Gino Raymond and Matthew Adamson (Cambridge, MA: Harvard University Press, 1991), 126.

10. Nietzsche, *The Will to Power* #516, 279.

11. Samuel Beckett, "First Love," in *The Complete Short Prose*, ed. S. E. Gontarski (New York: Grove Press, 1995), 45.

12. Harry G. Frankfurt, *Necessity, Volition, and Love* (Cambridge: Cambridge University Press, 1999), 139.

13. Ibid., 141.

14. Martin Heidegger, *Nietzsche*, vol. 3: *The Will to Power as Knowledge and as Metaphysics*, translated by Joan Stambaugh et al. (New York: HarperCollins, 1991), 34.

15. Texts of the two Walsingham ballads can be found in various printed collections and online at www.walsinghamanglicanarchives.org.uk.

16. Eamon Duffy, *The Stripping of the Altars: Traditional Religion in England c. 1400–c. 1580* (New Haven, CT: Yale University Press, 1992).

17. Julia Lupton, *Afterlives of the Saints: Hagiography, Typology, and Renaissance Literature* (Stanford, CA: Stanford University Press, 1996).

18. Hans Blumenberg, *Shipwreck with Spectator: Paradigm of a Metaphor for Existence* (Cambridge, MA: MIT Press, 1997).

19. John Donne, *The Complete English Poems*, ed. A. J. Smith (New York: Viking Penguin, 1976), 47–48.

20. Michel Foucault, *The Use of Pleasure*, trans. Robert Hurley, vol. 2 of *The History of Sexuality* (New York: Viking, 1985).

21. Nietzsche, *The Will to Power* #516, 279.

22. Étienne Gilson, *The Spirit of Thomism* (New York: Harper & Row, 1966), 64–65.

Why Is Death in Arcadia?

1. I. A. Richards, *Principles of Literary Criticism* (New York: Harcourt, 1950), 57.

2. William M. Ivins Jr., *Prints and Visual Communication* (Cambridge, MA: MIT Press, 1968). See especially chap. 2, "Symbolism and Syntax—A Rule of the Road—the 16th Century."

3. Barbara Herrnstein Smith, *Poetic Closure: A Study of How Poems End* (Chicago: University of Chicago Press, 1968). See chap. 4, "Thematic Devices: Closural Allusions," 172ff.

4. Frank Kermode, *The Sense of an Ending* (New York: Oxford University Press, 1967), 54ff.

5. The reader will recognize here as elsewhere a coloration of thought from the important work of the late Ernst Becker.

6. For constitutive rules, see Roberto Mangabeira Unger, *Knowledge and Politics* (New York: Collier-Macmillan, 1975), 68–69. In addition, it's my view that Unger's concept of "total criticism" is vital to the definition of a new restoration of literary theory and literary fact to a significant place in the central enterprise of human value studies, to which his work is a remarkable contribution.

7. Erwin Panofsky, "*Et in Arcadia Ego*: Poussin and the Elegiac Tradition," in *Meaning in the Visual Arts* (New York: Doubleday, 1955), 295–320.

8. It is, I think, obvious that displacement from idea, archetype, schema, pattern, competence, paradigm, or whatever is the major description of creation that unites in one loose theory broadly diverse fields, such as the history of science, political theory, linguistics, structural anthropology, the psychology of art, et cetera, in the modern world. The addition that I make to these concurrent systems is the observation that the process of displacement is not a neutral process—is in fact a catastrophe—or, as in Plato, a death.

9. For the annihilative character of political rhetoric, see Karl Mannheim, *Ideology and Utopia* (New York: Harcourt, 1985), 38.

10. J. J. Gibson, *The Senses Considered as Perceptual Systems* (Boston: Houghton Mifflin, 1966).

11. John Hollander, *Vision and Resonance* (New York: Oxford University Press, 1975).

12. Virgil, *Aeneid*, XII.203ff., trans. H. R. Fairclough, rev. G. P. Goold (Cambridge: Harvard University Press, 2000), 314–15.

13. For synonymity in this sense, see E. D. Hirsch Jr., "Stylistics and Synonymity," *Critical Inquiry* 1, no. 3 (1975): 559–80.

14. E. H. Gombrich, *Art and Illusion* (New York: Pantheon, 1960), 5 and *passim*.

15. Ludwig Wittgenstein, *Philosophical Investigations* (Oxford: Blackwell, 1958), 178e.

16. Jacques Derrida, *Speech and Phenomena and Other Essays on Husserl's Theory of Signs*, trans. David A. Allison (Evanston, IL: Northwestern University Press, 1973), 97.

17. J. Hillis Miller, "Stevens' Rock and Criticism as Cure," *Georgia Review* 30 (1976): 5–33.

18. See Unger, *Knowledge and Politics*, 215–17.

The Passion of Laocoön

1. In figure 1, the title page to George Chapman's *Odyssey*. Teiresias is represented with the face of Homer. The legend (my epigraph) corresponds to *Odyssey* X.612ff. in Chapman. It reads in full *Solus sapit hic Homo / Reliqui vero Umbrae moventur* (The only wise man is this one. / The rest are moved as shadows are). Cf. *Odyssey* X.490–95 in the Greek text. A. T. Murray in the Loeb edition (Cambridge, MA: Harvard University Press, 1919), 1:381, translates the conclusion of Circe's speech to Odysseus as follows: "But you must first complete another journey, and come to the house of Hades and dread Persephone, to seek soothsaying of the spirit of Theban Teiresias, the blind seer, whose mind abides steadfast. To him even in death Persephone has granted reason, that he alone should have understanding; but the others flit about as shadows."

2. Alexander Nehamas, "Nietzsche, Modernity, Aestheticism," in *The Cambridge Companion to Nietzsche*, ed. Bernd Magnus and Kathleen M. Higgins (Cambridge: University of Cambridge Press, 1996), 232.

3. Pliny *Historia Naturalis* XXXVI. Andreae notes that the Renaissance, absorbed in its imagination of the exceptional work, very likely misread Pliny. Bernd Andreae,

Laokoön und die Gründung Roms (Mainz am Rhein: Philipp von Zabern, 1988). What is not in question is the status category of the exceptional work assigned to the *Laocoön* by the Renaissance and very likely by Pliny. However, Andreae's position is approved by Simon Richter, whose book is far and away the most interesting argument about the Laocoön image; see *Laocoön's Body and the Aesthetics of Pain: Winckelman, Lessing, Herder, Moritz, Goethe* (Detroit: Wayne State University Press, 1992).

4. My point will be that transcendence, practically speaking reference to a god-term, is inevitable, because it is an indispensable component of the necessary building up of generality by which human knowledge (communication, the self-description of persons) is obtained, and thereby human recognition that is "the human interest." "Transcendence" is functionally whatever grounds, or makes believable, discourse about persons and the world, and discourse about that discourse. The single most characteristic "poetic" act is the construction of generality. Cf. Steven Knapp, *Literary Interest: The Limits of Anti-Formalism* (Cambridge, MA: Harvard University Press, 1993), p. 139.

But it must be noted that, anthropologically speaking, before God becomes a term, there is no category of the poetic. At the first moment "God" enters into the psalmic imperative as a vocative term, the category of the poetic is inaugurated. Cf. "The poem is the fatal declension of the name of God." Jean Baudrillard, "The Extermination of the Name of God," in *Symbolic Exchange and Death*, trans. Iain Hamilton Grant (London: Sage, 1993), 210.

5. My sense of the word interest (as in "the human interest") will be similar to that of Jürgen Habermas's "*Interesse*." I suppose the poetic to mediate a fundamental "knowledge-constitutive interest." I do not adopt Habermas's conception of critique. Nearer to hand is Steven Knapp's exemplary *Literary Interest*. For example: "The object of *interpretation* is necessarily the meaning intended by some agent or collectivity of agents. But the object literary *interest* is not an intended meaning; in fact, it isn't literally a *meaning* at all. The object of literary interest is a special kind of representational structure, each of whose elements acquires, by virtue of its connection with other elements, a network of associations inseparable from the representation itself" (104). My concern is with a "special kind of representation structure."

6. I note at this point that while Lessing knows the material constraints upon representation in the plastic arts, and accordingly raises questions about the constraints upon depicting of materials in all the arts, including the arts of language, he nonetheless is disposed to promulgate a view of the exemption of language in this respect that my analysis contradicts. For example, Lessing's assurance that "the whole infinite realm of perfection lies open to [the poet's] description." Gotthold Ephraim Lessing, *Laocoön*, trans. Edward Allen McCormick (New York: Bobbs-Merrill, 1962) 13, is contradicted by my argument. Such is this *new* Laocoön.

7. For scholarship on portraits of Homer, I rely primarily on G. M. A. Richter, *The Portraits of the Greeks* (London: Phaidon, 1965). I illustrate and comment on two of Richter's four or five types (figs. 2 and 3). The particular copy of the *Homer* illustrated is owned by the Huntington Library, San Marino, California. The dates given for this artifact vary from 300 B.C.E. to 100 B.C.E. Richter's several portrait types—sighted and blind—identify Homer in markedly different ways. There is a much more conspicu-

ous diversity among the types of the Homer image than is the case among the various types of images of any particular god in the Greek pantheon. It appears to be fundamental to the economy of images in the Greek world that the many images of each of the many Greek gods be consistent with one another in a way that the many images of persons are not. The imaging of the gods expresses the powerful appropriative hold of divinity on the value of the personal image in Greek civilization.

Note the abridgement of Richter's *Portraits* (Ithaca, NY: Cornell University Press, 1984), 139–50, where association with the Pergamon image to which I refer (fig. 8) and the *Laocoön* is suggested.

8. See Emmanuel Levinas, *Difficult Freedom: Essays in Judaism* (Baltimore: Johns Hopkins University Press, 1993). 196. Levinas speaks often without distinction about the poet and the Jew. For Lessing, the Jew (as in Nathan the Wise) is the archetypal poet whose otherness (to the same of the gentile order) constitutes the autonomy of the indeterminate (i.e., the self-determined or self-described other).

9. In order to reconsider poetics, I do not ground my argument exclusively in the poetic *text* itself, for two reasons: first, for the reason that the self-characterization of the poetic text, inasmuch as poetic text repeats itself as structure in its meanings, is not in my view an unqualifiedly useful, certainly not an exclusive, witness to the human interest in poetry; second, because communicative language does not include everything that is properly called poetry, or for that matter everything that is called language. Poetry is inextricably part of the social history (and prehistory) of human beings and should be seen as a finite historical practice among other practices, such as religion, that are engaged with recurrent unproblematic human needs, and in particular the need of persons—a general human necessity—to imagine and acknowledge one another. Insofar as poetry engages with experience, it does so on the ground, not fundamentally "poetic" of the *human interest* in knowing and valuing persons.

10. By "practice" I mean to indicate the continuously renewed, rule-governed activity of the making (with reference to the principle of Poetry [fig. 9] and the resistance of materials) of the poem. It is the logic of this activity that is the subject matter of poetics.

11. The best work on this subject is Paul Zanker, *The Mask of Socrates: The Image of the Intellectual in Antiquity*, trans. by Alan Shapiro (Berkeley: University of California Press, 1995). The "portraits" of Homer are discussed, pp.14ff. "The sculptor imagined Homer as a blind old man, turned slightly to one side and listening to his own inner voice. . . . True knowledge is ancient knowledge. The composing of verse is conceived in this portrait as a gift from the gods, akin to that of the seer, a form of revelation. Greek mythology is full of seers and poets whose powers are directly connected to their blindness. This is true, for example, of Demodokos, the singer at the court in Phaeacia, whom the Muse loved above all other men, and gave him both good and evil; of his sight she deprived him, but gave him the gift of song. The prophetic power of the blind is generally considered as a kind of compensation. The great seers like Teiresias and Phineas went blind because they had seen the gods, because they knew too much and revealed their knowledge to men. . . . According to a saying of the Delphic Oracle, memory is the 'face of the blind.'"

12. For the state of affairs called "constituted of," see below. *"'Constitutive of' implies identity of substance, and hence identity of the structure of substance. What is constitutive repeats the structure of the constituting circumstance or substance."*

13. *Eidos* is used throughout this essay to indicate, as in Homer, the form or fashion of the person, the wonder of the presence of the person. Consciousness in fact of human presence. (See p. 86 in the text.) I understand poetics to be the eidetic science.

14. By "manifestation" I mean that visible difference that "makes up" or constitutes (see note 12 above) consciousness and that by its hierarchical structure (a structure it reiterates as representation of "the real") determines the intentions of consciousness. *It is the struggle for control of this logic of manifestation that expresses itself as the warfare of the religious upon the poetic institution.* When Marsyas is flayed, it is manifestation that is atrociously torn from him.

15. The idea of indeterminacy is a more accurate account of the condition of meaningful voluntarism than are (let us say) adjacent notions such as constructivity and undecidablity from which indeterminacy must be discriminated. In my use of the word, "indeterminacy" must mean *unilateral undecidability by the other*. In an intricately qualified sense, indeterminacy means autonomy. The subject matter of *poetics* is the exploration of the qualifications of this autonomy. *Hence, the subject matter of poetics (eidetic science) is the exploration of the resistance of materials.* Since we think about these matters analogically, consider the well-known Perry-Lord account of Homeric composition-in-performance, the production of infinitely variable instances of discourse from finite always-already-determined elements. The outcome (which I do not understand very well) should be an openness of the person to "laws of its own making" (Coleridge), subject to the constraint of materials *including the structure of "law" itself.*

There is much talk about indeterminacy in contemporary poetics. In Marjorie Perloff, the term is mistakenly put in play as a synonym of undecidability. *The Poetics of Indeterminacy: Rimbaud to Cage* (Princeton, NJ: Princeton University Press, 1981); for the literary application of the term, she cites Tzvetan Todorov, *Symbolisme et Interpretation*. But there is no artifactual undecidability. In addition, Perloff employs the term as appropriate to one party or school of poetic practice since Rimbaud. But indeterminacy in my sense is a characteristic of poetry as such. A functional outcome *structurally* like the practice I am concerned with is found in Steven Knapp's *Literary Interest* (cited above), for example, p. 139: "For what makes the literary artifact 'literary,' in the sense I have been developing is precisely the way its typical elements are particularized by their insertion into a structure whose tendency toward full concreteness they nevertheless frustrate."

16. Unlike Homer's blindness, the blindness of Teiresias is narrated. The specific emphasis of the narrations of Teiresias's blinding is on the substitution of prophecy for sight at the moment of transgression. Teiresias knows and reveals the secret of the god (that is to say, he presents the inner as outer, as, for example, in the case of the woman's pleasure in sexuality). He sees the primordial signified by the sexual—the copulation of snakes (the primal scene, the scene of his own begetting).

In this context, sexuality expresses the eidetic relations of the powers of the world, for it is eidetic and not sexual satisfaction that is the need that requires signification.

Hence, Teiresias's physical androgyny constitutes a fundamental refusal of determinate form.

17. Il faut être absolument moderne.

Point de cantiques: tenir le pas gagné. Dure nuit! le sang séché fume sur ma face, et je n'ai rien derrière moi, que cet horrible arbrisseau! ... Le combat spirituel est aussi brutal que la bataille d'hommes; mais la vision de la justice est le plaisir de Dieu seul.

Arthur Rimbaud, "Adieu," *Une saison en enfer,* in *Rimbaud: Complete Works and Selected Letters,* trans. Wallace Fowlie (Chicago: University of Chicago Press, 2005), 302–3.

18. Of the Pergamene style in ancient sculpture, Spengler remarks: "Apollonian art came to its end in Pergamene sculpture. *Pergamum is the counterpart of Bayreuth.* . . . [A]ll Nietzsche's charges against Wagner and Bayreuth, the 'Ring' and 'Parsifal'—decadence, theatricalness and the like—could well have been leveled in the same words at the Pergamene sculpture. A masterpiece of this sculpture—a veritable 'Ring'—has come down to us in the Gigantomachia frieze of the great altar. Here is the same theatrical note, the same use of motives from ancient discredited mythology . . . the same ruthless bombardment of the nerves, and also (though the lack of inner power cannot altogether be concealed) the same fully conscious force and towering greatness. To this art the Farnese Bull and the older model of the Laocoön group certainly belong [as well of course as the 'Hellenistic' portrait of Homer with which we are concerned]." Oswald Spengler, *The Decline of the West,* vol. 1, *Form and Actuality,* trans. Charles Francis Atkinson (New York: Knopf, 1940), 291. The "baroque" style, to which all our ancient images belong, is characterized by a theatricality (in Schillerian terms, a sentimentality) representing enactment (the conscious articulation) of *consciousness*—in terms of this essay, disclosure by poetic means of the structure of experience.

19. Cf. Robert Lamberton, *Homer the Theologian: Neoplatonist Allegorical Reading and the Growth of the Epic Tradition* (Berkeley: University of California Press, 1986).

20. Homer *Iliad* XXIV.528ff., trans. A. T. Murray, rev. William F. Wyatt (Cambridge, MA: Harvard University Press, 1999), 2:603.

21. Ibid., 1:607–9.

22. Ibid., 1:105. Virtually all of the alternative narratives produce a rational account of Laocoön's suffering by introducing some grounds to attribute his pain to his guilt. The cultural disposition to disable narratives of unqualified theodicean disappointment (such as the story about Job) in the defense of a dominant regime of the real is discussed elsewhere in this essay.

23. Cf. Peter Weiss on the elder son: *"Der ältere Sohn aber gehört noch einer Belebten Welt an, er bricht sich aus dem Statuarischen heraus, um denen, die ihm vielleicht zur Hilfte, Bericht zu erstatten."* "Laocoön oder Über die Grenzen der Sprache," in *Rapporte* I, Rede über Lessing (1965): 180, 181.

24. Gregory Nagy, *Pindar's Homer: The Lyric Possession of an Epic Past* (Baltimore: Johns Hopkins University Press, 1990), 197.

25. The young Marx read Lessing's *Laocoön.* See W. J. T. Mitchell, *Iconology, Image, Text, Ideology* (Chicago: University of Chicago Press, 1989). Mitchell calls attention to,

among much else, the positioning of Lessing's text and the Laocoön image in a crisis among cultural understandings of the *status* of the artistic as over against the religious "image." "There is more than a little irony in Marx's invocation of the Laocoön as an image of the iconoclast become idolator. It is as if Marx were turning Laocoön into an emblem of Lessing's attempt to free art from superstition. . . . As long as Laocoön strives against the serpents, he symbolizes the iconoclastic struggle against fetishism, the valuers of Enlightenment aesthetics against primitive superstition. But the Laocoön also symbolizes, in that very struggle, a new fetishism, the bourgeois cult of 'aesthetic purity' . . ." (201–2).

Crucial instances of twentieth-century fine art enact the incompatibility of that scream with the well-formed human image and the oriented world (e.g., Edvard Munch's *The Scream*, Picasso's *Guernica*, Bacon's screaming popes, etc.). Such a breaking of the category of the intelligible by the countenance in pain is seen as pathologized in the psychology and attendant images of the nineteenth century by Simon Richter in his exceptional book cited above.

26. Cf. David Wellbery's discussion of "the disgusting" (*das Ekelhaft*) in Lessing's *Laocoön* as "non-sublatable" experience, that is, experience not conformable to the criteria of the intelligible (the beautiful), and the association of *das Ekelhaft* with the scream of Laocoön as the transgression beyond the theodicean powers of the culture of the beautiful. David E. Wellbery, "The Pathos of Theory: *Laokoön* Revisited," in *Intertextuality: German Literature and Visual Art from the Renaissance to the Twentieth Century*, ed. Ingeborg Hoesterey and Ulrich Weisstein (New York: Camden House, 1993).

27. Benedict Spinoza, *Ethics*, in *A Spinoza Reader*, trans. Edwin Curley (Princeton, NJ: Princeton University Press, 1994), 217. Hence Spinoza's critique of the Old Testament as "god-term," in the spirit of Maimonides' relentless deconstruction of figuration in *The Guide for the Perplexed*.

28. On the history of restoration, see Margarete Bieber, *Laocoön: The Influence of the Group since Its Rediscovery*, rev. and enlarged ed. (Detroit: Wayne State University Press, 1969).

29. William Blake, *All Religions Are One*, in *The Complete Illuminated Books*, ed. David Bindman (New York: Thames & Hudson, 2001), 21.

30. Louis Ginzberg, s.v. "Cherubim," in *The Jewish Encyclopedia*, vol. 4 (New York: Funk and Wagnalls, 1903).

31. Lessing, *Laocoön*, 35.

32. Virgil *Aeneid* II.795–812, trans. H. R. Fairclough, rev. G. P. Goold (Cambridge, MA: Harvard University Press, 1935), 357.

33. Ibid., 331.

34. Ibid., 313.

35. A useful introduction to the linguistics to which I refer is Thomas A. Sebeok, "Toward a Natural History of Language," in *A Sign Is Just a Sign* (Bloomington: Indiana University Press, 1991); and Ray Jackendoff, *Patterns in the Mind, Language, and Human Behavior* (New York: Basic Books, 1994). The medieval preoccupation of contemporary literary studies with Saussurean concern for sign/signified relationships and reference uncertainty ignores the profundity of language function that must concern

poetics. Jakobsonian language-function analysis should alert us to *phatic aspects* of language not includable in the shallow game of message transmission. An evolutionary history of language is implied by Chomskian notions of innateness, and such notions are confirmed by the requirements of poetic analysis as I indicate. The powers of the Horatian Orpheus display this logic.

36. Cf. Orpheus-Christos in, for example, John Block Friedman, *Orpheus in the Middle Ages* (Cambridge, MA: Harvard University Press, 1970).

37. Jean-Jacques Rousseau, *Emile; or, On Education*, trans. Allan Bloom (New York: Basic Books, 1979), 294, 290. Emphasis mine.

38. Robert Nozick, *The Nature of Rationality* (Cambridge, MA: Harvard University Press, 1993), 176.

39. Cf. Allen Grossman, "Holiness," in *Contemporary Jewish Religious Thought*, ed. Arthur Cohen and P. Mendes-Flohr (New York: Scribners, 1987), 389–97. Here the relationship of holiness, human value, and the absolute abstraction as consciousness as such (the container—*shekhina*—divinity) is worked out in the Hebrew (biblical and liturgical) context.

40. Plato *Symposium* 215b.

41. Ovid *Metamorphoses* VI.384–401.

42. Edgar Wind, *Pagan Mysteries in the Renaissance* (New Haven, CT: Yale University Press, 1958), chap. 11, "The Flaying of Marsyas," 142–46.

Figuring the Real

1. Jacques Derrida and Christie McDonald, *The Ear of the Other: Otobiography, Transference, Translation: Texts and Discussions with Jacques Derrida* (Lincoln: University of Nebraska, 1988) 149.

2. Dorothy Wordsworth, *Journals of Dorothy Wordsworth*, ed. E. de Selincourt, 2 vols. (New York: Macmillan, 1941), 1:356.

3. Sir Walter Scott, *Rob Roy* (Boston: DeWolfe, Fiske, 1870), v–vi.

4. Rainer Maria Rilke, *The Selected Poetry of Rainer Maria Rilke*, ed. and trans. Stephen Mitchell (New York: Vintage International, 1982), 303.

5. Wordsworth, *Journals*, 380.

6. William Wordsworth, *Poems in Two Volumes, 1807*, ed. Helen Darbishire, 2nd ed. (Oxford: Clarendon, 1952), 414.

7. Ibid., 336.

8. I quote an Irish historian of the period: "When England would a land enthrall, / She doom'd the Muses' Sons to fall. . . ." Joseph C. Walker, *Historical Memoirs of the Irish Bards: A Facsimile of the 1786 Edition* (New York: Garland, 1971), 139n. Cf. also Sir Walter Scott's "Lay of the Last Minstrel."

9. William Wordsworth, *The Early Letters of William and Dorothy Wordsworth (1787–1805)*, ed. E. de Selincourt (Oxford: Clarendon, 1935), 547.

10. Pierre Bourdieu, *Language and Symbolic Power*, ed. John B. Thompson, trans. Gino Raymond and Matthew Adamson (Cambridge, MA: Harvard University Press, 1991), 126.

11. Wordsworth, *Early Letters*, 525–26.

12. Ibid., 526.

13. Ibid., 527.

On Communicative Difficulty

1. See Allen Grossman, "Holiness," in Arthur Allen Cohen and Paul R. Mendes-Flohr, *Contemporary Jewish Religious Thought* (New York: Scribner, 1987).

2. Consider Chomsky's high-comic (integrative) conception of the universality of the language faculty or competence, the Bridge or Tower that never breaks, an innate material, value-bearing fact, the ground of the poetic principle that secures the value of all selves. In *Cartesian Linguistics*, Chomsky speaks of the prestige of poetry in terms of this "creative" aspect of language that is innate and specifies the person without exception: "The poetic quality of ordinary language derives from its independence of immediate stimulation . . . and its freedom from practical ends. The characteristics along with the boundlessness of language as an instrument of free self-expression are essentially those emphasized by Descartes and his followers. But it is interesting to trace in slightly greater detail the argument by which Schlegel goes on to relate what we have called the creative aspect of language use to true creativity. Art, like language, is unbounded in its expressive potentiality. But, Schlegel argues, poetry has a unique status among the arts in this respect: it, in a sense, underlies all others and stands as the fundamental and typical art form. We recognize this unique status [of poetry] when we use the term 'poetical' to refer to the quality of true imaginative creation in any of the arts. The explanation for the central position of poetry lies in its association with language. Poetry is unique in that its very medium is unbounded and free; that is, its medium, language, is a system with unbounded innovative potentialities for the formation and expression of ideas. The production of any work of art is preceded by a creative mental act for which the means provided is language. Thus the creative use of language which, under certain conditions of form and organization constitutes poetry, accompanies and underlies any act of the creative imagination no matter what the medium in which it is realized. In this way, poetry achieves its unique status among the arts and artistic creation and artistic creativity is related to the creative aspects of language use." (Chomsky is paraphrasing Schlegel's *Die Kunstlehre.*)

3. Crane put it this way in a 1925 letter Eugene O'Neill—a letter Crane designed to describe his project, in view of an introduction O'Neill was to write for *White Buildings*. (An introduction that was finally written, very successfully from Crane's point of view, by Allen Tate.) The following paragraph is from Crane to O'Neill, unpublished in his lifetime (a text now called "General Aims and Theories"): "It is my hope to go *through* the combined materials of the poem, using our 'real' world somewhat as a springboard and give to the poem *as a whole* an orbit or predetermined direction of its own. I would like to establish it as free from my own personality as from any chance evaluation on the reader's part. (This is, of course, an impossibility, but it is a characteristic worth mentioning.) Such a poem is at least a stab at a truth, and to such an extent may be

differentiated from other kinds of poetry and called 'absolute.' Its evocation will not be toward decoration or amusement, but rather toward a state of consciousness, and 'innocence' (Blake) or absolute beauty. In this condition there may be discoverable under new forms certain spiritual illuminations, shining with a morality essentialized from experience directly, and not from previous precepts or preconceptions. It is as though a poem gave the reader as he left it a single, new *word*, never before spoken and impossible to actually enunciate, but self-evident as an active principle in the reader's consciousness henceforward."

Crane then goes on to say: "As to technical considerations . . . the entire construction of the poem is raised on the organic principle of a 'logic of metaphor,' which antedates our so-called pure logic, and which is the genetic basis of all speech, hence consciousness and thought-extension." And further: "These dynamics often result, I'm told, in certain initial difficulties in understanding my poems."

By these words, Crane undertakes to explain and justify to O'Neill his own classification of the poetry he writes as difficult, presenting "difficulties," by which term he justifies the otherness of the mind he knows his poem presents to his reader, his poet's gift to the reader of "a single, new *word*, never before spoken and impossible to actually enunciate. . . ." What is clear is that this difficult "new" word ("never before spoken and impossible to actually enunciate") that Crane as poet intends to contribute to the "reader's consciousness henceforward" as an active principle is *valuable*, "worth it," a kind of truth. At this point, I note that Crane was for a time an advertising copy writer (for J. Walter Thompson, among others). These words addressed by Crane on his own behalf to O'Neill are certainly intended to supply O'Neill with some compelling "copy." They are an advertisement by Crane for himself, and for his project, in case O'Neill didn't get the point. It would be worthwhile to consider Crane's poetry in general from this point of view.

4. The bell tower narrative: Lesley Simpson, who read "The Broken Tower" when it was published, made the following note not long after Crane's suicide: "I was with Hart Crane in Taxco, Mexico, the morning of January 27, this year [1932], when he conceived the idea of 'The Broken Tower.' The night before, being troubled with insomnia, he had risen before daybreak and walked down to the village square. Hart met the old Indian bell-ringer who was on his way down to the church. He and Hart were old friends and he brought Hart up into the tower with him to help ring the bells. As Hart was swinging the clapper of the great bell . . . the swift tropical dawn broke over the mountains. The sublimity of the scene and the thunder of the bells woke in Hart one of those gusts of joy of which only he was capable. He came striding up the hill afterwards in a sort of frenzy, refused his breakfast, and paced up and down the porch waiting impatiently for me to finish my coffee. Then he seized my arm and bore me off to the plaza, here we sat in the shadow of the church, Hart the while pouring out a magnificent cascade of words."

In the photograph that we have of Crane in the tower, we see Hart Crane, the Mexican sexton who admitted him to the bells, and the shadow of Peggy Baird, who took the picture. In the photo she took, she casts a shadow on the lower part of Hart Crane's seated body.

5. "The logic of ecstasy" is an expression Crane found on the title page of the American edition of P. D. Ouspensky's *Tertium Organum (The Third Organ of Thought): A Key to the Enigmas of the World* (1920), which Crane read in 1923 and remarked on in a letter to Allen Tate. Ouspensky's logic is of the same "inclusive" nature as Whitman's. Cf. Allen Grossman, "The Poetics of Union in Whitman and Lincoln: An Inquiry toward the Relationship of Art and Policy," in *The Long Schoolroom* (Ann Arbor: University of Michigan Press, 1997), 58–84.

6. Poetry and closure: Poems are written in both lines and sentences. Line and sentence are radically different structures. There cannot, for example, be an interrogative *line*. Lines are invariant abstract structures each composed with an opening and close following metrical expectation but utterly different than sentences, which are grammatical systems governed by other rules. Sentences are not *materially* equivalent formal elements, but lines or groups of lines (stanzas) are. By reason of lines, formal closure is performed identically over and over until the poem ends. By reason of sentences, grammatical closure is performed non-identically. But at the end of the poem, the close as such, both (disparate) systems conclude simultaneously.

The reason all this needs to be said follows from the fact that Crane was a metrical line writer. His sense required the abstraction of measured line in a way uncharacteristic of what we call modern poetry, and the end of Crane's poem—this poem, "The Broken Tower" (its terminal closure)—requires a rationality (a meaning) consistent with the severely defined relation between line and sentence in accord with which the poem is constructed. The meaning of "The Broken Tower" is accomplished at the end (stanzas 9 and 10). Closure in this poem puts meaning in service to a liberation, not of the kind that defeats order, but of another kind. What is found is a liberation that sanctions order, the cure of poetic vocation by poetic means.

7. On Crane's sense of "brotherhood" as homosexual society, see this letter to Solomon Grunberg (February 8, 1932):

> Dear Mony:
>   . . . not as you surmise in constant Bacchic state. Not by any means. However, I happen to be in something approximating it at this present moment, since I've got to work on the first impressive poem I've started in the last two years. I feel the old confidence again; and you may know what that means to someone of my stripe!
>   The servants are all asleep—and I'm in that pleasant state of beginning all over again. Especially as I am in love again—and never as quite before. Love is always more important than locality; and this is the newest adventure I ever had. I won't say much more than that I seem to have broken ranks with my much advertised "brotherhood"—and a woman whom I have known for years suddenly seems to "have claimed her own." I can't say that I'm sorry. It has given me new perspectives, and after many tears and groans something of a reason for living.

8. Christian Science was the religion of Crane's family. Crane employed for his final language (Mind is God) Mary Baker Eddy's text *Science and Health with a Key to the*

Scriptures. The scriptures in question are Genesis and Revelation. From the Eddy glossary: "MIND. The only I, or Us; the only Spirit, Soul, divine Principle, substance, Life, Truth, Love; the one God; not that which is *in* man, but the divine Principle, of God, of whom man is the full and perfect expression; Deity which outlines but is not outlined." "FATHER-MOTHER is the name for Deity."

Index of Names

Franklin Pierce University

00176972

DATE DUE

GAYLORD

PRINTED IN U.S.A.